also
by
Dorothy Rodgers

MY FAVORITE THINGS
THE HOUSE IN MY HEAD

---

also
by
Mary Rodgers

THE ROTTEN BOOK
(for children)

A
WORD
TO
THE
WIVES

A WORD TO THE WIVES

BY DOROTHY RODGERS AND MARY RODGERS

ALFRED A. KNOPF NEW YORK 1970

*To all husbands,
particularly ours,
without whom . . .*

ACKNOWLEDGMENT

As in My Favorite Things *and* The House in My Head,

Marcia Wallace has once again brought her own

special brand of comfort, wit, and style to the organization of

this book and we want to thank her

for her invaluable help.

This is a book for wives—a book to help them cope with living in the world today. Since these days a woman is expected to have all the wifely arts and skills of motherhood plus a lively participating involvement in community affairs, there is no limit to the subjects we could legitimately include. Obviously we have had to establish some limits, and so we have chosen those subjects that seem to us of primary concern. The book is about husbands and children, entertaining and decorating the people and things that are constantly with us in our day-to-day living. We have tried, too, to go into fields like choosing and remodeling a house, moving, careers and vacations—blessings or curses that come into our lives occasionally. Feel free to read the chapters in any order you like.

We hope that having two of us from different generations telling you of our experiences will give the book an extra dimension. Both of us have spent most of our lives in New York City, in rented apartments and co-ops, and each of us has also lived in the country, both in houses we have rented (furnished and unfurnished) as well as in houses we have owned. In addition to my professional experience as an interior designer, I have remodeled two houses and built a third for ourselves. We aren't marriage counselors or child psychologists or even chefs, but we have kept house, raised children, entertained our friends and lived with our husbands in a world that has changed more in the past twenty-five years than in any other comparable period in its recorded history. We would like to share what we have learned.

To realize just how much everything has changed, you need only glance at the chapter headings of guides written for young wives at the turn of the century. Books like *Mrs. Beeton's Household Management* and *The Household Guide or Domestic Cyclopedia* (1892) give us a fascinating

How do two people go about working on one book? When we started, we weren't quite sure. Were we supposed to closet ourselves in the same room and supply alternate words and sentences? That didn't sound very practical. Or write concurrent but opposing views on the same subject? That didn't sound very interesting. What we finally came up with was a "dualogue" in which we interrupt each other, frequently in some chapters, less frequently in others, with comments, embellishments, occasional gentle gibes, and a few arguments. Very mild arguments, I might add, because, oddly enough, neither the generation gap nor the mother-daughter relationship seemed to engender anything more violent than a little cozy badinage.

In some chapters the dualogue becomes a monologue for several pages at a time. This is because one or the other of us has no comment to make. On the subject of decorating, for instance, I have no comment to make. What I know about decorating would fit on the head of a carpet tack and still leave room for the Lord's Prayer. On the other hand, children—near and dear to my mother's heart but twenty years removed from her hearth—are a fit topic for me. I've been surrounded by them for eighteen years, and with a two-year-old in the nursery the end isn't even in sight.

We divided the book into two sections. The first three chapters are about choosing a place to live, moving into it, and fixing it up. It's conceivable, although unlikely, that you chose your house years ago, don't ever plan to change a hair of it, and don't ever plan to move out of it (in which case you can skip this section), but the majority of women do have to deal with these horrendous problems at some point in their lives. DR, having had a good deal of experience, has supplied you with technical advice about real estate, contractors, pipes, moving men, etc., in the hope that the more you know, the more minor the trauma. My pri-

picture of the life and manners of their day. They served their readers as a kind of bible-cum-book of etiquette, "how-to" and "cookery" book, covering a vast range of topics. The mistress of the house was expected to know how to do anything that had to be done in the home, even though she delegated the tasks to her well-trained staff while she acted in a supervisory capacity. In addition to more ordinary skills like "Flower Arrangement," "Cooking," and "Menu-Planning," the books dealt with such matters as "Health and Happiness," "Napkin Folding," "Diagnosis and Care of Illness," "Carving and Trussing," "Legal Memoranda," and "Pest Exterminating." The rules were explicit, and no room was left for doubts.

Mary and I have tried to be explicit about only one thing, and that is that there are no rules. In fact, we even thought of calling the book *It Depends* because the phrase crept in so many times. Not only are there no black-and-white rules of behavior such as existed in more orderly times to serve as absolutes, but we couldn't find any books that even attempted to deal relevantly with the problems that face young women today.

Because of the scarcity of live-in help (and the advent of TV), people are spending more time at home than ever before. And so having money makes less difference than it ever has. If you can afford help and can't get it, your situation is not too different from that of the woman who can't afford it and doesn't have it.

Never before has there been a time when convention was so unimportant. Behavior, clothes, the food you serve and the way you serve it, decor, whether you sit on the floor, on the newest inflated plastic chair, or on a Chippendale number—all these outward facets of our lives have quite suddenly become entirely a question of personal preference. You are free to do it your way. Some of our young friends manage to serve a delicious dinner with apparently no effort. You and I know that a great deal of planning, organizing, and work have gone into making it seem easy, but the point is that it's the planning and organizing that have made it possible. If the hostess loves to cook, her food might be of the gourmet variety, but if she hates cooking, she can

introduction by Dorothy Rodgers

mary contribution here is to tell you all about the trauma. I've had a lot of experience with that.

The second section is about people and, of necessity, contains fewer facts and more personal speculation. Children don't come by the square yard, there's no blueprint to follow, and I can't tell you what to do about yours. The best I can do is to tell you about what works, or doesn't, with mine. The same goes for husbands; they're a highly diversified breed, and what makes one man happy might make another man miserable. However, since this book would be peculiarly incomplete without it, we've included a chapter on husbands—what they can do for us and, more important, what we can do for them. DR and I are equally responsible for this one. I happen to start it, she dives in in the middle, and I complete it, but the sequence of contributions is purely arbitrary. Since entertaining is an absolutely obligatory concern for all wives (no matter how emancipated or individualistic we may be, we still have to feed our families and friends) we share our disparate views with you on this topic too.

The final chapter is about wives. *Not,* for a change, in relation to their many entangling alliances, but in relation to themselves as women. In other words, wives as human beings, who, like all other human beings, have a need to grow, change, and develop within themselves, as themselves, and by themselves, in order to be happier people (and better wives). DR and I are equally responsible for this chapter, too. She starts first, this time, and I dive in with the subject of the woman who loves her husband, her children, her home, *and* her job. (Most of you are probably not working wives, but a little advice for those of you who are: as you read the chapters on husbands, entertaining, and children, remember to go easy on yourselves. Select the practicable information and guiltlessly reject the Lucky Strike Extras that only non-working wives should consider.)

DR and I are very different types of people, and the contrast between us should be illuminating. Her type of recreation and re-creation is nothing like mine. To her, a happy home and a happy marriage is an art, and—I can say it, she can't—DR is quite an artist. To me, a happy home and a

introduction by Mary Rodgers

give her guests just as good a time by being ingenious in her use of store-bought food. There is no one "right" way any more. "Manners" in the sense of Victorian etiquette have lost out to "manners" meaning "basic thoughtfulness and kindness in your relationships with others"—which is what manners started out to be.

We believe that the greatest stabilizing influences in the world stem from family and personal relationships, and that home is where it all starts. Husbands, children, careers, and where and how you live—each influences and is in turn influenced by the others. They are the stuff a woman's life is made of. (This book is probably not for those ladies of the liberation front who feel that we are an underprivileged minority. Unfortunately, we are not a minority, and I have never felt that being a woman made me underprivileged.)

For some time we have been aware of the phenomena of the nervous hostess, and the wife who is constantly worried about not doing the right thing. We hope, in this book, to dispel some of their fears. God knows, there are plenty of things we should be afraid of in this fearful world, things that are of great concern to all of us. Some of them are frustrating because we are, or feel we are, powerless to act against them. But your home and the way you live in it should not be among them. If this book can help you to relax in your house with your family and friends, it will make me very happy. What's more important is that it make you very happy, too.

introduction by Dorothy Rodgers

happy marriage are dumb luck—and a nice husband. I seem to be enjoying both.

Speaking of types, this book, as I'm sure you've already noticed, is printed in two different colors, black for DR and brown for me. Actually, our writing styles are pretty easy to distinguish from each other, but there's always the outside chance that somebody, someday, might call me up and ask me to decorate a living room. We certainly wouldn't want that, and neither would you!

CONTENTS

A
WORD
TO
THE
WIVES

HOUSE
TALK

city
or
country

Obviously, one of life's basic decisions has to do with where you'll live. Everyone feels strongly about it. I, for instance, have always been a city type. I am happier with my feet hitting concrete sidewalks than walking on good soft earth. Sports have never tempted me, either for playing or watching, but I love all the things that go to make a big city lively and exciting: theater, museums, galleries, shops. Loving good food, I delight in discovering new restaurants and in living where I can track down odd ingredients, exotic spices, and imported goodies.

I think a city can be a good place to bring up children, too. Dick and I grew up in New York, and so did our daughters. Cities can be wonderfully stimulating. In the country and the suburbs children may be told about differences between people and their ways of living, but in a city, they actually see and get to know a much broader cross section. The kids they go to school with are far more likely to come from varied social, economic, and cultural backgrounds than those in suburban schools.

Undeniably, however, city life today is becoming increasingly difficult—even apart from the obvious horrors of violence, pollution, and general deterioration. The great cost and scarcity of private schools make them out of the question for increasing numbers of people who are unhappy with the quality of metropolitan public education. Day-by-day household service is harder to come by; and when you do find help, it is apt to be unprofessional or just plain bad because domestic jobs are considered so undesirable now.

They're considered even more undesirable in the country; nobody *ever* comes by there.

"And," I can hear some exhausted young mother say,

"What about having to bundle up small children and take them to the park, and then sit there watching over them for hours every day? How about not being able to let them go out alone, and what about coping with traffic and public transportation?" I have no answer. Possibly with small children life in the country is simpler. But it is not necessarily perfect.

Moving to the suburbs is not a panacea. In many areas, the population has grown so rapidly that the local school systems, for instance, have not been able to keep up. Recreational facilities for young children are often inadequate; and what is even more important, not nearly enough has been done for teen-agers. Children are not always happy to play with the kids next door, and then suburban mothers must spend extra hours chauffeuring them to and from friends' houses—to say nothing of the miles and hours of driving absolutely essential to country living: meeting trains, marketing, doing errands, taking kids to music teachers, dentists, and doctors, and taking animals to the vet. (With chauffeuring in mind, you may be wise to postpone dreams of acreage way out in the country in favor of being closer to the center of things—within biking distance of children's friends, schools, and appointments.)

Generally, the most important person to be considered in choosing between city and suburbs is the head of the family —his preferences and his attitude toward commuting. We have editor friends who actually find the hours between home and office very profitable, since their work demands a great deal of reading, and on the train no one can get at them and telephones don't ring. On the other hand, for many men the pressure of always keeping one eye on the clock, the constant scramble for the last good train or getting home in time to catch a glimpse of the children becomes impossible. A heart specialist once told me he thought that the stress involved in commuting was an important cause of many heart attacks.

I, too, have always been a city type. Until recently, I was also happier with my feet hitting the concrete sidewalks rather than walking on the good soft earth. But I don't have to tell you what New York or any other big city is like these days. On the West Side, where we live, there are holes in the concrete and good soft banana peels to walk on. There are people to watch—drunks, junkies, prostitutes, inmates of homes for the aged; they all sit on benches in the middle of Broadway and watch the drunks, junkies, and prostitutes. Shop windows aren't much fun to look into—everything is dusty, there aren't any art galleries, the nearest bookstore is too far away, and when you get there, they haven't heard of anything you want. We have lots of bakeries—anybody want a dusty Danish?

And with all this, I *swear* to you I know how well off we are. Compared to most other areas in Manhattan, let alone Ocean Hill–Brownsville, we live like princes on Park Avenue (which recently had rats, by the way, emigrating in a hurry from Harlem in the north). We have, two blocks from us, the best playground in New York, with vast free-form tunnels and turrets, tons of sand, and a paid playground supervisor who does arts and crafts with the children, reads to them, knows them all by name, and loves them. We have an apartment big enough to ride tricycles in. Our children go to private schools, and only one member of my family has ever been mugged—my son, when he was ten. That's a pretty good record for a family of seven, but it's bad news when you have to tell a self-respecting, scrappy little boy that he should be a coward. "Give them the bus pass, give them the fifty cents, give them the football and run." That's what you say to boys. "Never walk down the side streets, look out for doorways, and scream your head off," is what you say to girls. What a way to live! But in big cities it's the only way to live.

Yes, there are all kinds of restaurants in the city. The expensive ones are too expensive for the likes of us, and the inexpensive ones are often in out-of-the-way places. Taxis are hard to get and expensive, buses and subways are unreliable—it's easier to stay home. Theater is too expensive, movies are too expensive, and we are all choking to death in the fumes.

I don't like New York any more and I don't want to live here. New York is only good for the really rich. The rest of us, especially if we have children to support, cannot take advantage of its benefits; the city is too noisy, too dirty, too complicated, too sad.

Why don't we move? Two reasons: My husband is in the

theater; with his erratic schedule, I would never see him if he had to commute, because nothing awfully snappy leaves Grand Central at midnight. The other reason is, curiously enough, the children. Not the little ones, who would probably love the country, but the big ones, the teen-agers. There is one thing to be said for New York: You know where your children are, how they got there, and how they are getting home. They are not careening around country roads in their own cars.

I happen to know about one groovy town near New York —it's full of liberal, likable adults but it's also a free port for pot, pills, hash, and LSD. The place is wide open and the kids are bored; they have done their growing up in a community that is matriarchal by day and overindulgent by night when the men finally show up, too tired to tune in on their kids and too guilt-ridden to discipline them. Interestingly enough, these parents seem to be unashamed, unshocked, and uncritical about the scrapes their kids get into; they tell you about them, not with embarrassment, but with a kind of detached amusement.

In the old-world, charming, conservative towns (and their number is fast dwindling) the exact same things go on—with one exception. These parents hush everything up, which is probably why I don't have any first hand information about their children. I hear rumors, though, and as far as I'm concerned, the fact remains: No matter how many healthy activities suburban New York children have available to them in the daytime, there is still nothing to do at night. If you and your husband cannot stomach the thought of urban garbage-can living, or you can't afford it, you must be prepared to pay very close attention to your kids at all times.

One more thing. My mother is a chauvinist. When she says she is a city type, she really means she is a New York City type. To be even more explicit, a Manhattan type. By her own admission, she doesn't want to live in any other city in the country. She thinks San Francisco is lovely, and New Orleans is very pretty and the food is wonderful, but her feet don't itch for their concrete pavements. Chicago has a pretty good bunch of art, and so has Washington. She doesn't want to live there, either. She's a third-generation New Yorker and she simply loves the dirty old place.

This in itself is not remarkable. I'm sure there's at least one person in, let's say, Cincinnati, who feels the same way about Cincinnati. But one of the things about Manhattan that makes it unique is that it is an island; its suburbs, therefore, may be no further away from its midtown than other cities' suburbs—as the crow flies. If a father could take the five p.m. crow to Connecticut, arriving promptly at six, it would be different. But commuter train service is abysmal, the throughways are impassable at rush hours, and you can't park when you get to New York anyway. Our suburban communities are cut off from the city's art center, the entertainment center—everything, in fact, but the shopping center. They exist in virtual isolation from the very heart of the matter, husbands and fathers, for most of the waking hours of the week. Bad, very bad. Very dangerous for children, very lonely, difficult, and demoralizing for mothers.

And so, if my husband were not in the theater, if he worked in Boston, or Chicago, or Cincinnati, and could come home at a reasonable hour to play with me and beat the kids, or play with the kids and beat me—anything, as long as he's around—I would live in the suburbs and walk on the good soft earth. As it stands now, I'm sticking to banana peels and they're sticking to me.

The one really essential thing is that husband and wife agree on where and how they are going to live—in the city, the suburbs, the country; in an apartment or a house; whether they are going to buy or rent. It is unlikely that you'll agree on all these points from the beginning, but with an open-minded approach and flexibility on both sides, things will fall into place. Basic values must be agreed upon. Certainly, it is far more important to find a place in which your family can live comfortably and happily, with a certain amount of privacy for each of you, than it is to squeeze into a too-small space for the sake of a chic neighborhood. Today more than ever sacrifices for status symbols are ridiculous.

If your husband becomes tense at the very thought of commuting, then perhaps the two of you should sit down and analyze the situation to find out whether city living is possible for you. Do you enjoy it enough to make the sacrifices it demands worthwhile? And, frankly, can you afford it? That old rule of spending 25 percent of your income on housing doesn't hold these days; unfortunately, city rents are astronomical and going higher. It is less and less often possible to find your place at your price.

Can you find an apartment to rent that is big enough and well enough located to fit your family? Are you lucky enough to have a nest egg you can invest in buying an apartment— either a cooperative, in which case you own the apartment and pay a monthly maintenance charge subject to the direction and approval of a tenants' committee, or a condominium which you own outright and may sell or sublet as you please, but for which you are still obligated to share the expense of building upkeep? A condominium can be bought for as little as 10 percent down. In the case of a cooperative, on the other hand, you must pay the full purchase price in cash, unless you unearth the rare owner who is willing to set up time payments. The only rarer bird is the one who owns a town house in reasonable condition that he is willing to sell at a price you can afford—even *with* mortgage money. (Incidentally, if you do buy a house, don't forget a little item known as "closing costs." On a $50,000 house, it can amount to as much as $2,000 extra. This includes legal and surveyor's fees, title guarantee, mortgage insurance, and miscellaneous taxes.)

Whether it's financially better for you to rent or to buy an apartment will depend on real estate values in your own city. Your lawyer or accountant will have to advise you about that. But if you have a choice, I think there is a psychological advantage to owning an apartment rather than renting one. When you buy a co-op, you are making a fairly permanent commitment—it's comparable to owning a house in the country. You can knock down walls or put them up, install a whole new kitchen, build in bookcases—you not only can but probably will do several of these things because you are making the place more attractive to live in, and you are enhancing the value of your own property. But when you rent an apartment, you won't make any structural changes because the landlord has the right to make you change everything back again when you leave. This involves what the agents call a signed "treaty" that goes with your lease. Generally, you're required to return the place "broom-clean and in its original condition"—which is to say with all holes, cracks, and smears caused by anything you've hung up or screwed in repaired. Anything you've "installed"—built-in bookcases, dishwasher, *anything*—belongs to the landlord. You can't take it with you unless you have specific permission. (*N.B.* Window air conditioners, while they can't be used without the management's permission, are not considered "installations" and therefore may be moved freely.) So unless you have a fifteen-year lease (unheard of and unobtainable), you're not going to spend your money that way. After all, who knows? You might want to move out in three years. If you're lucky enough to find an apartment that suits you perfectly when you move in, fine and dandy. But unlikely. And maybe it's my acquisitive nature, but I personally like the feeling that the four walls my children are systematically destroying belong to me, not to some omnipotent and equally acquisitive corporation.

what to look for

In looking for an apartment, what questions should you ask? Whether it's a cooperative or a rental, what services are provided? Generally, the list includes garbage removal, heat, water and, in some modern buildings, electricity, gas, and air conditioning. Other managements even provide window washing. Will yours repaint when your lease is up or at specific intervals? Will they repaper or give you an allowance toward paper if you prefer it to paint? Will they contribute so much per room if you want to use your own painters instead of theirs? If so, my advice is to take the allowance whenever it's offered, because house painters and paper hangers hired on a contract basis are too limited both as to quality of materials and time allowed to do a really good job. You should be able to do better on your own—but be prepared to pay more than you will be allowed. If appliances break down and need to be repaired or replaced, who pays? Again, in the interest of efficiency, I would suggest you arrange for the repairs or replacements, but if it's the landlord's responsibility, he should pay a fair share of the cost. Sometimes he can save you money on a new appliance by getting it at the wholesale price. If it is a cooperative building, you should be especially clear about what you are responsible for and what the building will do.

You should check to make sure the wiring is adequate for any extra appliances you might want to install. How about air conditioners? Will they fit into the windows easily? (Casement windows present special problems.) And how soundproof are the walls and ceilings? The only sure way to find out is to make several visits at different times of day. Any big apartment building built in the twenties is probably pretty soundproof. Some buildings built in the thirties are okay, too, but anything built after that—well, the acoustics are fabulous! You can tell when your neighbors are showering, when their baby is crying or dropping marbles; sometimes you even run to answer what turns out to be their phone. If there is no washer or dryer in the apartment itself, is there a well-equipped laundry room in the basement? And is there a storage room where you can stash baby carriages, bikes, and other bulky items you're not using?

Some buildings give you the protection of doormen and elevators operated by humans rather than buttons. And the best-managed buildings not only have service cars, but someone to run them as well. Service entrances and traffic arrangements are especially important. A friend of ours who bought an apartment in a very fashionable new building designed by one of the world's foremost architects didn't realize until too late that there was no service door. So in her splendid expensive apartment, garbage must go out through the living room. It is not an ideal arrangement.

suburbs

On the other hand, if you and your husband both prefer the country to city living and he doesn't mind commuting, you have no problem. Having decided on the suburbs, the question becomes "which"? Obviously, many things will influence your final choice of a place. How accessible is it to your husband's work? How about train service? Or, if he prefers commuting by car, how good are the roads and how bad is the traffic? Can you expect to be plowed out reasonably soon after a big snow? What about school buses? And speaking of schools, how good are they? Is there a well-staffed, modern hospital nearby? Where are the churches and synagogues? How close are stores? Does the town offer recreation the whole family can enjoy? Is it the kind of place where you have to join "the Club" (and how do you feel about clubs)? Do you like the sound of the people, the look of the country?

When you're planning a permanent move, I think it is

house talk

enormously important not to commit yourselves by buying a house or a piece of land until you have learned, by living there, whether or not you are going to be happy in a specific community. Two townships near us in Connecticut help prove my point. Both are on Long Island Sound and are separated geographically by only a few miles, but their life styles are light years apart. One has the delightful quiet charm of a town that has changed almost not at all over the years. It is tight-knit socially, politically conservative, and, I suspect, not very cordial to newcomers—unless they are well connected. If I were asked for a one-word description, I think I'd call it "exclusive."

The other town swings along very nicely, thank you. New houses are going up constantly; there are marvelous small shops and large shopping centers so tempting that you always spend more than you should. The population is strong on writers, artists, and advertising people who usually welcome new faces and who tend to be liberal in their politics.

Given two such disparate towns so near each other, it is quite possible that a couple, having decided to move into the area, might be shown a house or a piece of property they like and can afford in the wrong town. Buying in haste, they may find themselves committed and utterly miserable.

finding a house

But how do you go about finding the right house and neighborhood for you? Once you have settled on a general area, the real house-hunting begins. Usually, since husbands are involved with office hours and business responsibilities, this turns out to be woman's work. And, since you are the one who must run the machine—the house, that is—this makes sense. Today, through nationwide or international home-locating services, you can even start your search without leaving your former home. Some companies make a business of finding houses in congenial neighborhoods for families who are being transferred to new headquarters. It's all done with a questionnaire to help discover the kind of living you like. Through affiliated local agents, the firm then finds houses that come close to your needs and screens them for your inspection before you arrive on the scene. Since the companies providing this service collect fees from their agents, you pay nothing for their help.

If you're lucky enough to have any friends in the area, you

pay nothing for their help either, and they'll be dying to give it. They may know about houses that are not on the market yet but will be soon, and they'll pass the word along the neighborhood grapevine for you. They can also tell you, better than any real estate broker or impersonal home-locating service, what the good school district is, what the local sentiment is on zoning—all kinds of underground information you can't get anywhere else. The prospect of enticing new blood to any small community seems to bring out the best in the old blood. Even people you don't know very well will be delighted to drive you around from one house to another, or just drive you up and down country roads showing you how pretty it all is.

If you are starting from scratch, get some road maps and drive around on your own to find out which areas appeal to you most, as well as which ones are undesirably close to industrial sections or noisy highways. Then, contact several real estate brokers who handle property in the areas you like, so that as you look you can cross-check their advice about neighborhoods and schools. If you're being transferred, the company your husband works for or a business associate may recommend an agent. Failing personal recommendations, scout the Yellow Pages and newspaper real estate listings for local names and numbers. Follow-up appointments and house-seeing expeditions come next. A good real estate agent can be of tremendous help, saving you legwork and time by sifting out the impossibilities and showing you only houses he honestly thinks may suit you. Although he works basically for the seller, in that the higher the price, the higher his commission, an interested agent can also be enormously helpful to you, not only when it comes to finding a place to live, but in supplying advice on everything local—from painters and gardeners and butchers to tennis clubs and day camps. How do you get him interested? Simply ask him at the start what size house sells best in the area; this tells him right away that he may have you back as a customer within a few years' time, and chances are he will make a special effort to please.

Don't let your dreams soar with the deathless prose you'll read in newspaper ads. Words like "breath-taking," "rambling," and "enchanting" almost always gloss over shaky floors, corroded plumbing, or some such disenchantment. Distrust anything labeled "prestige" or "executive"; the neighborhood may be the best, but the mansion is missing something. And read *all* the words—one, two, three times. It may not be till the third reading that you accurately picture that "parklike half-acre lot."

See if you can locate a house-hunters' guidebook covering the part of the world you are interested in. Local bookstores often sell them, and some considerate corporations, whose executives transfer frequently, even supply copies to employees on the move. The most helpful of these books compare neighboring communities as to schools, shopping, recreation, and so on. They explain town taxes and assessments which could, although your tax rate is higher, result in your paying less than a friend with a comparable house in the next town (the key is assessment ratio).

if you're transfer-ring ...
If yours is a transfer move and you expect to be transferred again within two or three years, you should keep that in mind—not for the sake of profit so much as to avoid loss or difficulty in selling when the time comes. Unromantic as it sounds, this is not the time to shop for your dream house.

Years ago, during World War II, Dick and I decided that we had to move to the country. One dreary March day we were shown a very ugly house that had not been lived in for months. The chill was such that I felt Death clutching at me as we walked through its rooms. Neither of us could wait to get out. It wasn't the house for us. But somehow, by the time we reached home, we had decided to buy it for several excellent reasons. It was cheap; it had the right number of rooms; it was solidly built; and the scale of the rooms would accommodate the furniture we already had. It served us well for eight years.

What you want is a standard house in a stable neighborhood—ideally, a well-financed place with a mortgage you can take over to minimize your cash investment. The best house for you is one that is reasonably right the way it is, probably with four bedrooms rather than three because, in the country, people want to have a guest room. (In the city, a three-bedroom apartment can be just as salable.) Consider location carefully: What looks like a delightful house out in the country may seem inconveniently distant from stores and

13

schools to a buyer two years later. You should keep remodeling to a minimum, and what you do should be the kind of thing that will seem practical to an average family later. Kitchen improvements? a new stove? a freezer? Yes, by all means. They'll enhance the house's value. But this is not the moment to replace all the bathtubs with stall showers, no matter how shower-addicted your family is. There'll be time for all that later when your transferring days are over.

*if it's
a permanent
move ...*

When that time comes, be prepared to keep looking until you unearth a place or places that feel more than just acceptable. This is a time to put living first. Resale becomes unimportant. And until the time comes to move again (which you hope it won't), the only worthwhile return for the money and time and effort you have invested in finding a house is the joy you find in living in it. And that is profit enough.

Ideally, you are looking for a house you might like to own, but one you should rent first with an option to buy if possible. This sort of arrangement works all in the renter's favor: It sets a purchase price you can live with, protects you from rising prices, and leaves you room to negotiate before a final sale. Most important, it gives you a chance to learn the house's charms and drawbacks firsthand by living with them. A year of living in the house during all four seasons gives you time to assess the condition of the roof, fireplaces, and cellar; of weatherstripping, wiring, floors, pipes, and such salient items before you own the house and all its problems.

In the water problem department, I qualify as a veteran. Some years ago when we bought a house in Connecticut, we discovered acute sclerosis in the eight hundred feet of main pipe linking us with the town system—but not until the day we took possession of the house. The merest trickle squeezed through when we turned on the kitchen tap; and when we opened the one in the basement, the tap in the kitchen went completely dry. One gigantic mess and several thousand dollars later, we had learned our lesson: Never again would we buy a house without a thorough examination by disinterested professionals.

*old house
or
new?*

Can an old house be a practical investment? Certainly. To a large family, a big old place often offers room for privacy they could not have otherwise. A house of a certain age has character and, usually, a great deal more charm than newer,

14

house talk

rather jerry-built homes with cardboard walls, tiny rooms, low ceilings, and no halls. (Halls are immensely valuable, especially when they can serve as a sometime buffer between you and the crashing noises of young children.) Many older places lend themselves especially well to remodeling. My example is no less an architectural authority than the late Eero Saarinen, who designed such superb contemporary buildings. He and his wife, Aline, bought a great stucco house in Connecticut because he felt its interiors could be opened up beautifully to create the clean spaces he had in mind. And it worked.

Investigate any house that seems like a serious contender. You can count on friends to be more than eager to share their own horrendous experiences. Town records may list former owners who live in the neighborhood and whose firsthand knowledge could be valuable, but what you need is more professional advice. An architect will judge the present condition of the house and can also suggest improvements. Insurance inspectors are quite candid about structural weak points, and you should have an exterminator check for termites and rodents. Engineering firms throughout the country offer prospective buyers over-all inspection service at a predetermined charge. So even in a new neighborhood, you can find help to count on.

While the experts survey, ask questions of the agent and the owner. Keep a pencil and pad by your bed to jot down thoughts that occur in the night. What's an average winter month's heating bill? Big old places, Victorian ones in particular, are notoriously difficult and expensive to heat. The people who are trying to sell you their house may go all vague on you when you inquire about the oil bills. Look out for answers that begin, "Well, I can't remember exactly, but . . ." or with words like "roughly," "approximately," or "lemme-see-now." If you can track down the people who sold the house to its present owners, you may find out that the atrocious heating bills were part of their motivation for selling it. Where is the well and does it produce enough water? Are there outlets for the garden? Where's the cesspool? "Where's the cesspool?" is a fascinating question. They may tell you it's over the hills and far away or right under the front porch, but no matter where it is, you won't know what condition it's in until it stops working altogether. Then you'll know. And it will be the Fourth of July weekend, when you have a house full of guests.

Not everybody is as stupid as we were when we bought our summer house. We forgot to ask about a cesspool. Everything flushed along merrily for two years, and when we finally had to call in the septic-tank man, we couldn't even tell him where the dumb thing was. Considering the fact that he had two acres of wooded territory to search, he found it pretty quickly (I guess those guys have special divining powers or something) and he fixed it pretty quickly, too, but when we asked him how often we should call him in as a prophylactic measure, he said, "Gee, lady, how should I know? Ya gotta lotta big trees around here, and when them roots start chokin' up the pipes, ya gonna have trouble again."

"But how will I know when the roots are choking up the pipes?" I asked.

"Same way ya knew this time. So when it happens again, call me. Here's my card." The card was a stunner. It had on it his name, his telephone number, his profession, and a slogan: "Your s--t is our bread and butter!"

Try a few tests of your own: Turn on a tap on the top floor to check water pressure . . . and the color of the water. Is it rusty? Ask your plumber to check for galvanized iron pipes, because when the present owners tell you the pipes are copper, that may mean that only some of the pipes are copper. Check the placement of electric outlets, and inspect the cellar for dampness. Is there enough storage space? If not, can you steal room for more?

Sooner or later you will find a place where, in spite of minor jarring notes (unsteady front steps, dreary living room, ancient freezer), you can actually picture yourself, your husband, the children, and related livestock moving in and feeling at home. And that, if you're lucky, is it.

Whatever you do, don't try to lower the price of the house by downgrading it to its owner. Most people come to love their houses the way they love their children—faults and all. I've known people who refused to sell to buyers they felt didn't like the place enough, and others who even took a little less money for their property from a couple whose enthusiasm and affection were obvious.

house talk

If your husband approves, he takes over the business and paperwork while you take a deep breath and prepare to tackle such practical items as remodeling: where? and how much?

Even considering the cost of remodeling and the built-in follies you have to live with, I think most couples moving to the country find that an existing house offers the most practical solution. It is always less expensive to buy than it is to design and build a house of your own, not counting the bonus of landscaping that is part of the bargain when you buy a house that has been lived in and cared for.

However, I love to dream about building. It's my personal and extravagant eccentricity. I delighted in every minute (almost) of the thinking and planning and work that went into our new house in Connecticut, and we've loved living there. But I cannot in good conscience recommend building from the ground up to anyone who has to consider a budget at all seriously. In short, whether you remodel or build from scratch depends on scratch.

In addition to the cost factor, I would like to suggest two other arguments against building your house too soon. As the years pass and your needs change, the ideal adjacencies or relations between the rooms change. When children are small, parents want to be within hearing distance in case of emergencies at night, but when the children become teenagers, they don't want to be all that close to their parents, and the parents will probably enjoy the peace and quiet of the distance that separates them. Also, if you are building a house, the essential requirement is that you and your husband know and agree on the type and size of the house it's going to be. This will be far easier if you have had the experience of living with other people's mistakes. No matter whether you plan to build or to buy in the future, keep notes on the features you've liked in the houses you've lived in. It is equally important to remember the things that looked good at first but simply didn't work out. Then, when you finally plan your own house, you will be able to avoid some of the pitfalls.

There are, it's true, developments where you can buy land and order a house from a builder's stock plans. You save on design costs, and you can make minor changes to suit your tastes and needs. But to me, this system offers all the headaches of building (the delivery delays, material changes, the waiting) , with none of the creative satisfaction and none of the real excitement of ending with a house that is uniquely yours.

neighbor-hood

However, if this sort of scheme seems to fill your needs best, do check up on the builder before you commit yourselves. It should be relatively simple to get references from people in the neighborhood whose houses he has built. Find out how they have stood up and how dependable he is when maintenance problems arise. Make sure all the materials and equipment to be used are clearly described in the contract. And have someone experienced in the field advise you before you sign anything.

do you need an architect?

You can usually make minor remodeling changes with the help of a good contractor. But if you are building from the ground up or if your remodeling is extensive, and if you can interest an architect in it, he can be immensely helpful in making and carrying out plans. (I say "if" because architects today can make so much more money working on large office buildings that they seldom take on small private projects.) An architect knows construction—what walls can go and which must stay—and the newest materials. More important, his imagination is finely tuned. Where you may see only one way to use a space, he may see two. Often he will find a method of making a single area do several jobs. Not the least of his talents is creating storage space where none existed. He cares about visual harmony, which isn't really what a contractor is trained to do. He can plan for the future —not only by suggesting the groundwork that will make additional improvements less costly, but also by designing spaces whose function can change with the years (a child's bedroom becomes a den; an attic, a guest room) .

finding an architect

How do you go about finding an architect? If you're planning to build your own house, you do a lot of looking—at photographs in magazines, architectural trade journals, museums, and libraries. You buy books on contemporary architecture, and you keep your eyes and ears open for news of new houses you might be able to see. A call to the local chapter of the American Institute of Architects outlining your ideas and needs can put you in touch with several likely people.

If you have a tight budget and are adventurous, you might do what some young friends of ours did. Having bought a big barn and considerable country acreage, they had dreams of a ski and summer house, but no money to spend on architects. In fact, their budget ruled out professional labor wherever willing and reasonably capable amateur hands could do the work. Still, they didn't want to settle for anything conventional. So, on a whim, they wrote the director of an excellent college of architecture near them. Their description of their house and hopes caught the imagination of three young students who not only took on the design project, but followed through by doing a lot of the physical work themselves. They were paid for their labor, but the costs were way below what the owners would have had to pay ordinarily. And the results were charming and extraordinary enough to rate national magazine photographs and a feature in *The New York Times*.

When you find an architect whose work you like, make an appointment to meet him and discuss your plans. From the very beginning you should feel a special kind of rapport. Since a house is such a personal thing, this is a time to judge with your feelings as well as your head. He must be someone you like and whose basic approach is the same as yours. And of course he must be eager to do your job. (If he dreams of building museums, he will be bored doing over your garage.) Do you both feel that design should follow function? Or should you decide on the outside appearance and make the interior space conform? If your house is to be successful, you and your architect will be spending a great deal of time together, discussing every phase of your life. Is he easy to talk to? Is he sympathetic? Do you and he agree about the way a house should work? Do you feel he will stay interested and really care about the job until the last detail is completed? And does he live near enough to the site to be able to supervise progress closely?

I would be wary of a "name" architect; a man whose style and reputation are established is more likely to be guided by his own theories and tastes than by your personal preferences and prosaic needs. The result might easily be a house that is more recognizably his than yours, one into which your family must fit rather than one built to fit your family. The other possibility is that he will turn the whole project over to a junior member of his staff whose work may or may not resemble what you had in mind. The more prominent the man, the less you will be involved in the actual planning. For some people, this would be ideal. But I would have been miserable not taking an active part in the work on our house, and we would have been miserable living in a place that bore more marks of a given architect's style than our own. We were very lucky. We already knew our architect—John Stonehill, a brilliantly talented young man who is a cousin of mine. Not yet famous, he had designed some exciting buildings and he was enthusiastic about working with us. The relationship between client and architect frequently ends unhappily, but Dick and I love the house John designed for us, and we still love John. What more can I say?

choosing a contractor

Your contractor should not only be a man whose work you like, but also someone you trust. It is possible that your architect will know someone he works well with. Neighborhood friends or your real estate agent may be able to make suggestions. Failing these, there's the classified directory to give you a starting list.

In any case, your best source of information will be the people he has already done work for. Call or write them to ask how his work has stood up and how pleasant he is to deal with. Once the project is complete, will he continue to be easy to reach and cooperative when you call? Does he stand behind the materials and equipment he has supplied? Are his charges fair? If you are satisfied with the answers to all these questions, and your architect, if you have one, okays your choice, you have found your man.

But don't start the work without getting every possible detail and responsibility spelled out on paper: the jobs to be done, the materials to be used, the cost. And while things are in progress, if extras are added (and they always are) have the documents amended to show the changes on paper. But keep additions to an absolute minimum. Not only are they expensive, but they cause delays.

Try to arrange for a contract clause that sets a penalty if completion is late. (I don't know why I say "if"—the word is "when.") Then make it stick if you can, but realize that as long as you want and need the house he is working on, any builder has you over a barrel. You can cry; you can plead and cajole and scream. You can also pray a lot. But it isn't likely to help. The only effective speed-up scheme I have ever known calls for moving into the unfinished house at the earliest possible moment and applying pressure from there.

But that comes later.

Building a house is tantamount to giving Dracula a free swipe at your throat every night for a year. Go back and reread my mother's pages on finding an architect. The John Stonehills are rare. Unless you're related to him, too, finding his equivalent will take you six months of active research. *Active!* That means phoning, reading, writing, interviewing —who's got the time? Maybe my mother, because her children are out of the way and she happens to be a super-efficient woman, but you haven't got that kind of time. You want to cry and plead and cajole and scream at the washing machine repairman, the phone company, your children, your local P-TA board *and a builder?!* May I presume to tell you you do not? Later, maybe, but not now.

remodeling

First, you've got plans to make—probably for remodeling a house that already exists. It is rare to find an existing house or apartment that, without any changes whatever, suits your family life exactly. Chances are the place you finally settle on will have been built for other people, for another era, and for another way of life—that once-upon-a-time when butlers polished silver in their pantries and maids' rooms had real maids in them. Old houses are often well built and appealingly roomy (sometimes they're also appallingly gloomy). But that very appealing roominess can, if not redesigned for today's uses, make them inefficient and difficult to live in. So almost certainly you'll have some remodeling to do.

I've had a good deal of experience in remodeling houses, both for ourselves and for clients in my professional life as a decorator. And I know that, whether it's a house or an apartment, the first essential step is for you and your husband to sit down and decide what you really would like to do —what you'd like to keep and what to change. Let your minds wander through the fields of "I wish we had . . ." A family room? A sewing room? An all-new kitchen? Desk space for a study area near the kitchen? Parking space for strollers, bikes, and other such bulky objects? Obviously,

21

house talk

some apartments and some houses are more flexible than others. But dreams don't cost anything, and some of them even come true.

exteriors of country houses

Sometimes it happens that a house has everything going for it, but its exterior is unattractive. Don't despair. Improvements can often be made with quite simple measures. Your aim is much the same as that of a woman who tries through the skillful use of make-up to emphasize her best features and play down her worst.

It may be possible to give a house a fresh look by removing a lot of the gingerbread that has been added over the years —by taking off a porch, adding shutters, giving it a handsome new front door. In suburban and rural areas, houses are often made of wood. But wood or brick, stucco or brownstone, color is your best friend or your worst enemy. Changing the color of the house is certainly easy enough to do. White, gray, or pale yellow houses leave you free to use any number of colors for contrast in the doors and shutters. And window boxes planted with evergreens for winter and successively blooming flowers from spring through fall can do a great deal.

Our first house in Connecticut, built around 1920 (a particularly ugly vintage) was white clapboard with a red tile roof, a large porch, and a porte-cochere. We painted the roof and shutters black, which was a big improvement, but the cost of tearing down the porch and porte-cochere made that idea impractical. Besides, we learned to love them in spite of their looks because they were functional. In summertime, the porch provided shade that kept the downstairs rooms cool. And in the winter, the porch and the porte-cochere sheltered us from snow and rain while we were getting in or out of the car. Besides, it was pleasant to be able to go outside for a little of that fine crisp cold New England air without having to put on boots.

landscaping

Landscaping, too, can do a great deal for a country house, especially around the entrance or approach where planting can be designed to draw your eye away from the house's weak architectural features. But it should be considered early. Otherwise, what may be only a large budget item becomes an enormous one. Terrace planting costs more if you've neglected to leave holes for it and to provide for drainage in your original plans. Outdoor lighting bills escalate if you don't make advance provision for wiring.

Whether or not you consult a landscape architect will depend on how big the job is. Unearthing the right person involves roughly the same steps as finding a man to design your house: first, recommendations of friends, or finding out who has planned a garden you've liked, then visits to places where he has already worked. If your garden is small, you'll probably do your own designing with the help of a good local nursery man. Decide what you want to do. Are you trying to provide privacy or do you want to plant a specimen tree as a focal point? In either case, one thing to guard against is the temptation to have everything burst into full-scale full bloom *now*. Trees and shrubs don't work that way. Mature specimens are difficult and expensive to transplant, and all things need room to make themselves at home, space to breathe and grow in. Planting too many full-grown plants too close to your house or to each other results in choking, dying, and eventual replacements—none of which is fun or cheap. On top of all that, your house will grow darker as the trees grow larger until it is actually gloomy—a process so gradual you may not even be aware of it.

exteriors of town houses

In cities, some of the handsomest town houses have had their façades lifted. A Victorian house can be made to look completely contemporary, and there are many architectural firms that specialize in this kind of work. Window boxes of greens are a special treat on city streets, and there are some hardy blooms that manage to grow in spite of the soot.

Newspapers and magazines are constantly doing stories (complete with "before" and "after" pictures) about houses that have been restored or restyled, and they may give you ideas. However, even if the outside of the house you love is invincibly ugly, you can still live happily in it by concentrating on its good points inside.

exterior halls in apartments

There's not much you can do about the ugly exterior of an apartment building (except to complain to the management, which will get you nowhere), but if you have your own private, or semiprivate elevator hall, there is something you can do about that. Elevator halls are often ugly for two reasons: 1) They have no windows in them, and they are illuminated by five-watt bulbs stuck in the ceiling. Very depressing. 2) They've been painted Coney Island Mustard, and not recently, either. The tile on the floor matches the paint. The doors are dark brown or psychiatrist green. They have no furniture in them—not even a table for mail.

But for very little money, you can change all this. Good lighting, bright paint or washable wallpaper; an inexpensive table with an ashtray on it (I've seen ordinarily considerate people put out cigarettes on the floor—they wouldn't do it in your apartment, but the elevator hall apparently isn't the same thing) ; a couple of bright prints on the wall, and maybe an indoor-outdoor carpet. If you have a neighbor, check with her about your plans; she'll probably love the idea, she just never got around to it. And since she never got around to it, she's not going to be too opinionated about the decorating scheme. Furthermore, she'll split the cost with you (maybe) and if she doesn't, it's still worth it because these halls are never very big anyway. (I may take my own advice. What I just described with the Coney Island Mustard is my own entrance hall, and it puts me down every time I take the elevator!)

planning structural changes

No matter how large or small the inside job, get yourself a floor plan and look at all its areas with an open mind and a fresh eye. If no such plan exists, you'll have to make your own, using graph paper, measuring exactly, and drawing to scale. Yes, it's a lot of work, but it really is worth it. Look for all the unused spaces and see what they can do for you. Take a "mental walk" through the rooms and see how you like the arrangement.

The diagrammatic plans on pages 26–33 for the living-dining areas of old New York apartments illustrate the problems in old houses as well. The "befores" show space originally designed for a household with two or three live-in servants; the "afters," the way it might be used by a family today. What you do with the space depends on what you need. Is it more sleeping space for the children? Do you want a family room instead of the dining room on the original plan? Would you like an informal dining area off the kitchen? Or play space for the children?

As you'll see on these floor plans, many of the things you might like to do can be accomplished with a few simple shifts. These days a butler's pantry, which almost always lies between the kitchen and the dining room, is usually expendable. Where it once served as a buffer between servants and family, now it merely isolates the lady of the housework. It is a good idea to keep one maid's room and bath for come-in help to change clothes and it's wonderful for a child with a sick roommate or for an unexpected overnight visitor. The other maid's room (or rooms) might become children's rooms, or storerooms for seasonal clothing and sports equipment, or a sewing room-laundry much closer and more convenient than one in the cellar.

multiple-purpose rooms

Not so long ago, a dining room was a dining room and a living room was a living room, and the two never met. But a room that is simply and solely dedicated to eating seems to me a great waste of space and an anachronism today. Multiple-purpose rooms make more sense. The trick is to plan combinations that suit your particular way of life. For some families, a kitchen-dining room is the answer. Others would rather keep cooking separate and set aside part of the living room for eating. The best plans are made by putting down everything you dream of having, then shifting and re-shifting, pairing and re-pairing to find the combinations that do most for you. You won't be able to squeeze in every single thing you'd like. But I think you'll find that beginning this way, you can have a great deal more than you thought possible at first.

possibilities and limits

Structure imposes limits, but probably not as many as you'd think. Some walls do hold the house up, while others can be eliminated. (When in doubt, ask your contractor which are which—falling ceilings are embarrassing.) In the kitchen areas of these plans, I have suggested moving sinks only when there is existing plumbing in the new location. And I have taken advantage of every jog I could find to create extra storage space. The possibilities are infinite, and almost always you will end with a more attractive and efficient space than you had before.

Local ordinances also lay down rules. Be sure to find out what they are and meet their requirements because ignoring them can mean costly changes and inevitable delay.

When you've done your dreaming, it's time to get together with an architect and/or contractor and find out how much of what you hope to do can actually be accomplished—

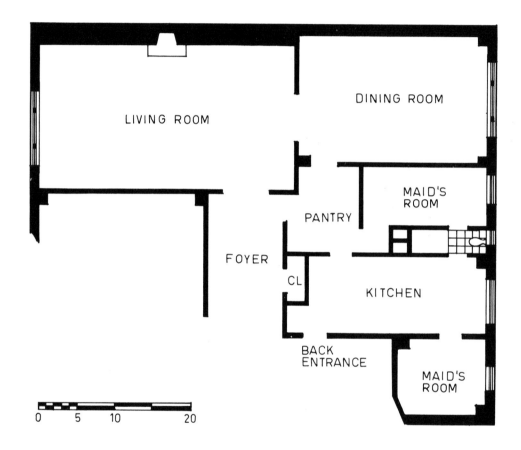

LIVING ROOM

DINING ROOM

MAID'S ROOM

PANTRY

FOYER

CL

KITCHEN

BACK ENTRANCE

MAID'S ROOM

0　5　10　　　20

PLAN A

original

In Alternate 1 for Plan A, one maid's room and the pantry have been eliminated to provide a large family room–dining room.

In Alternate 2 for Plan A, one maid's room and the pantry have been eliminated to provide an informal dining area in the kitchen and space for laundry equipment.

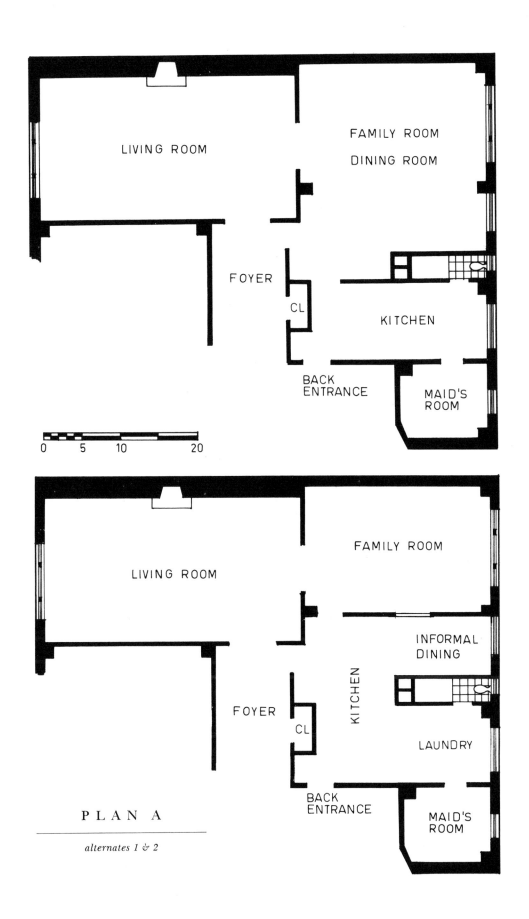

LIVING ROOM

FAMILY ROOM

DINING ROOM

FOYER

CL

KITCHEN

BACK
ENTRANCE

MAID'S
ROOM

0   5   10   20

LIVING ROOM

FAMILY ROOM

INFORMAL
DINING

FOYER

CL

KITCHEN

LAUNDRY

BACK
ENTRANCE

MAID'S
ROOM

PLAN A

alternates 1 & 2

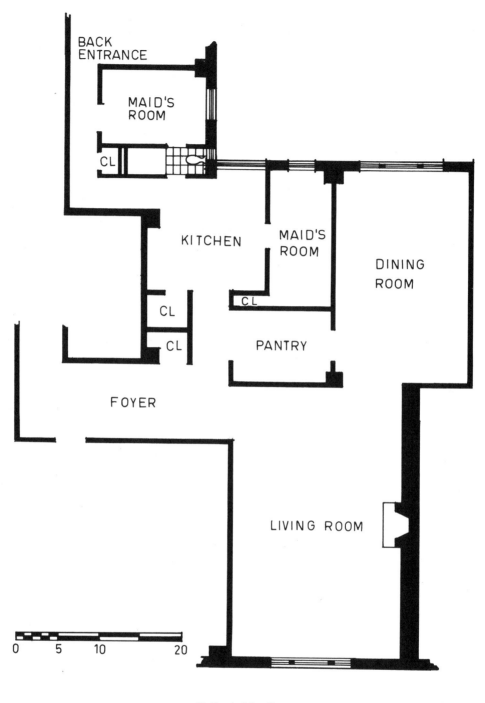

BACK
ENTRANCE

MAID'S
ROOM

CL

KITCHEN

MAID'S
ROOM

DINING
ROOM

CL

CL

CL

PANTRY

FOYER

LIVING ROOM

0   5   10   20

PLAN B

original

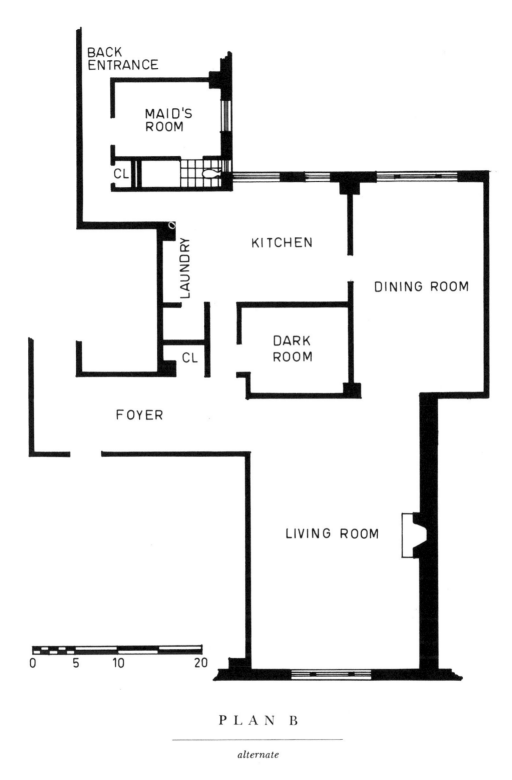

BACK ENTRANCE

MAID'S ROOM

CL

LAUNDRY

CL

KITCHEN

DINING ROOM

DARK ROOM

FOYER

LIVING ROOM

0   5   10   20

PLAN B

alternate

By eliminating one maid's room in the original Plan B, the kitchen has been enlarged to ensure enough space for laundry equipment. A door has been cut through to the dining room. The pantry has been converted into a darkroom by closing it in and installing a door for access from the foyer or kitchen.

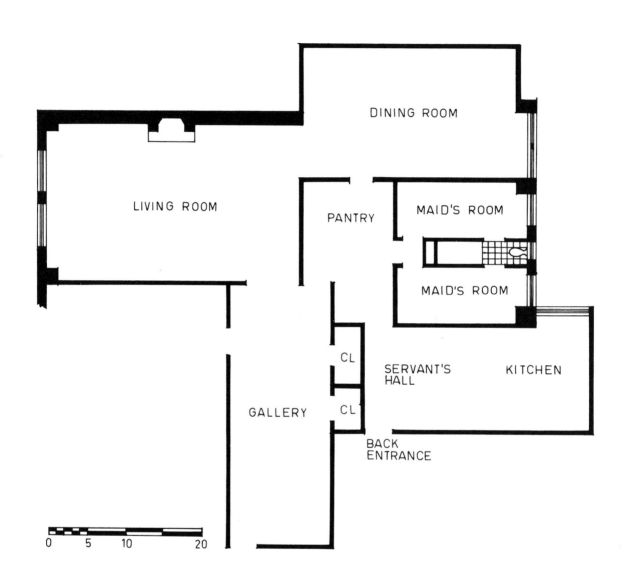

DINING ROOM

LIVING ROOM

PANTRY

MAID'S ROOM

MAID'S ROOM

CL

SERVANT'S
HALL

KITCHEN

CL

GALLERY

BACK
ENTRANCE

0   5   10   20

PLAN C

original

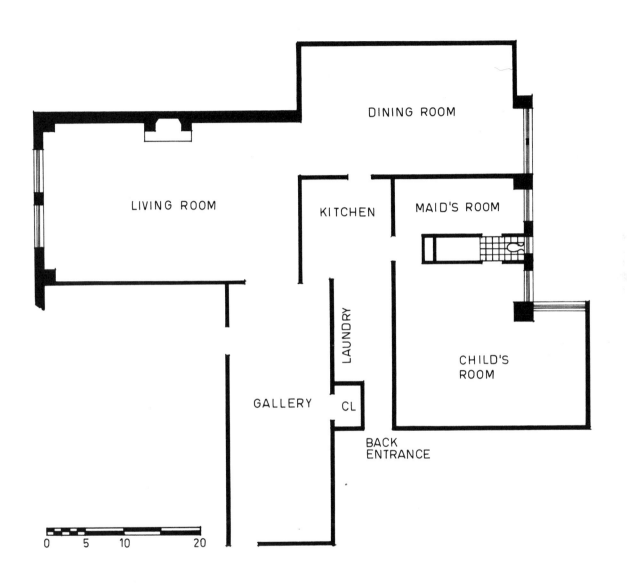

DINING ROOM

LIVING ROOM

KITCHEN

MAID'S ROOM

LAUNDRY

GALLERY

CL

CHILD'S ROOM

BACK ENTRANCE

0   5   10   20

PLAN C

alternate

By eliminating one maid's room in the original Plan C, a large room for a child has been created.
The pantry has been converted into the kitchen.

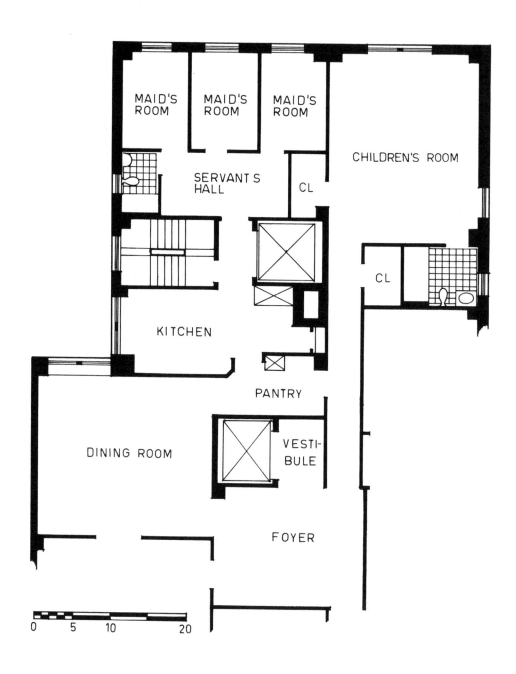

MAID'S ROOM

MAID'S ROOM

MAID'S ROOM

CHILDREN'S ROOM

SERVANTS HALL

CL

CL

KITCHEN

PANTRY

DINING ROOM

VESTI-BULE

FOYER

0   5   10   20

PLAN D

original

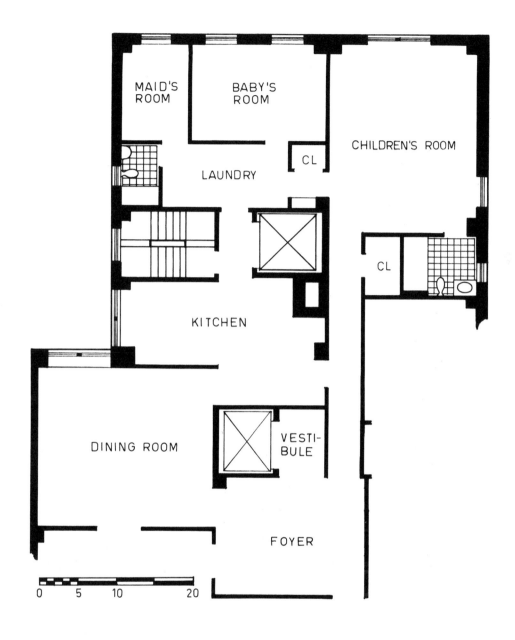

MAID'S ROOM

BABY'S ROOM

CHILDREN'S ROOM

CL

LAUNDRY

CL

KITCHEN

DINING ROOM

VESTI-BULE

FOYER

0   5   10   20

PLAN D

alternate

In Plan D, by removing a wall between two maid's rooms and closing off one of the doors, a good-sized room for a child has been made possible. The former servants' hall becomes an ideal area for laundry equipment. A doorway has been cut through a closet to provide access to the children's room. Elimination of the pantry space enlarges the kitchen.

what's possible and what you can afford. If you are planning to do a radical remodeling job, you'll get best results with the help of both an architect and a contractor. Firms that manage buildings can often recommend competent people.

If the work to be done is practical rather than aesthetic, a good contractor should be able to handle it. He will know what's possible and what isn't, and he will also know the best subcontractors for your job. But his absolutely essential skill is coordination: scheduling the comings and goings of the electricians, the carpenters, plumbers and others in the proper order, a feat that is beyond even a super-average lay-man. Finally, when the contracts are signed, *he* is responsible for seeing that everything is done as it should be. Carpenters, electricians—all the specialists—report to him. And when, as always happens, a dispute arises as to who is responsible for a problem, he copes. You have only one person to deal with.

remodeling "musts"

To some degree, you will be limited by the amount you have to spend. And inevitably, the moment comes when you have to decide what can be postponed and what should most sensibly be done right away. When you are remodeling, I urge you not to delay work that you might consider "op-tional," but which will eventually have to be done and which will cost more in money and inconvenience if it is put off. Frequently it entails doing additional plastering and painting, which means more plaster dust, more splattering and more nuisance—not to mention the expense. So, install plumbing lines for appliances you expect to buy; repair cracked walls; provide extra electrical lines and outlets where you think they will be needed. Installing a good system of lightning rods will probably reduce your fire insur-ance premiums. In many parts of the country, air condition-ing is no longer thought of as a luxury; if you plan to have a central system someday, have the ducts built in even if you don't install the machinery. Fixing ill-fitting windows and doors should be listed with the "musts," too. Apart from the noise they make shivering in the wind, they let in draughts and, in cities, that very special brand of oily dust—thereby adding considerably to maintenance and cleaning problems. Most serious of all, they keep heating or cooling systems from working efficiently. (Obviously, I'm assuming that horrors like needing a new roof, having to get rid of termites, rewir-

house talk

ing the electrical system to remove fire hazards, having to replace the furnace or the main water pipes do *not* come under the heading of "optional" and that you have very sensibly included their cost when you started out on this project.)

professional advice

Let the professionals advise you, of course, about engineering matters and any technical points you may not understand. Consult them about the amount of heating or cooling and ventilation you'll need and the electric power supply required to operate all the pieces of equipment you want. The professionals are the technical experts, but you are the expert on arrangement. So don't hesitate to tell them how you want things.

Now is the time for me to remind you that in the midst of this bewildering array of structural and mechanical possibilities, you may not *know* what you want! My mother recommends taking a mental walk through the new rooms before you do anything else. I've tried that. I am a mental paraplegic. On the assumption that there are more of me than my mother around, may I suggest that you approach the remodeling enigma in the following fashion:

1. Try the mental walking anyway—it can't hurt—and then if you still can't make a list of what you would like, make a list of what you find inconvenient in your present house.

2. Call in a contractor and tell him what you don't want. The only other information he has to have is the number of big appliances you want now and eventually. Tell him to come back in a week with a blueprint and an estimate, and let him know you're getting comparative estimates.

Before he returns,

3. Call in another contractor and repeat step two.

4. Repeat step three.

5. Now you're beginning to get somewhere! You've seen three estimates and three plans. Contractor #1 has a couple of nice ideas, but he can't begin work for six weeks. Contractor #2

has a lot of nice ideas, but his is a small retail outfit, and he marks up instead of down on the appliances. Contractor #3 also has nice ideas, but he calls you Mary (or Honey or Helen), calls you up in the middle of dinner and smokes cigars. The price is right, though, so how do you decide? Here's how:

6. No one plan is perfect, but now that you've seen all three, you suddenly have a clear picture of what you want: It turns out to be a little bit of this and a little bit of that and by combining the best features of #1, #2 and #3, you've got it. Contractors do not consider this practice dishonest or unfair. As long as you don't actually show one man's blueprint to another, they take it for granted that you are comparing plans as well as estimates.

7. Since the best plan is no longer a factor, you only have to decide on the man. Can you wait six weeks for #1? You definitely don't want #2—he's a waste of money. So #3 is probably your best bet. If he understands and likes your little amalgamated creation (by now, it's really and truly more yours than anyone else's), never mind his personality; it's not like an architect who's around for a couple of years. As a matter of fact, I began to get rather fond of our #3, and what do I really care if he calls me Mary—it's my name, isn't it? Besides, I got a great kitchen out of him, and I actually contributed a few original ideas of my very own.

kitchens   In any building or remodeling, the kitchen is the most important and costliest part of the job. But for most women (who spend so much time there these days) an efficient kitchen is worth every penny invested in it. Here, again, start with paper and pencil. Then do some mental walking: Imagine yourself at work cooking a meal. Go through all the steps you would take in fixing a casserole or baking bread. What do you use for each? In what order do you use the sink, the counter, the refrigerator, the freezer, the stove? I like a chopping block next to the sink so I can sweep the crumbs directly into it. If you want a chopping block, be sure you put it on the side best for you. (Are you right- or left-handed?) Is there a heatproof surface next to the oven where you can put down a heavy roast while you carve it? How about a counter next to the refrigerator? In fact, is there enough counter space, and are the cabinets adequate? Have you left wall space for a can opener and paper towel holders? I like both near the sink. There is a very expensive, set-in-the-wall paper towel, wax paper, and aluminum foil dispenser on the market now. Your kitchen man will try to sell it to you on the grounds that it saves space and looks nicer than the old-fashioned paper towel rack. This may be true, but it doesn't accommodate extra fat paper towel rolls or extra long rolls of foil which you end up stuffing in a drawer somewhere. There is also a very expensive mixer-blender that kitchen designers like to recommend. Its electric insides are embedded in your counter, which means if they break, you are in for a lot of trouble—major carpentry and a gaping hole for months. Also no mixer-blender. Don't get it!

Putting all these things down on paper may seem like an enormous waste of time while you're doing it, but it will do wonders to clarify your thinking. It will show you where to fit your appliances into your scaled floor plan. And this, I firmly believe, is the single most helpful thing you can do to insure yourself an efficient kitchen.

When it comes to getting plans on paper officially, resist any changes that don't make operational sense to you, but which will, for example, "put all the tall things together" or "give you a nice center island" (maybe, like me, you'd rather have a good old-fashioned kitchen table than a range in the middle of the floor). A small desk with a phone is a great help in a kitchen—you can order groceries and check bills while you are waiting for something to bake. And, if possible, put up a few shelves for cookbooks. For the enormous forty-cup percolator, tall vases, thermos bottles, big soda bottles, you'll need a couple of tall cabinets; and for storing trays, carving boards and platters, a cabinet with narrow vertical partitions.

While it is quite possible that you won't be able to afford to install all the equipment you'd like to have at the very start, don't let this stop you from planning the space and installing the power and plumbing to take care of them eventually. Let the contractor know how many electric outlets you will need and where you want them. Work of this kind done after you're all settled in and using your kitchen is nothing but mess, confusion and cost. So if you should decide that for the moment a washing machine and dryer are more important to you than a dishwasher, have them put in, but provide the electric outlet and plumbing for the dishwasher and leave the space you have allotted for it empty. (Give it a false front of plywood for the time being. Paint it to match the cabinets; you'll lose the missing-tooth look.) When the dishwasher comes, you'll be ready for it.

Let your contractor know about your personal likes and dislikes. If you have a favorite kind of work surface, tell him. If you are above average height, would you like your counter tops and work table raised? If you are small, make sure that the wall cabinets won't be placed so high that you will only be able to reach the bottom shelves. And if you, like me, think fluorescent light does terrible things to both food and people, specify incandescent light only. Now is the time to say what you want and stick to it.

major appliances

Choosing the major appliances you'll be living with for years is a very important business, especially if you are going to be doing most of the work yourself. Start by combing the market to discover exactly what is available and what stoves and ovens and refrigerators and washers have learned to do since the last time you shopped for them. Then, having digested all the miraculous promises, investigate performances—not only by talking to friends about their equipment, but by reading all the objective research material you can find. (Magazines that accept advertising tend to recommend advertisers' products, although they're not always the best.) It is also important to ask about the speed and competence of authorized service people in your area.

Decide what you really want each appliance to do for you. Today when equipment is programmed for more and more sophisticated functions, I refuse to buy any machine unless *I* feel up to *its* intellectual standards. I am put off by extravagant advertising. In highly competitive markets, companies far too often make totally unjustified claims about the talents of their brain children. And two months later when you complain because none of it is true, they will cheerfully admit that they have discontinued the model or product because—as you said—it's no good. But you've already paid the bill, and just try getting them to give you a replacement! This happened to me last year and, would you believe it, it even also happened to my *mother*. (We both got the same new floor covering at the same time). So . . . it may hurt your credit rating a little, but wait a while before you pay the bill. And before you make a final commitment, ask the dealer for the names of satisfied customers with whom you can talk. You may save yourself considerable frustration and expense.

appliance priorities

In the large appliance department, a good dependable washer and a trusty dryer probably come first on any family list. I'd steer clear of washer-dryer combinations until they are more thoroughly proven—their works are so complicated that they are subject to frequent nervous breakdowns, and service men loathe them. What's more, if one function breaks down, you've lost both till repairs are made on the ailing cycle. The best reason for not buying a washer-dryer combination is that it won't wash and dry at the same time. In a big family with children—and a great deal of laundry —this makes quite a difference.

placing equipment

These days the placement of equipment is worth a good bit of thought. Obviously, if you have a choice when it comes to placing noisy appliances like dishwashers, dryers or garbage disposers, avoid putting them on the wall common to the dining or living room. Years ago, when Monday was washday and everything had to be dried in the yard, washing equipment was relegated to the basement where it would be out of the way the rest of the week. Now, thanks to indoor dryers and no-iron sheets, shirts, tablecloths and pants, the laundry almost does itself—in daily loads. Soiled clothes don't accumulate. (Incidentally, you don't have to stock such stacks of clothes and linens as you once did.) Whether you live in a house or an apartment, you may want to promote your washer and dryer to a place near the kitchen or even— if you can plan or find space for them—near the bedrooms where most of their work originates and to which clean sheets, towels and clothes have to be returned.

Yes, yes, you absolutely would want to promote your washer-dryer to the kitchen. Apartment basement laundry facilities have about forty terrible things the matter with them. Here are just a few: The machines are ancient and don't work very well; they devour your dimes and quarters, and you'll spend half the day running to the corner drugstore for more change because the elevator men don't have any or don't want to give it to you; the other half of your day will be spent waiting your turn to use the no-good machines or waiting for your wash to get done (you don't dare go back upstairs because if you're not there when it's finished, some considerate soul will take it out for you and dump it on the floor).

You can avoid all of these problems by doing the laundry yourself at five a.m. (the corner drugstore won't be open— maybe your kids' piggy banks have some hard currency), but if I were you, I'd make a place for the equipment somewhere in the apartment. A combination washer-sideboard in the dining room? A dryer-dressing table in the bathroom? Anything as long as it's not downstairs somewhere.

In my book, the next most useful big appliance is a freezer —a vertical one, please, or as large a refrigerator-freezer as you can fit into your kitchen. If you can't have it in the kitchen, it won't be nearly as useful. Whether or not you like to cook, if you like to entertain friends, it can be your greatest help. And even if you don't care about entertaining, you and your family still have to eat.

A small freezer in the kitchen is worth two down a flight of stairs. Frankly, it was only a few years ago when our freezer first moved upstairs that I found out what a joy it could be. It is true that for it to give you its best, you must be willing to give it some thoughtful planning, but the rewards are tremendous. And in a later chapter, I'll tell you some of the things I've learned that have so endeared this piece of equipment to me.

Next on my list of priorities would come the dishwasher, and then I would opt for a self-cleaning oven. They do come built into stoves, but if space permits, I would choose the built-in-the-wall kind plus separate surface burners because it leaves you free to place the components where they can be most helpful. Electric ovens and gas surface burners seem an ideal combination to me because I like the flexibility of having two kinds of fuel for cooking. (And, in the country, an electrical storm won't leave you starving.) If you can, avoid the type of stove that has one of its ovens above the burners. Reaching across steaming pots can result in nasty accidents. Also, don't forget about fire extinguishers in key places, and be sure to have them serviced once a year.

As soon as possible I would install warming drawers—not only because they keep food crisp or hot and moist so beautifully and for so long, but because they are also useful as plate-warmers and great for raising dough if you like to bake bread. Or if you're a theatrical producer. Perhaps by the time you buy yours, they will be making warmers with drop-fronts and sliding shelves instead of drawers, which would be a big improvement.

minor appliances

A garbage disposal unit built into the sink is a tremendous help provided you watch its diet (it can't digest artichokes or dishtowels). But in some cities like New York, it's illegal to have one. And in rural areas you are almost always required to have a separate cesspool if you want one installed.

As a matter of fact, there are a lot of other things you shouldn't invest in, and they have nothing to do with local laws. In my house, for instance, there are many labor-saving devices that don't. Some of them don't even work. Most of them are electric. Most of them were given to me (by my husband), and the rest were given to my husband (by my husband—wouldn't you think he'd have learned by now!). Many of them probably work, but I don't know how to use them because I hate to read instructions, especially instructions that have been crayoned on. Take our very expensive, very fancy German mixer-grinder-beater-squeezer-vegetable juicer. Yes, I really mean *take* it. I'll leave it outside the door. It does everything but dispose of garbage, but I don't understand it at all. And now I've thrown out my nice old blender because the German thing was supposed to do it all better.

My own recent experience with a blender (as a matter of fact, with three blenders) has left me unnerved. I've been teased so much about using store-bought mayonnaise that I decided to break down and make this delicious sauce since my three blenders assured me it was a lead-pipe cinch. I don't know anything about lead pipes, but homemade blender mayonnaise was no cinch for me. I started out by reading several recipes and choosing the one that "tasted" best. It was to make two cups of sauce and it involved the use of 2 cups salad oil, 2 egg yolks, ½ teaspoon of salt, 1 teaspoon of dry mustard, a pinch of cayenne and ¼ cup of wine vinegar. I chose my newest blender, a marvel given to me by a friend. As you doubtless know, dear reader, the oil is to be added slowly to the beaten egg yolks and seasonings. Well, I was getting along splendidly. There I was, standing on my tiptoes to watch the miracle of the oil being incorporated into the egg-yolk mixture. The cover of the blender container had to be left off in order to add the oil. So I patiently accepted the globs of incipient mayonnaise that lodged on the wall cabinets and in my hair, but when they clouded up my glasses, I felt things had gone too far. They had. The mayonnaise had, in fact, gone round the bend and had liquefied (the blender was too powerful). So I threw the mixture out and started all over with the blender whose motor resides under the counter. This time all went well and the mayonnaise took on a beautiful color and texture, but the motor groaned before I had had time to add the last half cup of oil, and I had to turn to a higher speed, and—guess what—we were back to a liquid in no time at all.

Being a stubborn woman, I tried a third time—this time with my true blender friend on low speed. *Forget it* is my message to you. At this point Ellen Rostad, a woman obviously skilled in the art of mayonnaise-making, suggested putting two egg yolks in a mixing bowl and adding the soupy mess very slowly to the egg yolks while using a wire whisk, nonstop. It worked and I had two beautiful cups of mayonnaise at last.

Then there are the devices that work pretty well, but most of the time who remembers to use them? The shoe-polisher, the steam pants presser, and the lint-picker—all of them electric, all of them lint-pickers; they're just sitting around the apartment being tripped over, falling off the wall and picking up lint.

The worst device in our house is an automatic boiled-egg cooker; it cooks up to six eggs at a time. All six come out different, running the gamut from rock-hard to ooey-gooey. I absolutely *loathe* it. The next worst device in our house has lethal metal teeth and is supposed to open your soft-boiled egg for you. It does, but you need lethal metal teeth in your mouth because you get an awful lot of shell in your egg.

We have acquired, just this fall, a gadget that puts buttons on mechanically. It says on the box that the buttons never come off because they are attached with plastic instead of thread. This is 50 percent accurate—overcoat buttons never come off, but the plastic melts in the washer when it comes to shirts and overalls—well, I guess you could do those by hand, you don't *have* to use the washer! Or you could use a cold-water wash.

(It's interesting to note, at this juncture, the number of things in our house that end in "er." Washer, dryer, polisher . . . by actual count, we have twenty-four electrical appliances and all but three end in "er." Those three, the Water-Pik, the electric toothbrush and a gorgeous machine to make coffee, *always* work. I wonder what it all means.)

Anyway, to finish off the subject of minor appliances, mine are major nuisances, and I don't want them around. I almost wish we didn't even have a toaster; it doesn't work very well either, but have you ever tried getting a toaster fixed? I'd rather make toast over a cigarette lighter than go through that again.

As for major appliances, I really love mine a lot. The most exciting thing that's happened to me in years is our new fridge with the automatic ice-maker. Granted, it cost a hundred dollars to hook it up, but if it breaks, I have a promise from the manufacturer that they will fix it. This promise, otherwise known as a service contract, only cost me ninety dollars so I think I'm coming out ahead, and I don't have to get the ice any more.

I also love my washing machine, dryer, dishwasher and freezer, which work extremely well, even for a mechanical retard like me. Like most women. If you're one of the rare geniuses who understands the difference between Perma-Press, Drip-Dry, semidry, almost dry, sort-of-wet, and when to use cold wash instead of lukewarm or hot, don't be insulted, be proud. But most of us don't, and most cleaning women don't either. When we finally did our kitchen over, I bought the simplest, most *un*complicated, *un*gadgety machines I could find; I urge you to do the same. As it is, there is one dial on the washer that throws me—the bit about heavy wash, medium wash or light wash. How do you weigh your wash? On the meat scale? Do you weigh yourself on the bathroom scale and then get on again with an armful of sheets and towels and subtract the difference? What I do is stuff it in and hope for the best; I also have a service contract on the washer.

storage space

What else do you want to plan for? Storage space—all kinds of it—will certainly be high on any woman's list. For starters, you'll need an area for storing seasonal clothes, for blankets and sports equipment. In predetermining just how much storage room you will need in a new house, your most valuable clues will come from measuring your old closet space, your cupboards and bookshelves. But I also highly recommend Rodgers' Rule of Thumb: *i.e.*, list *all* the assorted items you find in your closets now, decide how much space it will take to store them comfortably in the new house, *then double it,* and see where you can steal room.

Is there a structural jog that could be evened out with a faked wall to hide valuable shelf space? Has the space under the stairs been used? If not, consider the possibilities. Even if it is awkward to get at, it could hold things you're saving for emergencies: extra rolls of wallpaper, remnants of carpet. Closing in the space under washstands provides a good place for storing bathroom supplies. If you can take fifteen inches along the whole wall of a room or hall, you'll give yourself an enormous space which, used ingeniously, will hold all kinds of things. We once built such a wall in the large entrance hall of our apartment, and it was almost like having an attic. We used one section for table linens, one for games, cameras, tennis rackets, bridge tables and general miscellany. One served to hide a filing cabinet (placed sideways) , and a large section became a bar concealed by a pair of good-looking white leather doors when it was not being used. The wall was broken at two places by doorways; strip lighting over them was not only decorative but provided light for the closets as well.

When you find space, think in terms of what needs to be used and therefore kept nearby, and organize accordingly. Check the dimensions of drawers and shelves. Often, I think, you'll find shallow drawers, about four inches high, yield far more serviceable space than deep ones for gloves, belts and handkerchiefs. Similarly, in a kitchen, narrow, adjustable shelves—to hold at most two rows of average size cans or jars

—work very well. If you cherish lots of small bits and pieces, scour ten cent stores and notions departments for those ingenious new organizers that hang on the insides of closet doors, sit on closet floors or shelves, or help partition drawers. It's a joy to be able to see what you want and pounce on it—especially if you're in a hurry.

In our New York apartment, I discovered I could add storage space in my bathroom by taking four or five inches from a wall above a counter and faking a new wall that opens to reveal shallow glass shelves—a hiding place for anything small from nail polish to prescriptions. Use spring latches or unobtrusive hardware on the cupboard doors, and no one will even know that they exist. The same trick might work well for kitchen spices, and it is something any contractor—or a husband who's clever about carpentry—can do for you. If you can't steal space, or your husband is an idiot with a hammer, buy one of those plastic lazy-Susan gadgets for your spices.

*speeding
the job*

As I've said before, the only way I know to hurry a construction job that is late is to move into your house as soon as it is remotely habitable. When work on our new house got behind schedule and stayed there, Dick and I finally "occupied" the maids' rooms even though the living room and our bedrooms still hadn't been closed in. Stepping from the bright finished kitchen hall into the sawdust and open air beyond it was a novel experience in nonelegance. But the move did have its advantages: Work seemed to speed up considerably, and also, I had a chance to try things out and have adjustments made while the workmen were still on the spot. When a cupboard door stuck, I could ask the carpenter in the next room to come and fix it. When a drain wouldn't close properly, I could call a plumber. It was a delight to be able to get them fixed instantly! After the men have packed up and gone off to other jobs, they're always hard to get back and little niggling things niggle on for months or forever.

supervision

Then, too, when you are right there, you can catch mistakes when they are made and sometimes, if you are really lucky, even before. Some seem incredibly simple-minded. I happened to be at the house the day a man was installing a toilet paper holder in one of the bathrooms. Without giving it much thought, he was about to anchor it to a wall across from the toilet (obviously, he wasn't planning to have to reach it himself). When I stopped him, he explained that the fixture couldn't be placed where the architect's plans indicated because of some air-conditioning ducts behind the wall. Together we found a better spot, and that day was saved. But I wasn't always so fortunate. The towel bar in my bathroom was already attached at head height on the newly papered wall before I saw it. Lowering it left holes that had to be plugged and later covered with two little pictures. Clearly, things like that are going to happen since you can't haunt the premises twenty-four hours every day—or even for the eight working hours the men are there. Some things will slip by, but the more you can be on the scene when it's time for those last-minute touches, the more trouble you will save yourself.

Even though I found building our house one of the most exciting and satisfying experiences I've ever had, there were times when I felt I couldn't make one more choice—in spite of the fact that professionally I'd been making such decisions for years. There are always compromises to be made, for whatever reasons, and the agony lies in whether you've made the right ones. Even painting your house can be a traumatic thing. But unlikely as it seems when you're in the midst of it, in most cases the anguish is well worth it. You will undoubtedly live to enjoy the results for years.

Few people can afford to hold onto one place indefinitely while decorating another. Besides, if yours is a long-distance move, you won't be able to hop back and forth casually while you're doing your decorating. But moving in early is not the worst thing that could happen to you. It will show you how the house actually works, how the traffic flows, where your furniture should go and what should be first on your list of things to buy. So as soon as you have a kitchen to stow your pots in and a working bathroom (these would be my own non-negotiable demands), move in and watch and learn.

IT'S
YOUR MOVE

People move for lots of reasons. For more room, for less room, because they're richer, or poorer, from city to country, or vice versa. And, of course, for business reasons.

Perhaps your husband has been transferred. If so, the chances are you'll have to move a fair distance, which brings special problems and considerations. If you own the house or apartment you are leaving, you will have to sell it, and here are some suggestions that may help to make the job easier.

selling your house

First of all, make a list of your house's good features and selling points and give copies to the real estate brokers through whom you hope to sell the house. If it's at all possible, take the time to go through the house with any broker who sounds particularly interested. Answer his questions and listen to his advice about what you can do to make the house more attractive to prospective buyers. While the house is being shown, plan to be out because it's less embarrassing for everyone. Have your house looking its best—which may even mean doing a little painting if a particular area looks grubby. One coat of paint on kitchen or hallway walls can make a great difference. Don't jam everything into closets to make the rooms look neat because would-be buyers will jump to the conclusion that your storage space is inadequate. Instead, consider packing some of the things you won't be needing before you move; put them in cartons and store them out of the way in the attic or cellar. Freshen up your closets; make sure shelf paper isn't torn or dirty. Silly as it may seem, women have been known to buy houses because the linen closet looked pretty.

learning about a new town

If you are moving to another part of the country, tell everyone where you are going—you may get help from the most unlikely sources. The owner of your drugstore might turn out to have a sister-in-law who runs a baby-sitting service, for instance, or the principal of your child's present school may know a teacher in the new place. Accept all offers of names and contacts. Write to your school or college class secretary and to the alumnae association office for latest membership lists giving names and addresses to see whom you might already know. And if you or your husband belong to any national clubs, find out about local chapters in your new town.

Most cities have a Chamber of Commerce. Write to the one in the town to which you're moving and ask for the names of publications about the area, for local maps, lists of recreational facilities and calendars of special events. These should tell you about theatrical or musical programs, lecture series and sports events to which you may want to subscribe in advance.

If you are lucky enough to be able to make a surveying trip with your husband to your new suburb or city, you can probably investigate the school and neighborhood situations while you are looking for your house. In real estate sections of local papers, you will often notice ads that mention school districts along with other selling points of a house. If you see one particular district mentioned frequently, it's safe to assume that it's considered especially desirable, and it's probably the one you should aim for.

A marvelously organized young friend of ours who is married to a doctor gave me several valuable suggestions about moving, based on her own experiences. Carolyn and John were able to choose their town themselves for the outstanding professional opportunities it offered John and the attractive way of life it offered the family. A scouting trip resulted in finding a house they liked well enough to buy in the school district they liked best. Through John's associate, they began to make friends in the community they would be moving to.

learning
about
schools

When they returned home, Carolyn wrote to the principal of the new school and asked what records he would need and what the curricula would be in the three grades her children would enter. (When people move, their children's educational continuity is frequently interrupted. If this is a problem for your children, and the public school is not equipped

it's your move

to give them the help they need, a private school with smaller classes and access to tutoring services may be able to fill the gap.)

John wrote to a vice president of a local bank, deposited some money and established credit in advance of their move. He also arranged for the contents of their safety deposit box to be mailed by one bank to the other. (This is much the safest way to transfer valuables.)

taking over the new house

Carolyn asked the former owner of the house they bought to leave appliance instructions, warranties and a list of the service companies she had used. The former owner also gave them the structural plans of the house, invaluable for any kind of remodeling. It is also very important to make sure that the house and all its contents are fully covered by insurance from the moment you take title. I remember the anguish of a friend whose uninsured Long Island place was swept away by a hurricane on the very day he signed the papers.

Often when you buy a house, you also buy appliances, floor coverings, and curtains. This makes sense because it saves you considerable money at the beginning, especially in the case of wall-to-wall carpeting, which has been cut to fit the rooms. Replacements can always be made later. The one thing Carolyn says she forgot to do was to have the carpets cleaned before the furniture was moved in. It would, she says now, have made life easier. It is also a good idea to get an exterminator to go over the house and yard and do whatever is necessary. Also arrange as early as possible to have phones installed so that they will be there when you move in.

executive transfers

Another young friend of ours, married to an executive in a large corporation, had similar but slightly different advice to give. Cynthia and Mac have lived all over the world, wherever they were assigned, and without the freedom of choice that Carolyn and John had. While this gives Cynthia and Mac a certain feeling of impermanence, they do have the advantage of help and advice from local members of their corporate family whenever they make a move.

Companies differ in how far they will go to help their people move. Some give an allowance for new furnishings and will even buy your house if you have trouble selling it. Cynthia tells me that most corporations choose the moving company and pay for packing and transporting the whole household, including the family car. This means that it is to the advantage of corporate wives to take everything with them. (For a gourmet cook, replacing a full set of herbs and spices is costly and sometimes impossible.) A number of moves has also taught her to keep receipted bills for important household purchases as part of an up-to-date detailed inventory to be used in case of loss.

before you move out

Other things Cynthia suggests doing before leaving your old town make sense for anyone's move. Buying shoes which can be a problem as far as lasts are concerned is a good idea, but she advises stalling about other clothes until you know more about the way people, adults and teen-agers especially, dress in your new community.

Ask your doctor and dentist to recommend colleagues, but don't have your records sent on until you have met the doctors and dentists yourself and feel reasonably sure they're the ones for you. (Do the same with your lawyer.) If your doctor doesn't know any physicians personally, it will be difficult for him to make recommendations. True, he can look up a name you give him in his directory to learn what training the man has had, but there is no way for him to determine how well the doctor has kept up with new developments in medicine or what his personality is like. In a strange place, the best way to get a qualified physician is to ask at the largest municipal or voluntary hospital for the names of men or women who head their services. The county medical society will furnish names, too. Then ask your "old" doctor to look them up and give you his preference among the names submitted.

Get medical and dental checkups and shots out of the way before you move. And be sure to take supplies of prescription drugs and copies of the prescriptions themselves—including those for eyeglasses.

Don't forget to close or transfer charge accounts, discontinue milk and newspapers, and notify magazines of your change of address. Leave a forwarding card with the post office. It is also thoughtful to let friends know what your new address and phone number will be.

Since you want to arrive looking your best and not having to worry about what a strange hairdresser might do to you,

it's your move

have your hair cut, styled, rinsed, bleached, dyed, waved or straightened before you leave home. If you use any special products, get their names or take samples with you.

moving the family

If you can choose the time of year for your move, the end of summer, shortly before school begins, is ideal. And if your husband can arrange to take his vacation just before and during the moving period, you might consider a cross-country drive that would give everyone a chance to enjoy the trip while the furniture is in transit. Probably you will have to spend some time in a hotel or motel before you can move into your new home; unless the stay is a very short one, try to get a place with kitchenette facilities—especially if you have children with you. (This is a fine time for grandparents or other loving relatives or friends to have your children visit them, leaving you and your husband free to get on with the job of moving in.)

When time is short, however, and you must fly, remember that delays are all too frequent, and it's not very comforting for a hungry twelve-year-old to hear the stewardess say, "We'll be serving cocktails as soon as we take off." Take some food—cookies, dried fruits and crackers—with you for emergencies.

In seventeen years of adult living, I have moved four times. I've always found it a loathsome business—but then, who doesn't? Oh, the moving-in part is kind of exciting, the smell of fresh paint and all that. It's the moving-out part that's so terrible. And since in this book I seem more often than not to be the harbinger of horrid things to come, I think I'll tell you about how to get out of the rotten old place, and leave the happier aspects of getting into the new one to my mother.

what not to pack

You know the story about the farmer who had to separate the good apples from the bad—it wasn't the work that got him, it was the decisions. Well, that's moving for you. The first time I ever moved—from 74th Street in New York to 78th Street, which is tantamount to moving from Newark to San Diego (how far you move has nothing to do with the amount of work it entails) —I couldn't face the decisions. My husband was away, I didn't know which of his belongings he wanted and which he didn't, I couldn't even make up my mind about my own things. Besides that, I was pregnant and feeling very languid. So I simply waved a weary arm at the moving men and instructed them to move the contents of the entire apartment. It was like a close-out sale on 42nd Street. Everything must go, is what I told them. Well, when those guys do your packing for you, they really do it. Ashtrays with cigarette butts still in them were lovingly swaddled in tissue. The garbage can arrived intact—with garbage. Nevertheless, I thought it was all lovely, until a few days later when I discovered that the new apartment was riddled with something nasty called miller moths which had been reproducing themselves at an alarming rate in a jar of my husband's malted milk health food. Naturally, they had been packed, too.

So for subsequent moves, I evolved another theory—everything must go, but not necessarily to your new house. Some of the stuff should go to the local thrift shop, some of it to the Salvation Army, and some of it, I daresay a lot of it, should go just plain out. Places like Goodwill Industries take things that can be repaired—furniture, equipment and toys, for instance. The rehabilitation job they do provides work for unemployed people, and the objects acquire a second useful life.

This means making decisions, and we're right back to the farmer with the apples. Here are some things you don't need: duplicate kitchen equipment—how many vegetable peelers do you have right now? I bet you have more than one. Unless you have three hands or two cooks, you don't need more than two wooden stirring spoons, either. (DR tells me she needs more than two, but have I told you about her third hand?) Two meat grinders with their parts all mixed up together. How about five frying pans—one with the Teflon all scratched off, one with a loose handle? Flower vases. Most of us can't afford to buy flowers for ourselves very often, and when people send flowers, they usually come prearranged. So what do you need with seven vases? Four will do. Any electrical equipment that has been out of commission for more than a few months. If you haven't gotten it fixed by now, you're probably not going to. Empty record album covers, records you never listen to, current novels you've already read, and paperbacks, unless they are beloved or classics that you are saving for your children. (Somewhat irrelevant, but never tell a child he's reading a classic. He'll

it's your move

put it down immediately. Tell him it's juicy.) Books are often welcomed by settlement houses and public libraries—especially in small communities—and hospitals.

Pictures and prints that have never been hung because you don't like them. They won't look any better on the new walls. Crinkly rolls of water color paintings executed by your ten-year-old when he was in the first grade. Likewise crumbling clay handprints from kindergarten. All broken toys, outgrown tricycles, ragged sheets and towels, unidentifiable raincoats and umbrellas that your guests left behind last year or the year before. Take back those unidentifiable raincoats and umbrellas. They are great for lending to friends trapped by sudden showers.

Half-empty cans of paint, old crib parts, dull scissors. All ornaments and serving equipment in the backs of closets and on the tops of shelves. They are all where they are because you don't like them or because you don't use them often enough to justify the space they take up. Example: If a copper chafing dish complete with Sterno falls out of somewhere and hits you on the head, who needs it?

The hardest thing of all is to bring yourself to part with heirlooms, wedding gifts, or other things that you are sentimental about, even though you know you'll never use them. This is not the era for grandmother's sterling silver tea service. No one will polish it, and it is undoubtedly packed away, taking up valuable shelf space. If it's a real treasure, keep it, if possible, until your children are old enough to decide whether they want it. But if you know your children won't cherish it, give it to a museum or a local historical society. If it's not special enough for that, sell it. Or better still, trade it for something you need or want. A dealer will always give you a better break on a trade than on a sale; because he can make money on both ends, he can be content with a smaller profit.

And so on. It all takes time, but, boy, is it ever worth it when you arrive at the other end. I can think of only one more thing you don't need—your little children on moving day. Give them to your mother, give them to an understanding friend, board them at a kennel, but if they're hanging around, they'll drive you crazy, and at least one of them is going to get mowed down by a grand piano.

Finding trustworthy moving men can be difficult, and the good ones are expensive. Estimates won't vary too much from one reputable company to another (and they very seldom bear any relation to the final cost), but here it often turns out to be true that the most costly is, in the long run, the cheapest. Choose an established firm whose reputation can be checked by calling former customers. Some so-called moving men, hired practically off the street, have no knowledge of how to protect valuable or fragile objects. Many large pieces of furniture must be dismantled and put back together, and it is important that this be done expertly. There is an art to crating and packing, and it takes a fair amount of experience to be able to maneuver an eight-foot sofa around a corner in a narrow hallway without scratching the newly painted walls. If you have a *very* neat painter, consider having the hall walls and doors given their final coat after the moving men have left. And in any case, be sure to save cans of paint for touch-ups.

If you are moving a short distance, you can save a good deal of money by moving small things yourself. Lamps, ornaments, books, china, glassware, kitchen equipment, silver and linens can be packed in containers which you can buy from your moving company. Today these containers are actually sturdy new cardboard cartons of various sizes, but moving men still refer to them as "crates" and "barrels." The moving company can also provide unbleached tissue paper, newsprint (newspaper without printing) and pre-cut corrugated paper that is marvelous for wrapping individual pieces of china or glassware.

In addition to saving money, one of the greatest advantages of doing some of the packing and moving yourself is that you can get things unpacked, washed and put away as soon as your cupboards and shelves are ready to receive them. The ordeal of moving is lessened considerably if, on moving day, your kitchen equipment, china, glass, silver and linens are all where they belong. If your bookshelves and record storage areas are built in, books and records can be off the floor and out of the way, too.

One word of caution. Don't hang pictures or mirrors in a hurry. Be sure, for instance, the sofa is in place before you make holes in the wall above it to hang a painting.

Clothing presents no problem in moving because movers supply large portable closets with bars for hanging things so that clothes can wait to be moved out on their hangers on the same day the furniture goes. Drawers can sometimes be used as cartons if their contents are unbreakable, but be sure to cover their tops with well-taped wrapping paper, and identify each drawer by number.

If your new home is near the old one, you will probably be making many trips during the last week or two before the move. Each time you go, take things with you, and bring back the empty cartons. (You won't have to buy so many.) If the new house is too far away for this system to be practical, but is still within reasonable driving distance, it would probably pay you to borrow or rent a station wagon or hire a small trailer to haul the cartons of small things.

On *the* day, don't count on leaving everything to the moving men. *Supervise* is the word. Have the things you will need first packed last—bedding, cleaning supplies, essential kitchen things and the vacuum cleaner. You'll probably be using them last in the old house, too.

supervising packing and loading

If you are moving a great distance, insist on a locked lift van so that your things won't be handled unnecessarily, even if there is a time lapse. Warehouse storage is incredibly hard on furniture. Once everything has been loaded onto a lift van, it is locked and, whether it travels by truck or rail or freighter or is stored, it will remain locked until it shows up in front of your new home.

protecting your possessions

Be sure to see that your possessions are covered by adequate insurance from the moment they are picked up until they are set down in the new place. Ask your own insurance broker to advise you about this because moving companies are not always equipped to get the best coverage for your needs. The hazards are, of course, breakage, damage, theft, loss and fire. In order to know what to insure, you will need to make a complete list of your things. This entails an enormous amount of work, but you can make the list doubly valuable by using it to clue you on the contents of the various cartons. As you pack them, give each carton a number. Mark the number in black crayon on the side of the carton, and add the room where it is to be unpacked. (Kitchen, master bedroom, linen closet, etc.) Enter each number in a notebook, and put down each carton's contents. That way, if one is lost or missing, you will know what it contains.

My final word of advice—don't pack the notebook.

words of caution

Most moving companies require cash payment before your things are unloaded, and, if you don't pay, they will cart everything off to the warehouse. Remembering that the final charge is always higher than the estimate, be forewarned. Don't be surprised if before they leave, the moving men ask you to sign a paper saying that everything is in better shape now than it was when the packing started. Don't sign anything until you have walked around with the head mover and examined everything. Be prepared to fight.

settling into a city: technical information for adults

When you're settling into a new city community, especially if you've never lived in a big city before, you'll find quite a lot to adjust to—some of it good, some of it bad.

You won't be able to use your car for hauling children and groceries and broken lamps because there's no place to park it. That's bad. But then, you don't need a car once you've got the hang of the public transportation system and markets that deliver. If you sell the car, you can save yourself a year-round expense (when you really need one, you can rent one). That's good. The transit company will mail you free maps of the bus or subway routes which you can tack up on a bulletin board where everybody can memorize them. You'll have to make some trial runs with your children to and from school until they can negotiate reliably on their own. That's boring!

If you decide not to sell your car, be sure that you never leave valuable things like television sets or typewriters in it when you park it on the street or even in a garage. This is not a case of *maybe* someone will break in and steal everything, it's a case of definitely, without any question, someone will break in and steal everything including your cigarette lighter. That's bad.

Markets that deliver save you going out in the pouring rain at six o'clock at night for the one loaf of bread you forgot. Good. But they'll charge you twice as much for the loaf of bread, so you can't afford to use them all the time for everything. Bad. This is equally true of bakeries, drugstores, delicatessens and dry cleaners, so what you need is two of

it's your move

each of these services. Keep a small running charge account at the luxury establishments—just big enough to make it worth their while on the rainy night. But do the major part of your business with the local chain stores. If you don't fancy lugging fifty pounds of staples home in a wire cart, you can always find a supermarket that will deliver for a slight charge.

If there are four bakeries, two delicatessens, several cleaning establishments, etc., in your neighborhood and you don't know which ones are best, ask your next-door neighbor or a friend who lives in your vicinity which she likes best. You may not end up agreeing with her, but in six months or so you'll be familiar with every store within a four-block radius and can make up your own mind about what you want.

While you're at it, inquire about a local toy store and a small clothing store; you don't want to make a trip to the major shopping district for one minor purchase like a pair of sneakers or a toy for a child's birthday party.

The moment you move into an apartment, especially if you're listed in the phone book, you'll be inundated with second class mail, leaflets, flyers and booklets about local services. Most of this is junk (I guess that's why they call it junk mail), but if you get a booklet about the neighborhood, hang onto it; it will tell you where to find the notions store, the shoe repair store, the electrical appliance repair shop where you leave your toaster for six months—all those niggling little places you forgot to ask your neighbor about.

I want to warn you that one of the most frustrating dilemmas of urban living is how to get something big fixed. A small lamp, for instance, you can carry to the hardware store, or the electrical appliance shop; they'll fix it. But a standing lamp at a rakish tilt or three dining room chairs with straw dribbling out of their bottoms? An antique sideboard with a broken lock, a ceramic sculpture of a horse with three legs? (The fourth leg, wrapped in Kleenex, is in a drawer with five mixed-up packs of playing cards where you'll never find it anyway.) There is no such thing as a man who will come to your house to remove and repair these horrible accidents. They just sit there for months, proof of your slovenly housewifeliness, until finally, in self-defense, you stop noticing that your apartment looks like a combination fun house and

it's your move

Appalachian shack. Of course, if you devote every morning to searching the Yellow Pages for broken ceramic horse-leg-gluers-on, you can probably find one, but the place will be eighty blocks away and won't pick up.

Big old apartment buildings have two storage areas: One is in the basement where each tenant has his own storage bin—a dusty Black Hole of Calcutta where you put trunks, Christmas decorations and smallish bits of furniture you're either not using at the moment but may need again (a crib), or things you don't know where to put now, but might someday find a place for (an extra end table). This room has a key which resides with the superintendent or the back elevator man and nobody can get in there to steal anything. Considering all the stuff that usually lands up down there, nobody's going to want to anyway. If you, yourself, want to keep track of which hunks of stuff you have, make a list of the things you've sent down and keep it current, adding and subtracting items as you go. This will save countless trips to the bin. Before you do any of this, however, make sure that the building doesn't have fire laws that will prevent you from storing anything that isn't fireproof.

The other big storage area is usually on the ground floor. It's for bicycles, sleds and baby carriages; it's not locked, anybody can get in there to steal anything, and quite frequently somebody does—good bikes in particular. I recommend the following safety precautions: If you have a big baby carriage, don't worry about it. Unless the thief comes equipped with a baby, he'll attract suspicion when he saunters out of the building with an empty pram. But I've lost two strollers in seven years, so I keep them upstairs. If you can find room in the apartment for a good sled, do so; it's a highly pinchable commodity. Keep tricycles upstairs, too, and if you have any big bikes, keep them downstairs, but locked up. If you have something fancy like a multi-geared English bike, add it to your insurance policy.

Unfortunately, most new buildings don't provide adequate storage space in the basement or anywhere else; if you're moving into one of these buildings, you'll have to cut down rather drastically on the amount of furniture and equipment you'd like to hang on to. Obviously, it's a good idea to check on the storage situation before you move, not after, when you'll be much too busy to worry about how to dispose of all those end tables and sleds.

Front and back doors should be locked at all times. It's a colossal bore, especially when you have several small children who lose their keys constantly, but I don't have to tell you about the crime rate in big cities.

Some buildings have house phones over which elevator and doormen have been trained to announce to you the arrival of anyone and everyone. The men are either super-careful or else they're not very discriminating; for five years, they'll squawk at you that your sister is downstairs, is it okay to let her up, thereby implying that maybe she's not really your sister. My Lord, wouldn't you think that after five years they'd recognize her? But don't discourage them; any amount of tedium is preferable to letting in an unknown lady junkie.

household help

Household help is a major concern for any woman, no matter where she lives, but apartment house living provides you with a variety of choices with which to solve the servant problem—one of the few advantages of urban life.

Building employees: If you have always lived in the country, you are undoubtedly more self-sufficient than we city mice when it comes to things like changing fuses, or disemboweling the washing machine to fish out a bobby pin from the lint filter. Even so, there will be certain things you simply cannot do for yourself, like fixing leaky faucets or making minor adjustments on the oven pilot light. The superintendent will be your best friend or the most extraordinarily unfeeling wretch, depending on how he estimates your tipping potential. Ugly but true, so tip him quite lavishly (approximately ten percent of one month's rent or maintenance)—not after you have moved into your apartment, but the very first time you set foot in the building. While you're at it, you might ask him what the tipping procedure is for the other building employees (elevator men, handyman, house electrician, plumber). The word will spread like wildfire that you are a lovely person, assuring you full cooperation on moving day and in subsequent moments of trial. If your building has none of these helpers, your neighborhood hardware store is a possible source of information about a handyman who can put up curtain rods, and hang pictures and mirrors.

If you have bought a house in the city, you may inherit the janitor from its former owners, who have either been his sole employers, if they were very lucky or very rich, or else they have been sharing him with several other house-owners on the block. He's the fellow who single-handedly provides many of the services that an apartment building gives you automatically (sweeps sidewalks, checks the furnace) so even though you're paying him a salary, if you expect him to do any special moving-in favors, be sure you tip him ahead of time, too.

Non-live-in help is quite easy to get in the city. Not necessarily good, you understand, but easy to get.

A part-time cleaning woman (one or two days a week, for instance), a man to do heavy cleaning—waxing floors, scrubbing walls, etc., or a laundress who comes once a week, can be found through employment agencies, friends or newspaper ads. Check all references carefully, especially if you're hiring a totally unknown quantity from the newspaper. You may end up with several duds before you find the right permanent person, but it's not fatal, it's just time-consuming.

Though domestic servants are scarce birds these days, it's still important to learn the subtle art of reading and writing references. Certain character traits, like honesty and sobriety, are not matters of opinion. Degrees of skill are. So since the standards of the writer and the reader of a reference may differ enormously, descriptions of skills have very little meaning. A woman who, to one employer, may seem a first-class housekeeper may seem second- or third-class to another. Certain things you must find out for yourself.

References should always tell you if the person is honest and sober, in what capacity he or she was employed, for how long, and from when to when. Read them very carefully— both the lines and in between them. If there seems to be a significant time lapse between jobs, try to find out why. Especially where children are involved, always speak to the former employer if possible. And when you do, be sure to ask whether there is anything you should know that you have neglected to inquire about.

In an interview, you should be very clear about what will be expected. Describe the work as accurately as you can, and spell out financial arrangements as well as those for time off and vacations. If uniforms are required, who provides them? As a rule, part-time workers supply their own, but employers usually equip full-time employees. When you have finished explaining the job's requirements, offer to answer questions: You may find you're being interviewed, and this can tell you a great deal, too.

If you find yourself completely without help and with a filthy house on a day when you're having a party, you can always call up a bonded maid service and ask them to send someone—anyone, as long as she has two hands and one head—to tide you over. This is expensive, but great in an emergency.

To find a Monday-through-Friday, live-out housekeeper, you go the same route—agencies, friends, newspapers. The price varies depending on the agency you call and the self-esteem of the housekeeper. The one thing it doesn't seem to depend on is the quality of the housekeeper, who can be a gem at seventy-five a week, or an ill-tempered sloppy harridan at a hundred and twenty-five. Eventually, you'll find someone who hangs in there for a whole year; these days, a whole year is a long time.

Baby-sitters are also easy to locate, but here you obviously have to be more discriminating. A little dust under the bed is a nuisance; a drunk, irresponsible or nasty baby-sitter is a trauma. To find a good one, you can try the following:

Is your housekeeper or cleaning woman nice with the kids? Ask her if she'll baby-sit—for extra money, of course. She already knows your kids and knows her way around the house. She might even rearrange her hours by coming in later and staying later so that it doesn't cost you more. (Pay for her taxi home if she lives far away.)

Is there a reliable-looking teen-ager or older lady in your

apartment building? If you haven't run across anything that looks possible, maybe the super knows of someone.

Call the dormitory of a school of nursing at a big hospital and ask them if they have any student nurses who want to earn some extra money. I haven't tried this lately, but I used to find it very successful; the price was reasonable, and I never worried about anybody getting sick.

There are part-time child care agencies, just like the bonded maid services, who will send you well-trained types on the spur of the moment during the week and, with advance notice, on weekends or big holidays. They are brutally expensive, charging more for each child after the first one, more for infants, more for day work than night work, and a whopping big commission on top of all that. But they're pretty reliable, and if you find a sitter you like, you can request her again.

Live-in help is, of course, much harder to find, but here again, the city has it all over the country. Importing *au pair* girls (girls from "good" overseas families who come to this country to learn the language and enjoy themselves—they expect to be treated as members of the family, not as servants) or semi-trained domestic workers has become almost impossible to do now that the immigration laws have changed, but I suppose it's worth trying. Bear in mind, however, that it will take a year to cut through the red tape, the girl may turn out to be a monster, and then you're stuck with her unless you can get some unwitting soul to buy out your contract. If she gets seriously sick, or decides to run up huge bills on your charge accounts, you are responsible for her. The only way to import someone is to know a lot about her ahead of time. (The sister of your best friend's housekeeper might be a good bet, but even then, you're only half safe—sisters don't always think alike.)

Local agencies and newspaper ads are really the best, and of the two, I prefer agencies because they are supposed to have checked references. With newspaper ads, you spend several days on the phone trying to weed out the maniacs from the possibles, and then half the possibles don't bother to show up for the interview anyway.

I have only one other piece of information for you: When you're leafing through the Yellow Pages or the newspapers to find an agency to call, beware of the ones that advertise "waitress, chambermaid-waitress or cook." These are high-class places with such high-class help that you'll end up waiting on *them*. In fact, they won't take the job in the first place if you expect them to do more than one, highly specialized little chore (bed-making and ironing Modom's lingerie). Actually, even the lady in the agency won't give you the time of day because what you want is an all-round houseworker, and she doesn't have any of those. The agencies that advertise "housekeepers" are what you should be looking for.

personal information for adults

Presumably you have already been given the names of new doctors, lawyers, dentists, oculists, and accountants by your old ones. Now, *before* you or the kids get sick or sued or cavity-ridden or go broke, pay a visit to each of these gentlemen to establish yourself as a face and a personality.

Friends: For you and your husband, the move from the country to the city, or from one city to another, will be hectic and intimidating. For the first few months, until you adjust to the pace, you will be nervous and jumpy and tired. On the other hand, you will never be bored, and you will never be lonely. **I disagree. You** *may* **never be bored, but you will quite possibly be lonely.** You're probably going to know at least one or two couples who already live there; they'll introduce you to others. You'll also be meeting business associates of your husband and their wives, and between the two groups, you may actually find yourself too busy with too many friends and too many dates.

The one category to look out for is apartment house or, if you have your own house, next-door neighbors. These people may be lovely—as neighbors—but uninteresting and leech-like as friends, hard to be rude to, but hard to get rid of; so go slowly.

technical information for children

Schools: Unfortunately, a great deal needs to be said about schools—most of it discouraging. If you have bought or rented an apartment partially on the basis of the good public school district it's in, you're in good shape. The only thing you have to do now is visit the principal and discuss with him your child's curriculum and in what grade he belongs. But if you have been forced to move into a bad school district and have decided to spend the money for a private school (whether or not you can afford it—and you probably can't) , you have your work cut out for you.

New York private schools are the only ones I know anything about, but in any big city, the situation must be pretty much the same: If you haven't made private school plans well in advance, your goose is cooked for at least a year. I have friends from the West Coast who sailed merrily into town in September, expecting to solve the problem immediately. I warned them way back in March that it wouldn't be easy, but they didn't believe me. *Believe* me! It's a terrible job. Here's what you have to do—in six nightmarish steps:

Step one: What kind of education do you want, progressive or traditional? Which schools are which? And how do you find out? Ask everybody you know who has children in private schools in your new city. They'll tell you about the schools their kids are going to, and you can often judge more by the recommendations of friends than you can by seeing the school itself. A tour of a school gives you a superficial glance only, but an intelligent friend whose children strike you as being well-mannered and well-informed (a traditional school) or slightly less well-mannered, total idiots in some subjects and brilliantly informed in others (a progressive school) will give you a pretty good idea of what that particular school is like. The information doesn't make it any easier for you to get your kids into the school, but you'll be able to eliminate a few undesirable ones from your list— at least for now.

Step two: Call all the schools on your list and speak to each director of admissions. He or she will tell you if there is any chance for this year (there won't be) . Make an appointment to see the school anyway because even if you've already made up your mind about it, it still has to make up its mind about you. Dress conservatively, even for progressive schools, ask all the questions you want, but don't drop any names or try to pull any strings. The time for that is later, if ever.

Step three: Have a qualified agency (ask one of the schools at the top of your list to recommend one) give your child the standard achievement and intelligence tests, and ask that transcripts of his records be sent to schools to which you're applying.

Step four: If a school is willing to consider your child at all, you will be asked to produce a few letters of recommendation written by people who know you and are known to the school, attesting to the suitability of you and your child. You're both expected to be charming, intelligent, imaginative—you know, everything wonderful. These letters are a big problem. First of all, if you've just moved into a new city, you may not know enough people to write them. (Take a look at the school catalogue; if it contains a list of members of the board of trustees, you might know one of them.) And even if you scrounge up enough letters, you're not yet out of the woods because although the schools insist on the letters, they never pay attention to them unless they're negative—nevertheless, it's a boring formality you have to go through.

Some schools, instead of asking outright for letters of recommendation, simply ask you to list the names of people who know you and the school on your application. Then the school contacts these people and asks them to write the letters. Under no circumstances do you send back your application without first informing your "names" that they've been listed. It's considered very bad form and will make your "names" mad!

Step five: Unless your child has an I.Q. of a hundred and eighty or is black or Chinese (these days, even Jews aren't considered a very interesting minority), you may have to resort to pull, if you have any. Some schools are influenced by influential people—like the aforementioned board member, or maybe the mayor of the city. Some schools are influenced by the *subtle* promise of large future donations. (The subtlest way to go about this is to have someone else do the subtle promising for you; a close friend of the school can always imply that you and your husband will be willing and able to take a lively "contributory" interest in the school's affairs.)

Step six: If steps one through five have netted you nothing, you'll just have to be patient. Put your child in a less good private school for this year, and try again next year. Eventually, you'll make it. Don't be surprised, by the way, if a bad private school costs more than a good one. The good ones are often the old ones, which means they are better endowed, and the bad ones exist for desperate people who'll pay as much as they have to in order to avoid public school.

One more thing: Whenever your child makes it into the good school, he may be asked to drop back a grade because the curriculum is more demanding in this school, or because he's lost ground during the transition period. He may object at first, but he'll get over it, and if he does well, he'll be advanced back up to where he was in a year or so anyway.

friends

For children, alas, there is almost nothing good to be said for the transition period when they are adjusting to a new city. Be prepared for depressed children. The confinement of an elevator existence will infuriate them. All that waiting around while you assemble the coats and the hats and the park toys and the house key, getting out the bicycle, putting away the bicycle—they're going to hate it, but as a new city mother, you're going to be convinced that fresh air at least twice a day is vital to their health. (Frankly, I don't believe this for a minute. The air in most cities is foul enough to be considered detrimental to their health, so unless they're clearly aching to get out to run off some excess energy, they're just as well off indoors, especially in lousy weather. And as for babies, they don't ever have to go out. When one of mine was a few months old, I used to put him in a snow suit in the carriage in an empty room with all the windows open. The poor, benighted thing thought he was in Central Park and slept blissfully all afternoon. At seventeen, he's in glowing condition, so I guess it didn't hurt him.)

And then there are the constant warnings: Look out for the lights, look out for the traffic, look out for what you're stepping in! don't feed the squirrels—they bite, don't lean out the window—you'll fall, if you get home before I do, don't answer the door to anybody. One long Ode on Intimations of Mortality is what you're going to sound like.

it's your move

Worst of all, the children will be lonely. They'll miss their old friends, as will you, but they don't have business associates to provide them with ready-made new ones, and becoming an accepted member of the school group may take longer than they think. It's not that city children are particularly unfriendly; *any* new kid coming into a class of old pals who have known each other for years is going to get the once-over several times over before he finally gets invited over to someone else's house. And invited over is what it will be; there's none of that casual biking around the neighborhood to see who's available.

And so, dear friends, on top of all your other settling-in chores, you will have to settle your children in, because until they have achieved some degree of social independence, you're going to be miserable. Here are some of the things you can do:

Don't wait for other children to initiate the action. Ask your child which kids in his class he likes, then call up the mother of one of them and invite him over for lunch and the afternoon. Don't make your child do the phoning and inviting; it's far too frightening for him, and establishing parental rapport is a good idea anyway. Plan a very good meal (hamburgers and potato chips) and something definite to do afterwards. Don't abandon the two kids with a baby-sitter or a maid. Later on, when the friendship is firmed up, they'll want to be left alone, but in the early stages you have to eliminate the added burden of:

> "What do you want to do now?"
> "I dunno, what do *you* want to do?"
> "Oh, anything *you* want to do."
> "Well, what *is* there to do?"

If this first encounter is successful, you'll know. For one thing, if you're playing with them and they begin to ignore you, it means you're not needed. Great! If the guest sort of doesn't want to go home, that's a very good sign. If the guest or his mother requests a return engagement, you've got it made. But if none of these things happens, or even if it does, don't stop there. Go on down the list of friends and invite several more of them over.

School friends alone won't fill your child's calendar, nor should they. An eclectic social life is as valuable for your child as it is for you. Plunge him into the Boy Scouts, the Sunday school, an afternoon play group, an ice-skating club; he's not going to keep up with all of these activities for very long because I've deliberately recommended a super-abundance of them, but after a few months, he'll be able to select the ones that appeal to him most. In the meantime, he'll have met plenty of new people.

City neighbors are obviously not like country neighbors. You can get to know a good deal about the family who lives one floor above you without ever actually meeting them— just by listening to the noises they make. (Squeaky crib = baby, hooting mechanical train = small boy, Clementi Sonatina = twelve-year-old girl with eleven thumbs, hard rock = teen-agers.) But why not meet them? We apartment dwellers are ridiculously insular; if the family upstairs has a seven-year-old boy and you have a seven-year-old boy, they could be making beautiful noises together on many a rainy day. So speak up: Introduce yourself and the kids. If they don't get along, at least it's a short trip home.

Last year, I suggested to the management of our building that they compile a list of children—with the parents' permission, of course—with names, ages, and phone numbers from which parents with children the same age could pick a rainy-day pal. The idea of this simple little service had apparently never occurred to anyone before and the management was positively thunderstruck with delight. I now have a nifty assortment of small people for Adam to play with, and I've begun to identify all sorts of others as well. I don't know how the rest of the parents feel, but I like to know who lives in the building with me; even if they never come over, it's fun to know who they are.

There are other ways to meet children. If you consistently run into the same woman and child in the park and the local market, you can assume she lives near you. Again, speak up, exchange phone numbers. Pretty soon you'll begin to amass quite a collection of local talent, and when your child has mastered the traffic lights and learned his way around the neighborhood, he'll be able to get to his friends' houses on his own.

it's your move

The question of when to allow your child to travel alone in the neighborhood is one of age and individual maturity. Any four-year-old can negotiate the trip from one apartment to another in your own building if the elevators are manned. If they are self-service, you'd better deliver him: He may not be able to reach the button for the seventeenth floor; he can't read to push the alarm bell if the elevator gets stuck; he may not be able to maneuver the gate or push open the door; and, most important of all, a lot of unsavory characters ride up and down self-service elevators these days—you don't want your child locked in with one of them.

Most kids, from the age of about seven on, are capable of navigating in, let's say, a five-block radius. Most, but not all. For years, one of my own daughters looked like a victim of the battered child syndrome; she was apparently more interested in where she'd been than in where she was going and I've always wondered why she was never mowed down by a Madison Avenue bus. With that kind of child, you have to rehearse for a while before you let it out alone.

Attention, mothers of all small children! It is possible to lose a child in a big store, on the street and especially at the circus, so never mind teaching your child nursery rhymes; teach him his full name, his address, his phone number, and what to do if he gets lost.

I think that's about it for the doom-and-gloom, murder-and-mayhem-in-the-city category. Please be advised that most of the horrible depravities you read about will not happen to you or your children. In seventeen years, nobody in my family has ever been raped, terrorized, or even lost, and we're not what you could call over-protective about ourselves or our children. Like everyone else, we simply take for granted certain common-sense precautions, and most of the time, we go our merry way without giving a thought to the evil that lurks in the hearts of men. So don't worry. After a few apprehensive weeks, you'll be just like us.

*settling
into
a suburb:
technical
information
for
adults*

When you're settling into a new country community, especially if you've never lived in the country before, you'll find quite a lot to adjust to—most of it good.

You'll be able to use your car for absolutely everything. It will haul your children and your groceries, and your broken lamps will all get fixed. You can park your car almost anywhere, and you'll only have to lock it some of the time. Of course, you'll be spending most of your waking hours in the car, and if your husband is commuting to the city, he'll have to have a car, too, but I have a feeling that maintaining two cars in the country is cheaper than one in the city. (You have no garaging problem, and you save a fortune in taxis.)

Markets, cleaners, delicatessens, drug stores, bakeries and even the movies are all cleverly lumped together in shopping centers. You won't have to ask your neighbors about any of these things; they're all five minutes away from your house, and whether or not they deliver is unimportant. The milkman does deliver, but you won't have to search him out— batlike radar will lead him to your house the day after you've moved in—and he can supply you with eggs, orange juice, cottage cheese, yogurt and a bunch of other goodies as well as milk.

You'll have plenty of storage room in the basement and in the attic if not in the garage. It's probably a good idea to lock all the doors at night, but during the day, you won't have to bother.

Here endeth the idyll and beginneth the trouble. There are no adjectives to describe what it's like trying to find help in the country. *Rotten* is the first word that comes to mind.

household help

Building employees: Obviously unless you live in an apartment in the suburbs, there aren't any. Learn everything you can about your labor-saving devices (maybe your husband can teach you about the lint filter) ; find out where the fuse box is and how to change a fuse; find out where the septic tank is; and try to dope out the vagaries of the furnace and the hot-water system. Assuming that you have judiciously placed fire extinguishers all around the house, learn how to work those, too.

If you're moving into an old house, the previous owners should have left you a list of service men (plumbers, electricians, furnace fixers, etc.) , and if you've remodeled or built your own house, you'll have your own list. When your amateur machinations fail you, you'll have to call these people up and beg them to drop by. It may take them a day or two to get around to you, but when they do, you'll find that they are much pleasanter than their city equivalents; they think of you as a person, not just a service contract, and eventually, they think of you as a friend. I've spent many lovely hours chatting with our plumber in the country. We talk about kids and schools, and plumbing, which he knows I don't understand, but he keeps trying anyway.

If the previous owners have left you a gardener, or a teen-aged lawn mower, take him on; just like the janitor in the city, he may belong solely to you, or you may be sharing him with your neighbors. But whatever he is, take him, at least for now. Your husband and your own sons will be too busy getting settled themselves to manicure your lawn.

Part-time help is almost impossible to find. There may be, if you're lucky, a local employment agency that for a gigantic fee will dig you up a couple of bodies to thoroughly clean your house before you move in, but it will take you months to locate a permanent part-time helper. She probably won't have her own car, either; you'll have to fetch and take her to the bus or to her home.

Baby-sitters are somewhat simpler. Your neighbor may know of one, or there may be teen-agers in the high school who are available—but be careful about stealing someone else's; it won't be appreciated. If your neighbor has generously recommended her own, you have to make it clear to her and to the baby-sitter that the neighbor gets first call if there is a conflict. And don't pay her more than she gets from the neighbor—that won't be appreciated either.

Live-in help in the country is *absolutely* impossible to find. You can promise own room, own bath, own TV, own car, a three-hour week, and six hundred dollars a month and nobody will take you up on it. I know of only two possible solutions: The first is to import some unsuspecting foreigner who, unless she's a total fink, will honor her contract for the year. (As soon as she arrives, start negotiating for another one because, as I said before, it takes a year to cut through the red tape.) The second solution will only work for you if you have extra bedrooms. Look through the newspaper ads, or place an ad yourself, for a woman with a child. There is never room enough in a city apartment for this kind of arrangement, but there seem to be quite a few widowed or unmarried women around who, although not actually "trained" to do housework, are willing and happy to do it in exchange for a small salary plus room and board for their offspring. And as we all know, housework doesn't take training anyway; it just takes energy and a certain talent for organization.

nontechnical information for adults

Because the community is small and there is no anonymity, friends are harder to make and harder to shake. When you first move to the country, you will be nervous, jumpy, tired, *and* lonely. You'll get to know your neighbors pretty quickly, and your husband will have some business contacts in the new town, but if you turn out not to like the people in either category, it's awkward to back out of the friendship. As a matter of fact, with business associates, it may be more than awkward, it may be downright damaging to his career.

Be a joiner. Don't join just anything, but somewhere there must be organizations that will interest you. If you went to college, is there a university women's club? If you like the theater, look for an amateur community theatre group. If you're a member of the Junior League, call them up and tell them you're there.

Join the P-TA and visit your children's school; you'll find women with common interests there, too.

When you come across a woman you like, have lunch with her before you invite her and her husband for dinner. It's somehow a less formal step and constitutes less of a commitment should you discover that you hate her politics, or that you hate *her* because she never stops talking and is an opinionated bore. If she turns out to be as nice as you'd thought, the dinner invitation will probably come rather naturally from one or the other of you . . . there's no rule about who invites whom—just play it by ear.

If your husband expects to be transferred within a couple of years, you can't afford to be too fussy, because even two years without friends for you or your children is an eternity. Just like a girl who's beginning to go out on dates for the first time, you'll have to smile a lot, and you'll have to put up with some nice but dull people in the hopes that through them, you'll meet some nice but interesting ones. Unless you are startlingly peculiar (if you are, do your best to conceal it!) people are going to like you. In fact, they may even love you, because you're a pair of new faces to see on Saturday night. Eventually, you'll be asked to join the country club, or the golf club, or the garden club, and if you are church-goers, you can join that group right away without waiting to be asked.

If, on the other hand, you are moving to the community for good, you're like a beautiful girl with four older brothers: You can be more discriminating and make your friends in a more leisurely fashion. You can even be a little eccentric if you want; if you live in a town long enough, you're bound to find some other eccentrics to keep you company.

Once you've settled in, there are a few other things you'll have to do.

technical information for children

Get the clothes that you have held off buying until now, because you wanted to see what was being worn in the town (blue jeans vs. corduroys for kids, pants vs. skirts for you, etc.) .

Ideally, you have settled the school situation ahead of time, but if not, go visit the public school in your district and discuss curriculum, the grade your child belongs in, and what books you need if your child is behind in some subject and requires extra help. Ask the principal of the high school what percentage of last year's graduating class went on to college, and how many National Merit Scholars there were; this will give you some idea of the school's academic standing.

As far as private schools are concerned, check their reputations carefully before you consider them. Unless you happen to be living in an area with an exceptionally good private school and abysmal public schools (unlikely) , it may turn out that the private school is a haven for problem children who don't fit into the public school system and for children of social-climbing parents. If you want to, you can always send your children away to prep school for the last four years, but these days, colleges are inclined to favor the top graduates of a public high school over a mediocre prep school student.

Friends are much easier to make in the country because they are so instantly available at your back door and your kids can bike around the block to find others. Life is much more informal; you won't have to spend weeks on the telephone, making social arrangements. And since you'll be quite used to hopping in and out of your car twenty times a day, it won't be an overwhelming nuisance to deposit your child at the house of a school pal who lives beyond biking distance. I'm taking it for granted that you have deliberately moved into a genuinely suburban neighborhood—a house, a yard, a shady, tree-lined street—on which there are plenty of other houses and yards . . . and children.

If you have moved into a house deep in the country because you detest what I've just described above, be prepared to cope with very lonely, very restless children. Once they've gotten used to the novelty of the brook and the tree house, they're going to drive you crazy unless you provide them with some friends. Once you've done that, they're going to drive you crazy because you're going to be hopping in and out of the car not twenty times a day, but all day long. In other words, if I were you, I wouldn't buy a house deep in the country until your kids are old enough to drive themselves. **At which time they'll drive themselves** *and* **you crazy.**

By the use of such subtle adjectives as loathsome, nasty, and lonely, I guess I've managed to convey my true feelings about the process of moving and settling in. But in case there is any doubt left, let me warn you once again—it's a loathsome, nasty, lonely, intimidating, messy, confusing, and b-o-r-i-n-g business, and I hope you never have to experience it. On the bleak assumption that you will, however, I offer my sympathy and a final pithy thought to cling to in your many hours of need: It's agonizing to live through, but you *will* live through it and, like pain, you won't remember it once it's over.

INTERIORS
AND HOW
THEY GROW

Decorating is a continuing process—not always the big job of "doing everything over," but replacing a worn fabric or rug, repainting or adapting a room as its use changes with the years. However, it always costs money, and frequently what you'd like to do costs more than you can spend. When this is the case, it's encouraging to remember that, enormously important as it is, money is never the single solution to any decorating problem. What really counts is how comfortable your house makes your particular family, how well and how specifically it fits them.

As far as money goes (which is never far enough), I offer you one cheering thought: Taking your time to find the things you want can be a delight in itself. Dreaming about what you would like to see where, imagining different ways of grouping your furniture, exploring auctions, browsing in shops, looking through magazines, and, most of all, picturing yourself and your family actually living in the house—all this will help to crystallize your thinking. I know the best rooms I have ever done have taken a long time because the process of seeing them clearly in my mind's eye can take quite a while, and when that's done, I still have to find the pieces I picture. Meanwhile, living with what you have until you can get what you want isn't all that difficult. So many of our problems today, I think, stem from impatience. We have to have it *now!* Well, we don't really, you know, and the pleasures of anticipation can add immeasurably to the joy of finally owning the things you want.

What do you want? First, some space where everyone can relax and the family can be together. And, although I do feel that "formal" rooms are obsolete, if at all possible every house should also have some room that is kept reasonably free of electric trains, stray livestock, and wandering sneakers. It's nice to feel that if you bump into friends at the movies or in a restaurant, you can invite them home for a drink or a cup of coffee without worrying about whether they'll trip over things or find a place to sit down. It's a pleasure I think parents are entitled to.

living rooms

A living room is basically a place for people to sit and talk. It should be comfortable, pleasantly lit, and the furniture should be grouped so that five or six people can talk together easily. Small chairs that can be pulled up to enlarge a group are useful, too. There should be a place to put a drink and an ashtray within reach of each person. (I hate coasters, and I find they're not necessary if surfaces are waxed from time to time and if glasses and the rings they make are not left to stand for hours.)

The chances are that your living room is furnished with a combination of things you have inherited, or been given, and things you have bought. Over the years, you'll be able to weed out most of what you dislike, and when you have the chance to buy something on your own, even without a decorator's help or sources, you still have several choices open to you. You can, of course, go to the most reliable furniture dealer in town and rely on his integrity. Or you can haunt the auction rooms and take your chances. Very often you can get excellent buys—especially on upholstered pieces. You should, of course, examine them as thoroughly as possible. But you can usually be reassured if they are part of an estate sale that includes pieces of generally high quality. If you're after real bargains and you know what you want, there are thrift shops and Salvation Army stores.

People are often confused when they see two chairs that are seemingly twins except for a vast difference in price. The difference is always in the construction—much of it out of sight. Both can be good value. If, for example, you are looking for something to go in an entrance hall where it won't get heavy use, you can very well use the less expensive one. But if you want a chair for years of comfortable sitting, you'll be better off investing in the more costly of the two.

Wooden pieces are something else again. Few of us today can afford true antiques (the United States Customs definition is one hundred years old or more). And almost no one

interiors and how they grow

can find or afford period pieces—those made at the time of the original design: an eighteenth-century table made in the eighteenth century, for instance, not a nineteenth-century copy of an eighteenth-century design. However, charming pieces of uncertain age may turn out to be just what you're looking for. Fifty years of use and care may have given them a patina that newly made pieces won't have, and even a piece with good lines and of the right scale but with surface damage beyond repair can often be painted or papered.

lamps

Lamps are among the most important accessories in a living room. Lighting should never be harsh or spotty. It should illuminate the room evenly, with overlapping pools of light. Most rooms can be adequately lit by four well-placed lamps. Lamps in themselves can be beautiful, but attractive ones can be hard to find. Fortunately, you needn't depend on those in stores because it's a simple matter to mount and wire almost anything—a vase, a piece of sculpture or porcelain, even a clock.

accessories and wall treatment

Small treasures you have collected and love will add immeasurably to making the room warm and personal. As for walls, there are so many choices. If you have paintings or graphics, you will probably have solid-colored walls. But if not, wallpaper, patterned or textured fabric, a handsome mirror and a beautiful tall piece of furniture will help create interest. Even if you have lots of paintings, it's a good idea not to have them on every wall.

window treatment

To me, some method of shutting out the night is also essential. How it is done depends very much on the architectural features of the room and its general style. Shutters, blinds, and Roman shades are often used, but my preference is for curtains or draperies, or a combination of the two, because they are soft and graceful.

changing the look of a room

There comes a time in every woman's life when she's tired of a room and wants to give it a new look without doing it all over. The most obvious quick change is to repaint the walls, but your choice will be limited by the fabrics and floor covering that are to remain. Upholstered pieces (those on which almost no wood shows) can be successfully slipcovered in a totally different color and fabric for much less than it would cost to reupholster them. However, if their springs are sagging and the down has flown, slipcovers will look sloppy.

Change merely for change's sake is a bad idea. While it's useful to try shifting the grouping of furniture, once you have found the way it really works for you, leave it alone. And that's equally true of fabrics and colors; I often reupholster a chair in the same fabric or one as close to it as I can get. Changing your pictures around, however, can do a lot to make you look at them with a fresh eye. If you leave them in the same place for too long, you very often stop seeing them.

family
rooms

But a real living room is only possible if you have another, a family living room where you can be sure of tripping over trains and shoes and books, where most available seating space is draped with parkas and miscellaneous clothing, and half-finished Cokes are part of the landscape. Again, it is a question of space, but a successful family room is also a matter of organization.

In the introduction, I warned you that there would be several areas about which I know nothing. Remodeling a house is one of them. Decorating is also one of them. Come to think of it, decorating is my best one of them. But DR has generously suggested that I tackle the family room because I'm the one with the family. True, quite true, but in our house the troops are always in my bedroom or my bathroom, neither of which is a suitable site for mass meetings or entertainment or studying or whatever is supposed to go on in a family room. Of course, if we *had* a family room instead of just a hacked-up dining room, maybe everybody would be there—so out of my empty head, I'll try to construct one for you. (Construct, furnish, design? I don't even have the vocabulary for this job!)

MY FAMILY ROOM
by
Mary Rodgers Guettel

In my family, there are seven people: Tod, Nina, Kim, Adam, Alexander, my husband Hank, and me. So in my family room, everything is washable, unbreakable, and

interiors and how they grow

cheap. Not vulgar, just inexpensive and replaceable, because boys will be boys and girls will be girls and together they are destroyers. This room is soundproof, spotproof, fireproof, shatterproof, litterproof and eighty proof (there's a built-in bar, because my husband and I occasionally have to share this room with the destroyers). We have vinyl wallpaper, vinyl tile floor, vinyl chair covers, machine-washable scatter rugs, curtains, slipcovers, and pillow covers. We have several comfortable chairs and a sofa bed for overnight guests, a permanently set up bridge table at one end of the room, and a dining room table at the other end. The dining room table is made of marble, Formica, or stainless steel—I forget which —but it certainly isn't wood or glass, and there is no scatter rug under it because destroyers are also messy eaters.

Three out of four walls have built-in bookshelves and cabinets to house TV, hi-fi, FM, trains, games, puzzles, a left-handed first baseman's mitt, and one sneaker. I don't visualize the fourth wall too well, but I guess there's a door or a window in it somewhere and maybe some blank space for posters.

A nice imaginative use of color—red, white, and blue, for instance. Black is out, too gloomy. Doesn't show the dirt, though—but red, white and blue is nicer. Besides, everything's washable. I forgot that.

This is a lovely, big room, twenty-five feet square, good for teen-age dances, children's birthday parties, pitch and putt, informal banquets. The whole family enjoys it.

THE END

For my next theme, I'm going to do MY SUMMER VACATION, but before I get to that . . .

You sound like every client a decorator ever had, and now I'm going to sound like every decorator!

First of all, I need to know exactly what you and Hank want to use the room for. Then let's see if I can give you most of what you want. Since you're bridge players and accustomed to using points of the compass for identification, let's use that system: South is the wall with the windows,

West has a door at one end leading to the kitchen, North has a door that leads to the rest of the apartment, and East is reserved for the sofa and other pieces of furniture.

We'll assume there's no separate dining room, so in the West wall, let's open a pass-through to the kitchen. The pass-through should consist of a nice roomy counter, about three feet deep and nine feet long, with two sets of folding doors, one opening into the family room and the other closing off the kitchen. (To get the three feet, steal about twenty inches from each of the two rooms and allow two inches for each set of doors.) The counter's surface should be heatproof and, as you say, washable. The best height is the one most comfortable for most of the family, but I find forty inches just about right; it leaves you with good space below for cupboards on the family room side to store extra bridge tables, table tops, folding chairs, trays, and party equipment. Put your bar supplies next to the counter on shelves concealed by panels, and store wines and liquor in the upper section in honeycomb shelves.

Now let's add a few electric outlets so that you can not only keep food hot, but actually prepare it in the family room when you feel like it. So many wonderfully intelligent pots and pans have appeared on the market that you aren't limited anymore to dull chafing-dish items like scrambled eggs and welsh rarebit.

Now let's even out the wall by adding built-in cupboards. Since you, Hank, the kids, and lots of your friends love looking at 16mm films at home, how about providing a permanent spot in this West wall for the projector? Plug it in and set it on a pull-out track to make it easy to get at; focus it on the East wall, perhaps above the sofa bed (which I forgot to tell you I've upholstered in smashing shades of blue and white fabric treated to be soil resistant). Meanwhile, back in the counter wall, let's also install the TV—about forty inches above the floor on a track and on a turntable so the screen can be seen from all parts of the room. (Be sure to leave air space in back of it to reduce the fire hazard.)

To enjoy great stereo sound, get the best pair of speakers you can find (the same speakers will work for films, TV, hi-fi, tape recorder, and AM-FM) and install them one on either side of the pass-through (they can be put up high since you won't need to touch them once they've been set in place). Put the hi-fi turntable and AM-FM tuner in one of a pair of sturdy end tables flanking the sofa, which should be your best spot for listening. Use the other table for record storage and tape recorder, and add red Formica table tops and a pair of good-sized white lamps.

Since Nina likes to sew, find a place in the storage wall for her to plug in the machine, and remember to give her a good small light. A cutting table and an ironing board might fit in, too (don't forget an outlet for the iron!). Then, if there's any space left in the counter wall, use it for records, games, trains, and puzzles. Put Kim's easel in a corner near the window. Tod will be happy with his hi-fi, and Adam and Alexander can have their own fun without doing any damage.

Ha!

Since we've dreamed up windows in the middle of the South wall, build in some adjustable floor-to-ceiling bookshelves on either side of them, and frame them with washable white draperies tied back with thick red rope. Make the window shades of the same dazzling blue and white stuff used on the sofa bed, but this time have the shade-maker treat the fabric so that it can be wiped clean with a damp cloth. Since you're all great floor-sitters, get fifteen foam-rubber pillows (30″ × 36″ × 4″), cover them with red, white, and blue terrycloth slipcovers, and stack them in a triple row under the windows against the wall when they're not needed.

You asked for a vinyl floor, Mary, but I may try to talk you out of it. In a room where the quality of sound is important, I think you'd all be happier with one of those inexpensive indoor-outdoor wall-to-wall carpets. They wash easily, and they're less trouble to maintain than vinyl. After all, how often do you have a dance?

In either case, the floor color should be *red*. And I see the walls covered in a textured white vinyl with the trim done in matching washable paint. Because the warmth of natural wood is beautiful, and a waxed finish is so easy to take care of, how about leaving the paneling and the bookshelves unpainted?

Put your dining table near the North wall opposite the windows. Have the table marble-topped if you like, but please make it a round one (it's so much better for talk);

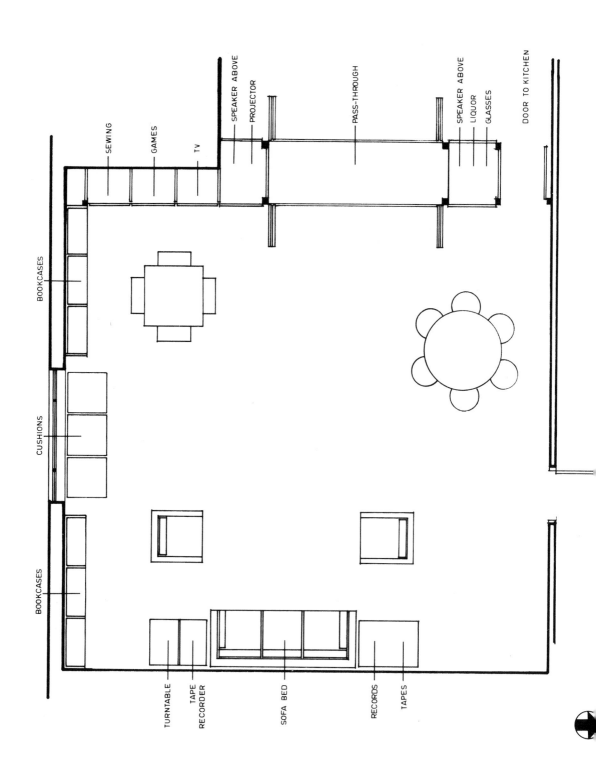

SEWING

GAMES

TV

SPEAKER ABOVE

PROJECTOR

PASS-THROUGH

SPEAKER ABOVE

LIQUOR

GLASSES

DOOR TO KITCHEN

BOOKCASES

CUSHIONS

BOOKCASES

TURNTABLE

TAPE
RECORDER

SOFA BED

RECORDS

TAPES

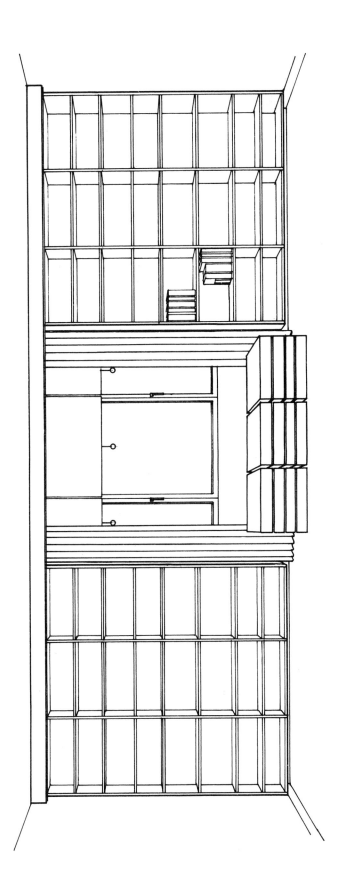

SOUTH WALL

Windows flanked by bookcases. Foam-rubber cushions stacked on floor below windows. Floor-length draperies may be installed from back of cornice to floor between bookcases and windows.

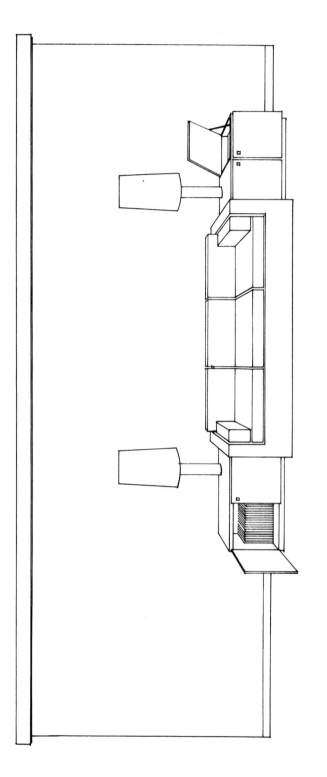

E A S T   W A L L

Pull-out sofa bed flanked by end tables holding record player, tuner, and tape recorder in one and record and cassette storage in other.

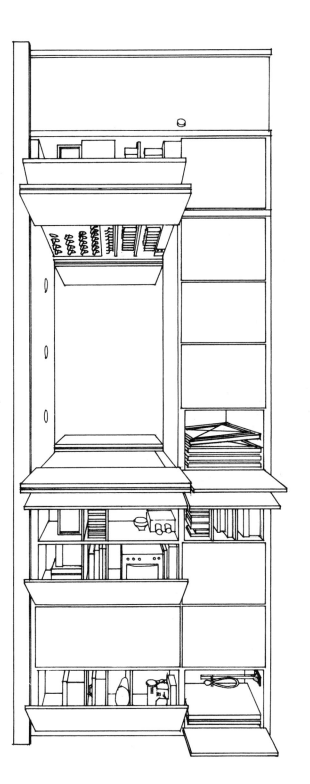

WEST WALL

Details of pass-through opening into kitchen. Storage space for sewing machine, TV, two amplifiers, film projector, bridge tables, bar equipment, games, and miscellaneous items. Door leading to kitchen is at right.

one that is forty-eight inches in diameter will seat six comfortably, but with a little crowding, you can manage seven. For any number over seven, let people serve themselves buffet style and sit all over the room. Get eight small comfortable chairs for dining, and four small (swivel, if possible) arm chairs to match for your permanent bridge table. Give them bright blue shiny vinyl seat pads. Cover the bridge table top with red felt, and set it up near the window. Now find a couple of big upholstered chairs on casters that will turn easily to let you watch television or that can be pushed out of the way when necessary.

Install some incandescent lights in the ceiling of the pass-through, and add strip lighting around all four walls. This not-very-complicated installation involves a cornice four to six inches deep and about five inches in from the wall, behind which are long incandescent bulbs shielded by translucent plastic strips; it will be particularly useful for reading book titles on the window wall. As for ceiling fixtures, I'm generally against them because they're not called "fixtures" for nothing. They're so "fixed" that your furniture groupings become totally inflexible. Two floor lamps should complete your lighting scheme. A few pillows for the sofa, posters for the wall, and, oh yes! ashtrays for the table.

Of course, most people will never have a real room that size, but no two families are alike, and therefore no two family rooms should be. If all this gets the rest of you started thinking about and planning a room of your own, it will have achieved its purpose. Meanwhile, there are other important rooms to consider.

bedrooms   Bedrooms are the most personal rooms in the house, and they should be as close as possible to the way their owners want them. Some people crave lots of gadgets—a refrigerator, a television set, an electric coffeepot. Others yearn for a cave with nothing but a large bed and dark walls. It makes no matter as long as it makes you happy.

I like bedrooms that are more than just a place to sleep. So my own provides me with desk space, bookcases, and it has a great big sofa where, when the children were small, they could curl up with their homework. There's something particularly cozy about a bedroom that has a sofa or a couple of comfortable chairs, some books and possibly a desk. Hank and I also have a bedroom that's more than just a place to sleep. With the child-traffic that goes on there, who could sleep? Actually, this is fine with us—we like having them around—but we've made one mistake: Our biggest, most lavish, unportable television set is in there. It's a color one, which makes it doubly fascinating for the kids, and I hate trying to talk over the phone and "Sesame Street" at the same time. Then there are some nights when I want to read in bed, but three lumpy teen-agers are lying on their stomachs on my stomach watching "The Bold Ones," which, they assure me, is no good in black and white. In other words, I strongly advise you to put your best set in the family room and keep a small portable one in your bedroom.

I gain extra space in my bedroom by eliminating a dressing table. (I like to fix my hair and do my make-up in the bathroom.) You can also make the room seem larger by using a minimum of storage furniture, and perhaps you can build some chests of drawers into a closet or gain an extra closet by stealing one from an adjacent room and breaking through the wall.

You'll want to check on the source of daylight, and if your windows face east, place your bed so that it doesn't face into the sun. And make sure you have opaque shades that fit properly to block out the dawn's early light. Check on electric outlets to see that there are not only enough for lamps and a TV set, if you like one in the bedroom, but one or two extra places to plug in small appliances that you use only occasionally—and for glorious things still to be invented.

children's bedrooms

Bedrooms for small children should be made as safe as possible, with a minimum of sharp points and hard edges on furniture. Small children in city apartments love to throw things out of windows. When Tod was three, he chucked several hard wood blocks, one each of two pairs of slippers, a pillow, and an aluminum footstool into the courtyard thirteen stories below. Luckily, nobody happened to be standing there, but somebody might have been; so in order to prevent an incipient Isaac Newton from dropping lethal objects (including himself) into the street, put bars on the windows. Good contemporary wall fixtures are available everywhere now, and for children's rooms I like them much better than lamps on small tables that tip over easily. Colors should be bold and rooms uncluttered—kids manage to do their own cluttering with almost no effort; there should be plenty of shelves for toys and books . . . and plenty of closed-in cabinets behind which you can hide all the nasty plastic bits and pieces that look messy on the shelves no matter how many times a day you rearrange them. And, for electric trains and such, how about a big sturdy table on very low legs and casters so it can be wheeled under the bed and out of the way (be sure to keep enough open floor space so it can be pulled out)? If two small children have to share a bedroom, as is often the case in an apartment, the best thing on casters that can be wheeled under the bed and out of the way is the second bed. Unpainted furniture stores have ingenious space-saving inventions for children's rooms—beds that pull out, double-decker beds, combination beds, and bookshelves —and they have designers who will help you figure out how best to use the space you have. You can also arrange to have them paint the stuff for you, but it's more expensive that way and more fun for a kid to do it himself. When the furniture arrives, put newspapers on the floor, slap a paint brush into his hand, and let him go to town with the primer coat. If he's spectacularly neat or older than eight, he can even help you with the two subsequent coats of enamel. Indoor-outdoor carpeting is fine for the floor: It's safer than vinyl, pleasanter to sit on, easy to clean and—for the people who live below you in an apartment—blissfully quiet. Finally, there should be a comfortable chair for you to sit in while feeding the baby and while reading to young children later. Make it a very large chair; kids always want to sit with you or on you while you're reading so they can see the pictures.

privacy

For children, and for grown-ups, too, privacy is at a premium these days when all buildings, apartments especially, seem to have been planned within a square inch of their lives. If you are stuck with one of those modern wonders that is all tiny rooms and no halls, I really don't know the answer. But fortunately, it isn't always that bad. Very often it is possible to partition a room in such a way that children can have small bedrooms to themselves as well as a larger shared space for play and homework.

The challenge of trying to create privacy when space is at a premium sometimes pushes you into a brilliant solution.

interiors and how they grow

When my niece, Judy, and her husband, Bob Crichton, bought and remodeled their house in New York, my sister-in-law, Wilhelmina, who is a professional interior designer, came up with just such a plan. The Crichtons, who have four children, wanted privacy for them as well as a place where the kids could do homework, entertain friends, and watch TV. The problem was fitting all this on a single floor of a rather narrow town house. The solution: Sarah and Susie—the oldest and youngest girls—share a room, because their hours are different enough to keep clashes at a minimum. Jenny has her own tiny room, and so has Rob. And a larger room has been turned into a living room-study for all the kids. (Its sofa becomes a bed for overnight visitors.) In Jenny's room, which is barely six feet wide, a chest of drawers and a desk, both with their backs upholstered, serve as head- and footboards for the bed. One wall has been left bared to the bricks—it makes a great background for posters. The floors are covered with indoor-outdoor carpeting. As it always does, the lavish and skillfully planned use of color (the ceilings are painted dark blue, orange, red, and yellow) has made a great contribution and added nothing to the cost.

When my two granddaughters, Nina and Kim, asked me to redo their bedroom, they made it clear that they wanted as much privacy as possible. Since there was no way to partition the room, I tried to give it to them by designing things so that the only shared pieces of furniture are a bookcase and an étagère. The beds, with their heads at opposite ends, are placed along one wall so that the length of both separates one head from the other. Each girl has her own reading lamp, dressing table-desk, and chest of drawers.

Fortunately, they had no trouble agreeing on general style and colors—a lot of white with tomato, orange, and yellow. First choice: those wonderful, bright, reversible wool bedspreads made in Spain (the girls picked tones of orange and white). Automatically, certain other decisions became obvious: For one, pattern had to be limited. Three walls are covered in a textured white vinyl and the fourth with cork, painted white, an ideal surface for tacking up all those things kids love to tack up. The furniture on the desk wall is painted white with white Formica tops; the beds are white wicker. The wall-to-wall carpet is tomato color, the curtains

interiors and how they grow

are a bold yellow-and-white cotton print, and the window shades are of the same fabric treated to make them washable. Lamps are contemporary in design—yellow and white plastic. There are masses of Op Art pillows on the beds. An étagère made of lucite stands in one corner, adding some glamour and providing a place to keep gay colored scarves, beads, and assorted pretty things. White fiberglass swivel chairs—two with arms and two armless ones at the desks—have orange and yellow patent pads, and the change from a room that started life with four-poster beds and rather drearily conventional furniture and colors is quite electric.

The room proves a point: It has been designed for its occupants, and it looks right for them. I had great fun doing it and I love it. But five years ago it wouldn't have occurred to me to do a room like it, because its strong hot colors and plastics are so much a part of today.

The room is now not only the prettiest one in the apartment, but also the cleanest. Because our apartment building has casement windows, which let in more greasy, grimy city filth than any other kind, DR made one important improvement: She had the whole window frame replaced. To redo all your windows is much too expensive an undertaking for most people, but I do urge you to install air conditioning in as many rooms as you can. That, too, is expensive, but you don't have to do it all at once, and when you've finally sealed yourself in hermetically, you'll find your cleaning bills are much lower, and the city noises will be less obtrusive. By the way, you need heavy-duty wiring for most air conditioners. If your apartment already has it, fine. If not, you may have to foot the expense of running a line up from the street, and depending on how high up you are, this may prove more expensive than the cleaning bills.

bathrooms Dull bathrooms needn't stay that way. Graphics, wall decorations, and even your children's drawings can brighten them. Even old-fashioned bathrooms look attractive with new wall covering or printed towels. If you're lucky enough to have white fixtures, you might try keeping floor and wall coverings neutral and, instead of buying all the same color bath towels, getting different sets—solids, patterns, stripes. That way just changing the towels changes the whole look. Many people like bathroom carpeting because it looks pretty

90

and feels so cozy to walk on, but, if you choose to have it, you should make sure it can go into the washing machine and dryer. Incidentally, if your bathroom lacks a shower, the "hand-telephone" kind is easy to install and makes a great substitute. I actually prefer it to a stand-up shower, and it's sensational for washing hair.

learning about decorating

Learning about decorating can be approached in many ways. Caring about your home is the first, the essential step —one you've already taken if you're reading this chapter. Beyond that, it's a question of looking, really looking. Think of the rooms you've liked and try to discover what appealed to you about them. Was it basically an appeal to the eye through the use of color and light? Or was it a quality—a particularly serene feeling about a room good for talk or reading or listening to music? Was it a mood of excitement and energy—a room for a big party?

Browse, too, through magazines and department store displays, but be a little wary. Though the colors and lines may be great, nobody really lives in those glorious model rooms at Gump's or Gimbel's, and the same can be true of the delightful "sets" they photograph for magazines. I've seen Louis XV wood and upholstered chairs photographed in an outdoor patio, where they would never survive. And, at best, rooms designed for imaginary people can never be anything but impersonal.

It isn't important for you, as a layman, to become an expert on antiques and periods; reputable dealers and professionals can advise you about them. Knowing clearly just what you want is much more important. Though you may not be able to bring it about by yourself, with the help of a good designer you should come pretty close.

working without a designer

Some women are quite capable of decorating their houses imaginatively and beautifully without any help. They love the planning, the shopping, the detail work. And from beginning to end, they're unworried and sure their families will be pleased. They wouldn't have it any other way—and that's wonderful. But most wives faced with the prospect of redoing a room—not to mention a whole house—find themselves bewildered and slightly terrified. There are so many decisions to make and so many subtle points to understand. Along with reassuringly tangible items like rugs and chairs and wallpapers, there are such disturbingly vague concepts as mood, texture, form, and scale. And the whole changing world of colors: How is one affected by another? by light? by the room's exposure? Should the curtains be long or short? lined or unlined? opaque or transluscent? to draw or not to draw? Should the walls be painted or papered or covered with fabric? Where is there room for books? the television set?

Buying a dress that turns out to be wrong is annoying and sometimes expensive. But it can't compare to the anguish and cost involved in the wrong decision about hundreds of dollars' worth of wall-to-wall carpeting or draperies that you can't afford to replace but that you are going to have to look at every day for years. So, for the average woman, I think it's safer, more comfortable and, in the long run, more economical to take advantage of some professional help. And for people who find it impossible to visualize the results, it is essential.

interior designers

Interior designers—which is what they like to be called, since house painters, paperhangers, and upholsterers all seem to be styling themselves "decorators" these days—are schooled in the mysteries of color and texture and scale. They know where specific fabrics, wall coverings, and furniture can be found. Most of the best places are "to the trade only" and are not available to the public without the services of a professional. Designers also know craftsmen who can do the work. The fact that their stock in trade is keeping up with (almost ahead of) new designs and materials, often gives them ready solutions to problems that may look unsolvable to you. And having been down the road before, they can help you avoid its pitfalls.

how to find one

Where do you look for a designer? Large department stores have professional staffs who consult with customers and plan purchases to solve specific problems. Friends' recommendations are helpful, especially if you like the work a particular designer has done for them. A word of caution: The right designer stands a good chance of ending as your friend, but don't start out with friendship as the basis of your relationship. The situation can get very sticky and lose you a friend besides.

In a new community, where do you go? You can window-

interiors and how they grow

shop and, when you find an interesting-looking room, find out who designed it and introduce yourself and your problem. Or you can contact the local chapter of the American Institute of Interior Design (AID) or the National Society of Interior Designers (NSID), give them some idea of the work you need done and any strong feelings you have about style or period, and ask them to suggest members who might work with you. Then call and set up appointments. Feel free to ask anyone you are seriously considering about seeing examples of his work. Photographs are useful, especially when they're in color. But a room you can walk into, with fabrics you can touch and chairs and sofas you can sit on, is a thousand percent more revealing.

working with a designer

A good designer can, with your help, design a room, or a number of them, that will truly reflect you and your family. The operative words in that sentence are "with your help." You can't drop ideas about furniture, floor plans, and a few sketchy thoughts in his lap and sit back complacent in the knowledge that he, or she, will magically produce a room—much less a house—that is "utterly you." It just doesn't work that way. When it comes to the real test of living in and with them, the only successful decorating schemes are collaborations between a client who knows what she wants and can afford and a skilled professional designer. He can show you the possibilities, but only you can make the choices that will please your family most. It takes patience and considerable conferring. So the man or woman you choose should be someone you like and with whom you feel easy.

Try to find a designer who makes you feel that he is not only sympathetic to your point of view, but that he welcomes your suggestions—and that he might even like them. The person you finally choose will want to know a great deal about you and your family: numbers, ages, and sexes, of course, but also what your hobbies are, how you like to entertain and how often and, when it comes to rooms the whole family uses, what activities the room should be equipped for. In short, he has to know how you like to live before he can begin to plan. He must also know, reasonably accurately, what you can spend before he can tell you what he can do. And the more realistic you are to start with, the better your chance of being really pleased with the results.

The how and how much of payment should be settled before work starts. Independent designers work in several different ways. Some make their profit by buying wholesale (from stores, antique dealers, wallpaper and fabric houses) and charging you retail prices for the things they supply. Others charge a flat fee for the whole job—in which case, the discount savings are passed along to you. Another group charges by the hour for consultation (here again, you are charged wholesale prices for the things they buy). And a fourth category works on a "cost plus" basis with a percentage of the wholesale-priced total added to each bill. You should agree on how often you are to be billed and what payment terms will be. Find out, too, about drawings ("renderings," the trade calls them). Will you be charged for them? If so, are they yours? This sounds like a strange question, but if you pay only for the mechanical labor of the draftsman, the "idea" and the drawings remain the designer's property. On the whole, I'm wary of renderings. They are generally expensive and often make the room look much prettier than it has any hope of being. I prefer to use "elevations"—blueprints of each wall—which are safely unglamorized and which, though they don't show perspective, give you a precise idea of exactly what will be where.

I've had people—nice bright people with reasonably straight faces—ask me to tell them how building, remodeling, and decorating costs can be kept from going beyond the estimates. My only answer to that one is: Dear reader, if you find out, please tell me. The only cost control I know is thinking ahead—because it saves changes, and afterthoughts are always expensive.

Many people fear that interior designers will tempt them to spend more than they can afford. It is true that a decorator will try to show you the full range of possibilities where your house is concerned. And many of them may be tempting. Should you be so tempted that you decide to do this *and* that rather than this *or* that, costs are bound to mount. However, if you ask your designer to keep a strict eye on the budget and on you, he will do his best. It is also a very good idea to minimize spur-of-the-moment changes—which individually seem to cost almost nothing, but taken collectively can total quite a sum. To guard against impulse changes, make it a rule that only the designer can give orders to painters, upholsterers, plasterers—anyone who works on your job.

The most valuable skills a designer has probably have to do with his knowledge of how to play down the structural defects almost every house has to some degree. He can make windows that are too small seem larger (by extending curtains beyond their true limits all the way to the end of the wall; by adding height with valences or cornices; by placing mirrors between or on either side of the windows themselves). He can smooth an effect by boxing exposed pipes or evening out a wall that has a structural beam in it and then building bookcases or cupboards. Or, if you can't afford a lot of custom cabinet work, he can suggest other ways to achieve the same effect. Most important, he can show you how to spend your money wisely on things that you'll live with all your lives, like good upholstered furniture, and where you can spend a little to gain a big effect. Even if he does nothing else, he will have earned his fee.

DR obviously feels that most of you will require some professional help when it comes to decorating and, reluctantly, I have to agree with her. No matter how confident you are in this department, there are still some things you can't do for yourself. You might, for instance, know exactly what *kind* of material you want for your couch, but only a decorator can get you into fabric houses where you can find it—or at least look for it. She also has access to carpenters, upholsterers, and painters, which you will not have, especially if you are moving to a new part of the country.

Now DR also says you should look for someone you really like and with whom you feel easy. That's very good advice, but very hard to follow. Even if you find a decorator you like, how are you going to feel easy with someone who, morning, noon and night, for weeks on end, asks you questions you can't answer and asks you to make decisions you don't know how to make? Well, be prepared: You're probably not going to feel easy until the whole job is done. What you're going to feel is indecisive and confused.

In my lifetime, I've had dealings with three decorators. The first, my mother, almost doesn't count because she knows full well how indecisive and confused I am and she also knows what I like. The second did a nice job, but she

95

interiors and how they grow

cost me my self-respect, my sanity (temporarily, anyway), and a great deal of money. The third decorator was adorable. She actually gave me back my self-respect, I loved working with her, and she saved me a fortune by hunting down carpet sales, getting a Formica top put on an old kitchen table, sewing bathroom curtains for me—she was an indefatigable Yankee bargain-hunter with a sunny personality who wanted to please me, not her.

This is not what you could call extensive experience with decorators, but it was enough to lead me to some conclusions about the way the average, confused, indecisive amateur ought to cope with them, and herself. For what it's worth, here they are:

You need *discipline.* When the decorator tries to elicit your opinion on esoteric trivia such as the kind of bathroom faucets you want, brushed chrome vs. shiny chrome, or the depth of the cornice from the ceiling, do not dismiss her and her question with a vague "Oh, I don't know, you decide." She'll decide for you, but it won't seem like such esoteric trivia when you hate the faucets or the cornice. A decorator is always asking you boring little technical questions, but in every single case, make her explain to you what she's talking about, make her draw you pictures if you still don't get it, and make her tell you why she prefers one thing to another.

You need *thick skin.* You have, let's say, a sideboard that's been in your family for years. You love it, but the decorator does not. If she's the overbearing, unsympathetic, intimidating type (which is something you can't always find out until you've hired her), she'll say, "Let's get rid of that tacky old piece, shall we?" If she's the nice type, she'll say, "I can't quite see where your lovely old sideboard fits into our dining room scheme. Don't you think perhaps you should store it—or sell it?" The answer is no. Don't let her embarrass you, and don't get hurt feelings. It's your sideboard, your dining room, your family, your nickel, and her problem to accommodate your desires.

You need, and this is paramount, the *courage of your convictions,* although there will come a time when you're positive you don't have any. This time is usually in the beginning. The decorator takes you to three fabric houses in one day, she flips through hanging racks of material with the speed of a card shark in Las Vegas, mumbling, "No, no, no, no! maybe, this one's nice, no, no, yes, yes." And what are you doing while she's doing that? You're just standing there, a numbskull, utterly baffled by this riotous profusion of colors and chintz and heaven knows what all—she went too fast for you to see what she picked. So ask her to go back over it more slowly, and if you see something you think you like, say so.

Now, take all the samples home and spread them around. Do not study them or think about them. Rely on pure instinct; if you find your eyes keep gravitating toward the same particular sample, that's the right one, no matter what the decorator likes. This rule works for all areas where choice is involved: The decorator will help you amass the various possibilities, but believe it or not, you *do* know what you want if you give yourself half a chance, and you most certainly know what you don't want.

I guess, when you think about it, the function of a good decorator is primarily to help you use your own instincts, to help you project your own personality and individuality beyond yourself to the rooms you live in. So just relax and decide what you like, what feels good to you, and you're going to end up with a nice house.

I'm sure some women dream of finding themselves in a naked house with nothing but a checkbook (unlimited funds, of course) and a designer. "Go," they would say, "buy, create. We'd like to move in in two months." And sixty days later, back they would come to a house that's all new and all divine. I happen to know a woman for whom that dream came true. Having lived happily with conventional decor for twenty-five years, she and her husband decided it was time for a change. So they bought a new apartment, called in a designer, and gave him carte blanche. A contemporary place was what they ordered. He was to do furniture, rugs, paintings, linens, china, silver, ornaments and vases— even supply instructions about what flowers to use and how to use them. Cost was not important, and everything was to be new. They went off on a trip, and when they came back they moved in, taking only their clothes with them. I must say it was a beautiful job, including the flowers on the dinner table, but I couldn't have let anyone do that for me. I could not bear to break so completely with the past and live in a place so entirely impersonal, no matter how attractive it was. The things you buy or keep because you love them give your house character that no one else can ever achieve for you.

So you have your house, and probably a designer. And you have assorted furniture that has moved in with you either because you love it or because, at this particular moment in your life, you can't afford to replace it. You start off by distributing it around the house. Fine. But where do you go from there?

making a start

Since no two houses or families or sets of decorating problems are alike, it's impossible to lay down an absolute step-by-step plan of attack. But although some of my suggestions may differ from your designer's ideas, perhaps they can serve as guidelines and be helpful if you are trying to cope with the job yourself.

To me, the best start has always been a scaled diagram of each room (using graph paper makes this very easy). Next, I cut out pieces of cardboard or Manila paper scaled to the floor plan to represent the furniture I have, and I label them "bed," "chair," "chest," or "table" and shift them around on the plan until I find where they fit best—it's lots easier than shifting real furniture.

What you tackle next will depend to some extent on the things you already own—a striped sofa in near-perfect condition, a strawberry-colored carpet, your favorite flower-printed draperies—each imposes its own set of limits on the patterns, the styles, and the colors you use in the room with it.

In a room with no inherited restrictions, you are free to start with a fabric you really love. When rug colors were limited, you almost had to do your planning from the floor up. But now, with so many stock colors to choose from—not to mention the ease of custom dying—you might begin with the upholstery or drapery material, or even with a fabric to cover the walls. (Be very careful with this last trick. It's been done to death in recent years, it's expensive to install if done correctly, and it's difficult to maintain. On the other hand, loosely hung fabric that matches your draperies is graceful and effective when it comes to masking structural defects in your walls.) Or perhaps you might find the perfect wallpaper—an especially good thought if you're short on pictures —and go from there. However, choosing wallpaper is a difficult business—having it surrounding you on all four walls is very different from seeing a sample or even a roll. That's why so many amateurs tend to go wrong with it, or end by "playing it safe"—which can be very dull indeed.

painting walls

When it comes to painting, colors are certainly no problem, with patience you can end with just what you want. Rightly or wrongly, painters are often suspected of taking the easy way out. If the shade you want is difficult to match, they probably won't bother. Samples won't necessarily save you. I remember one friend who watched carefully as the man stirred and dabbed until he had mixed just what she wanted. She returned to a finished job that to her eye looked (and was) a whole different color. But she was utterly frustrated because the ingenious painter had painted over the sample with the rest of the wall, and she couldn't prove a thing.

Professionals take precautions and so can you. Arm yourself with two pieces of plywood or board on which you ask the painter to put samples of the colors you've okayed and number them. (Don't use cardboard because it's porous and will soak up the paint and change the color.) Be sure the paint is dry before you approve the samples. Leave one board with him, and take the other home. This way there's no chance of his switching samples; you can also check the colors in both daylight and artificial light. Some colors are particularly tricky and, especially in a room you'll be using only in the evening, it is important to see how they look under incandescent lights (some yellows go quite green). Don't bother to test with fluorescent light—just don't use it.

Time was when the best paint jobs (certainly any on less-than-perfect walls) began with a layer of canvas that kindly hid the faults that lay underneath. Today, you seldom have to go to that expense. You can probably find a solid-colored vinyl wall covering in a texture you like and the color you want, and if you want to change it later, simply paint over it.

ceilings
When it comes to ceilings, I like mine on the simple side—unless, of course, Michelangelo happens to be available. Most often I choose a pale tint of the color that's on the walls, especially since most ceilings are low to begin with. But if yours are in the rare house where they are too high, you may want to paint them a darker shade to bring them down a bit.

lighting
In dark rooms, warm colors help a lot—I've used a combination of pale yellow and artificial lighting for walls and draperies to suggest sun. Incandescent strip lighting bathes the walls with a light that is as warm and flattering as lamplight. Some modern lighting is too cold for my taste—much of it is installed in the ceiling and quite unflattering. I have, however, seen several examples of lit-up plastic furniture that seem to glow, and that I think would make fine conversation pieces in the right rooms.

floors
Your floors may well be your best chance to splash some color around. How you do it will depend on the state of the floors themselves and, if you live in an apartment, to some extent on your neighbors. If your floors are beautiful, by all means let them be seen—at least in part. Polish them, and choose scatter rugs (all with non-skid backs or pads, of course). If you have people living below you, you should carpet most of the floor out of consideration for them. Painting and spattering are other possibilities where the wood is nondescript and noise doesn't disturb anyone. (I've even covered floors with paper and coats of varnish.)

Synthetic carpets tend to soil faster but can be cleaned more successfully than wool. For my money, however, wool is still the best choice: Its colors are more vibrant, it does not mat as readily, and it looks better longer. But unless you are reasonably sure that this move is going to be permanent, I think it's a mistake to spend a great deal for wall-to-wall carpeting which can't help turning into a misfit when it's time for your next transfer. What if you're already endowed with leftover carpeting? Just don't think of it as carpeting any more; have it made into a rug—rectangular, round, or oval. If it's good quality wool and not too worn, you can even have it dyed to fit a new color scheme. If your carpets are dark and you want a lighter color, they will have to be bleached first.

Vinyl covers so many floors these days that being against any form of it would be a little like being against children and dogs (especially since some of the best jobs it does are in rooms used by children and dogs!). But I hate floor vinyls (or any synthetic) designed to look like what they're not: wood, brick, marble, or tile, for instance. And I'm unalterably opposed to gold flecks, gold stripes, or the custard-in-aspic look. I like vinyl to look like vinyl.

ornaments

Ornaments or accessories add the finishing touches that make a room particularly yours, but don't rush out and buy them in wholesale lots. You can't make a list and go out and shop for them, because what really makes them effective is the special charm they have for you. You'll find them unexpectedly—on a trip away from home or during a walk around the corner. So be patient and, when it comes to necessities like ashtrays, buy the least expensive glass ones you can find. The ones that really go with the room—antique plates or pewter, perhaps—will come later.

Among the questions I'm asked most often is whether it's all right to mix periods and patterns in the same room. And my answer to that one is yes of course—if it's skillfully done. But lest that seems to leave you right where you started, let me add that I think this is one place where you need a professional's advice.

new ideas

From the start, the designer you choose will do a tremendous amount of legwork and research on your behalf. And in these imaginative times, it is more than likely that along with the expected in wall coverings, fabrics, chairs, tables, and what-have-you, he will bring you some things that are new. Some you'll hate, some will intrigue you, some you may even like. Although I'm against fads in decorating, I'm all for keeping your mind open to new ideas. It seems to me that the ideal approach combines an affection for the past with a lively interest in new things. You don't have to like it all. Some "now" phrases like "up tight" and "turned on" and "gross" that sound natural coming from Tod, Kimmy, Nina, and Peter sound all wrong coming from me. Decorating ideas can be like that, too: a color or furniture style you might find fun in a store's model room or somebody else's house might be all wrong for your home.

Yet tastes and ideas do change. It's amazing how quickly the eye accepts new things if you provide the exposure. To take a personal example, I now find a lot of the new plastic furniture exciting and beautiful. Only last month I bought a small table that is clear plastic and entirely geometric to go next to a Hepplewhite chair in our living room—a combination that would have been unthinkable for us two years ago. I think that kooky inflatable plastic furniture is great for people who are on the move (imagine deflating the living room and packing it in a two-by-three carton!), but I'm still not ready for some things. For instance, no matter how they praise it, I doubt that you'll ever find me laying carpeting in my kitchen.

While we may not be living in an age of great art, we are certainly exposed to some first-rate design. Things we use every day like pots, casseroles, toasters, high-intensity lamps, and clocks are often extremely handsome, and I find the local hardware store irresistible.

On another level, there are so many graphics available now—silk screen prints, lithographs, posters, multiples (limited editions supervised by the artist)—that even if you can't afford original paintings, you can still collect first-rate art that is valuable because the medium is part of the artist's total conception. I am fascinated by the new plastic constructions—sculpture that is not "sculpture" in the old sense, the kind of thing Louise Nevelson does so brilliantly.

With such new and old temptations everywhere, the amount you spend will almost certainly exceed your early estimates. But wisely spent, it will give you a great deal of pleasure. I rationalize it this way: The more chaotic the world gets, the more complicated our lives become, and the more we need restoring, the more we all need havens. That is what a house should be. And I can't think of a better investment.

HUSBANDRY

In a book for wives, there are all kinds of topics that don't absolutely have to be included. Decorating, for instance. If one of us didn't happen to know something about it, there wouldn't be anything about it. The same goes for remodeling houses, or vacations, or entertaining. Even children . . . there are, after all, a few scattered wives who don't have any; we could have written a book for them, thereby avoiding (and evading) that whole subject, too.

But husbands? There is no conceivable way to come up with a book for wives without mentioning husbands. Like it or not, they are the nitty-gritty of this book, and I'll tell you right now, from where I sit, I don't like where I'm sitting. It's a very hot seat. Here's why:

1. All husbands are married men.

2. All married men are one half of a profoundly complex arrangement called marriage.

3. All marriages are different (from all other marriages) because all men are different (from all other men, married or not), and so are all women (different, married or not). Q.E.D.: Any chapter that purports to deal with husbands is, in essence, a chapter about marriage, and I don't want to write it. I'm frequently quite baffled enough wending my way through the delicious intricacies of my own, and, like everyone else, my own is the only one I know anything much about.

All of which is to prepare you for a good deal of hedging. At the end or at the beginning of every paragraph on what you *might* do ("might" being a hedge word in itself), there will probably be a sentence that begins "on the other hand" or "not everybody." And even if the actual sentence isn't there, do we agree that the implication is? All right then. Ready or not, here come my thoughts on the Care, Feeding, and General Maintenance of Husbands—a catalog of wifely duties, obligations, and responsibilities.

general maintenance

Depending on how you look at them, there are certain details or loving services a wife is supposed to perform for her husband in order to keep the home machinery running smoothly. The supposition is based on the old traditional concept: A wife takes care of the home and its inhabitants; a husband provides the money to support it, and them.

There has been an enormous change in two generations in the kinds of things husbands and wives are or are not expected to do. Everyone's marriage is "special" but some marriages are more special than others—which makes me feel that there are few generalities that are always applicable. The sensitivity of a wife to her husband's moods, his fears and worries, should be her guide, and she must do a lot of playing by ear.

My own marriage to a man who is at once extraordinarily talented, sensitive, complex, and dear has its own particular set of requirements because Dick does his writing at home. And since he is not at all complicated about where or when he works, and has never wanted a work area set apart from our living quarters, he works in the living room. The only contribution I have been able to make is to do my best to see that the household runs smoothly, his piano is tuned regularly, lunch is provided for him alone or for him and a collaborator, and try to prevent interruptions, and give him the climate that makes it possible for him to work without distractions. (One rainy day when Dick was in the midst of writing the score for *Carousel*, I took the girls to the movies to get all of us out of his way. The result was spectacular—the Mr. Snow song.) In effect, I behave as though he were out of the house and at his office, where I wouldn't dream of interrupting him except for something really important.

Meanwhile, back at the more conventional ranches, wives don't have to pretend their husbands aren't around; they

husbandry

simply aren't, unfortunately, for many hours of the day. And even though DR is probably correct about the generation gap, there are still one or two tiny household responsibilities that most wives expect to assume.

Here is a list of things that husbands aren't supposed to have to do, or don't know how to do, or forget to do. The list is a compendium of trivia—but it takes a heap of trivia to make a house a home.

feeding

1. Feeding: This is almost too silly to mention! I know of very few conventional homes where the wife doesn't consider it her responsibility to plan the meals, shop for the food, cook it, and, unless she has a snappy serf in a uniform, serve it and clean up afterwards.

But even planning has some positive and negative aspects. Every once in a while, for instance, you might ask your husband if he has a yen for anything in particular; after months of dreaming up dinners, we all tend to fall into the rut of steak, chops, chicken (rich meals), and hamburgers, stew, tuna fish casserole (poor meals). Your husband may have a clever suggestion for you. If not, he'll still be glad you asked.

Unless you're awfully unobservant or your husband is awfully polite, you won't have to ask him what he doesn't like; he'll either say so, or you'll know by the look on his face. Whatever it is, obviously, don't serve it—or serve it on a night when he's out.

When one or the other of you is dieting, the double standard still obtains. In other words, if you're on a diet, you're supposed to go right on providing and drooling over mashed potatoes and rich sauces. If he's on a diet, you're not supposed to put those things anywhere near him because you'll tempt him. A case in point: For weeks now, my own adorable husband has subsisted on a most peculiar combination— steak and cottage cheese. After the first two days, my daughters joined him, leaving me and my already emaciated four-year-old son with some not too attractive alternatives: I can surreptitiously sneak a couple of baked potatoes and some creamed spinach in my pocket to the table, where we will then eat behind the evening newspaper. Or we can eat in the kitchen. Or go out to dinner. Or simply starve to death, which is probably what will happen. It's like the Siege of

Leningrad around here. But when it's all over, if two of us aren't in our caskets, three of us are going to look gorgeous and all five of us will be happy.

As for shopping, although it's technically not his province, there is the occasional husband who is mad for the supermarket. Let him go, by all means, but don't be upset when he comes home without the foaming cleanser. He couldn't find your brand, so he didn't know what to get instead, so he didn't get any. What he got instead was a lot of stuff that wasn't on your list—like one Mexican TV dinner, chocolate kisses, and a giant bottle of mouthwash that won't fit in your medicine cabinet.

For last-minute shopping—bread, milk, butter—if your husband just happens to phone from the office at the end of the day, it's okay to ask him to pick those things up for you, but I wouldn't make a special call to him for that purpose, he may not mind doing the favor, but he may easily mind the phone call.

Some men love cooking. Those who love it invariably do it very well and almost invariably do it very messily because they don't cook often enough to have evolved an orderly wash-and-put-away-instantly system. You can complain lustily about the profusion of gummy pots and pans, thereby ruining his fun and maybe his meal, or you can meekly and gratefully clean up after him. Fielder's choice.

Once it's cooked, getting a meal *on* the table is easy enough; getting your husband *to* the table is sometimes a problem. Nine out of ten men, when told that dinner is ready, will pick that very moment to wash up, fix another drink, or begin a long distance phone call. You can solve this by giving him a five-minute warning. If he's supposed to carve something, give him a ten-minute warning. Speaking of carving— traditionally a man's prerogative, and probably an atavistic remnant of prehistoric times when the he-caveman was better at ripping the mammoth apart than the she-caveman— anyway, speaking of carving, there are a lot of men who detest it and are terrible at it. If your husband doesn't like carving and you don't want your mammoth all hacked up, learn to do it yourself, with a carbon steel knife. Carbon steel can't be put in the dishwasher because it rusts easily, and it never looks as pretty as stainless steel, but it's much sharper and it can be sharpened, by you. Thanks to modern industry, stainless steel is too tough to sharpen once it gets dull. (In my spare time, I'm a metallurgist.)

All of the above, of course, presupposes that your husband is in the house at dinner time—or ten minutes before it. Many husbands are not; some of them arrive an hour late without so much as a phone call to warn you about it; some of them make the phone call—just as you're about to take the food out of the oven, which is all right if the food can be warmed up, but not all right if it's something like steak. And some, the enviable minority, will tell you at breakfast time that they are going to be late. Why enviable? Because they are in the enviable position of knowing in the morning what the end of the day will bring.

You see, I really do believe that late husbands aren't deliberately trying to drive you crazy. They want to get home just as badly as you and the children want to have them there. The poor, beleaguered men who don't phone at all probably can't find the time. In our darkest, least cooperative moments, we all think, "Surely there must have been a three-minute interval somewhere in the day; he's an inconsiderate slob!" but quite often, there is not a three-minute interval. Literally not.

As for the men who do call, but call too late—well, they're trying, and at the very least, we can curb the tendency to snarl "A fat lot of good it does to tell me now!" into the phone when they apologetically ring up.

So you can be charming, or you can be uncharming—but the problem still exists and how do you cope with it? If your husband is a totally unpredictable no-show, you go ahead, you and your ravenous children, without him, and keep his food warm as best you can. If he doesn't like to eat alone, plan to feed the children first. Two can be cooked for as easily as one, and it's a more companionable way of going about it. If your husband is the type who calls at the last minute, it's a question of whether or not the food and the children can wait. Yes? Then wait. No? Then follow instructions for the totally unpredictable no-show.

maintaining the house 2. Household Maintenance is another almost too-silly-to-mention category. We all know and accept, some of us more grudgingly than others, that it's our responsibility to keep the place clean and in fairly good repair.

Exactly how clean and how well-repaired depends on what you've found out about yourself and your husband. If both of you are neat and tidy types, you have no problem. If you're a meticulous housekeeper and your husband drops his clothes and his pipe ashes all over the place, you have a slight problem in that you'll have an insatiable desire to reform him. Control it—it's almost impossible to reform a full-grown clothes-and-ash-dropper—so you'll either have to adjust yourself to picking up after him or adjust yourself to the mess. It is, after all, part of "your job." What if you're the messy one? Well, then you have a slightly more serious problem, because messy people don't usually know how messy they are; their eyes literally don't see what neat eyes see. But since your neat-eyed husband is going to be driven crazy by what you don't see, you're just going to have to do something about your powers of observation. Then you're going to have to do something about your house—like picking it up, or hiring someone to pick it up for you. It is, after all, part of your job.

And what if you're both messy and blind? Congratulations! I happen to think most Americans are entirely too concerned with the Puritan ethic of cleanliness and godliness. One more slipper under the bed doesn't mean much in the over-all scheme of life. Once in a while, though, and especially if you're expecting visitors, you might *pretend* to be a meticulous housekeeper and straighten things up a bit —for appearance's sake and to prevent people from saying you're not doing part of your job.

And as for the question of whether or not your husband should help with the housework, I can either refer you to vast sociological tomes on the disintegration of the male image or to the more aggressively feministic viewpoints of Betty Friedan and Gloria Steinem. But I'd rather think of it this way: How desperate are you? If you've got one kid in the tub, another one leaning out the window, the washing machine needs emptying, and the stew is boiling away, I certainly think it would be nice if your husband pitched in. And if he has nothing better to do and reaches for a dish towel after dinner while he's talking to you, I wouldn't snatch it away with a "No, no, dear heart, this is woman's work." Those days are gone. I don't, on the other hand, think one should take it all for granted. Women have it pretty good now, and men do seem, more and more, to be expected to take over some of the female functions. For instance, today's father spends more time with his small children than his father would have dreamed of spending—I'm all for that—but while women are acquiring more and more freedom, it seems unjust to expect men to dry more and more dishes.

Here I suspect there actually is a generation gap. Young fathers never diapered the baby when our children were growing up. Helping with the dishes was unthinkable unless there was a major household crisis. Husbands usually bought the wines and liquor and served the drinks (as they still do), and sometimes they were even willing to fix something around the house. Cutting the grass and working in the garden was always considered okay for the man of the house to do, but today, for the helpless or for those with less help, there are many husbands who are perfectly willing to do a share of the household chores. In any case, welcome your husband's help when he offers it, but don't expect it.

I happen to be married to a man who established the fact, early in our marriage, that he was incapable of doing (for this, substitute unwilling to do) any little jobs around the house. Curiously enough, Dorothy Hammerstein says this was equally true of Oscar. One evening when we were visiting the Hammersteins, Oscar announced that he was thirsty. Someone made the daring suggestion that he might go into the pantry and get a glass of water. He did, and the entire Hammerstein family gave him a solid round of applause.

3. Husband Maintenance involves a hundred and one details of upkeep. Here are a few of them:

personal maintenance

The Cleaners: Getting your husband's clothes cleaned is simple enough as long as you know that that's what he wants. I'm not mentioning any names, but some husbands leave an assortment of pants and jackets all over the room and then expect me to guess which ones need cleaning, which ones only need pressing, which ones are merely lacking a button, which ones are merely lacking a hanger, and which ones are ready for the Salvation Army. With this kind of husband, you have to pin him down rather carefully before he leaves the house. And then I call the cleaners.

The Laundry: As long as their clothes are washed and put back where they can find them, most husbands don't think about laundry much—except where it concerns their shirts. Then, it seems, they care a whole lot, and I get positively faint-hearted thinking of the numerous catastrophes that can happen to a shirt—too much starch, too little, a tiny button off, a tiny whalebone missing or a tiny wooden stud, a tiny crease somewhere—as a matter of fact, the mystique of putting shirts away is just as complicated as sending them to the laundry in the first place. The back of the collar, folded and pressed in the wrong place, is one of your father's few but strong peeves. All that cardboard and paper and where do the blue shirts go and where do the dress shirts go, and there's never enough room in the drawer for all of them anyway—unless you remove the cardboard, and then the shirts get wrinkled. *I hate shirts!*

Oh well, I suppose all wives hate shirts, but unless we want our husbands in a continual state of rage and frustration, we'll have to continue the endless odyssey from one hand laundry to another, or from one laundress to another, until we find the right one. Or learn to do it ourselves.

While we're on the subject of clothes maintenance, it's a wife's job to find out what the expected clothes are for any social occasion and to see that they're in good shape.

Throwing things out for your husband is a much less perplexing chore. We all know torn shorts and undershirts when we see them. The same goes for socks with holes (unless you're one of the few remaining women alive who know how to darn and is economical enough to bother), torn handkerchiefs, and shirts with frayed collars. (I cannot seem to get off that topic.) The list ends here, though, because items like old jackets, sweaters, ties, slippers, ratty sneakers, and Adlai Stevenson shoes—what looks like junkpile material to you—may be regarded rather more fondly by your husband. To put it bluntly, if you throw out things like these without asking first, he may get good and sore. If the chipmunk collection becomes more than you can stand, set aside a free evening or Saturday morning and ask him if he really

husbandry

wants that old sweater any more, or if he'd like you to take the shoes to the shoemaker. (Taking the shoes to the shoemaker is a nice, wifely gesture, and it's easy. There's always a cobbler somewhere in the neighborhood.)

Buying new things for your husband falls into three categories: the first—shorts, undershirts, socks, handkerchiefs and shirts (unless he is in the process of changing his neck size or his mode of dress—there I go with the shirts again!), i.e., replacement items—can be replaced by you, over the phone, and probably should be. You have more telephone time than he. Check first with your husband to make sure he wants the old ones duplicated. Collars and colors change very fast these days.

The second category—sweaters, ties, accessories in general —can be replaced or supplied by you only if you and your husband generally agree about what looks good on him. Even then don't be hurt if he returns something once in a while; you can't be right all of the time. If he returns things often, you can assume you're losing your knack, or never had it in the first place. Be content with buying category one.

Category three—suits, jackets, shoes—obviously cannot be bought without your husband because they have to fit. Can they be bought without you? is more to the point. If you like the way he looks and he likes to go shopping alone, then they most certainly can and should be bought without you. Who needs you?

If, on the other hand, you think his taste in clothes is abysmal and might even be hurting his career (because deep down, you suspect that maybe clothes do at least help make the man or unmake him), you can try to change his self-image: "Jarvis, you're not the lumbering, baggy, slovenly, great, gray, greasy, green-elephant type of person! Goodness no! I've always seen you in soft blues and subtle browns." To which he might reply, "Is that so, darling?" and invite you to go shopping with him—or crack you across the face. It all depends. On the man, and on how tactful you are.

Miscellaneous, nonobligatory but friendly, little extra tasks you might consider performing for your husband are: replenishing his drugstore supplies before, not after they run out; organizing the papers and mail on his desk (Some women have been shot for less!) so he can see what he's got; renewing his magazine subscriptions; filling his lighter; finding his slippers and fetching his pipe.

keeping a husband healthy

Keeping your husband alive and healthy is very definitely your responsibility, because, unless he's highly unusual, your husband certainly won't consider it his. On the contrary, he'll do anything to avoid the whole subject; if there's anything the matter with him, he doesn't want to know about it. If you remind him gently about his annual checkup, to the doctor, or the dentist, or the oculist, he'll give you one of those "Oh yeah, I really ought to do that" answers and before you know it, five, ten, fifteen years later, he's either dead, toothless or blind. So, instead of reminding him gently, it's safer to *tell* him gently that you are going to take the liberty *tomorrow* of making some appointments for him, and would, therefore, like to know *tonight* when during the next two weeks or so, he thinks he'll be free. Then, make the appointments, tell him *and* his secretary when they are (there's many a slip 'twixt home date book and office calendar), and then after he's gone, inquire, ever so gently, about what the doctor, dentist, oculist had to say. If you have reason to believe your husband isn't telling you everything, be brazen and call the doctor up.

I don't agree. I don't think a wife should ever make appointments for her husband without being asked; that's treating him like a child.

(A small addendum—mental health is something else again. It makes no difference whether someone is a raving lunatic or merely mildly unhappy; there is no one anywhere, including your husband, who can be helped by psychiatry unless he wants to be. If you think your husband needs to be helped, the most aggressive thing you dare do is mention it—once, just to put the idea in his head in case it hadn't occurred to him. That's all you can do; the rest is up to him.)

relations with family and friends
Keeping your husband in the good graces of his family and friends is another wifely service to be rendered. Men are notorious for forgetting birthdays and anniversaries—there have been countless short stories and television episodes on the subject. The fiction may be funny but the fact, when it involves a mother-in-law, or a child, or a best friend, is not.

husbandry

These people get hurt, or mad, your husband's mother simply will not believe that he was all that busy, but aha! we know differently. He *was* all that busy; for the rest of his working life, he'll go on being all that busy, and if you don't want your husband to be in a permanent state of disgrace, you're going to have to do his remembering for him.

My mother, the only pretty elephant in town, never forgets occasions. Actually, it's her date book that never forgets occasions; on January first, she transposes all the pertinent data from her permanent birthday book to the new date book which is a sensational system provided you can remember, in October, to order the new filler for your date book.

You, too, can be a pretty elephant. The credit you get from friends for remembering their birthdays and anniversaries is enormous and it's really so easy to do. I also put down the year they were born or got married so that special dates get particular attention. It's a great way to keep track of friends' children's ages so you don't end up sending a stuffed animal to a sophisticated twelve-year-old.

I have a little trouble with that part; sometimes it gets to be February before I get around to it and all the Capricorns get a raw deal. My other problem, or failing, which for the sake of altruism I am willing to reveal to you, is this: I tend to write down my own family's birthdays—and I know them by heart anyway—but frequently forget to write down my husband's. Since they all live in Kansas City and we live in New York, this results in tumultuous last-minute activity with the florist and Western Union and our very unreliable postal services. (By the way, I think wiring flowers from one city to another is both unimaginative and risky. You order twenty-five dollars' worth of little red roses and freesia at your end. What arrives at the other end is probably man-eating tiger lilies with a couple of giant football mums. You'll never know for sure because most people are too polite to tell you.)

Needless to say, it's not nice to forget the members of your husband's family. So, on January first, write all those dates down, and unless your husband insists on doing it himself, think up a good present. Check out the choice with your husband first, if he has strong opinions on the subject, and send it well in advance. If your husband needs to be reminded to call up on the actual day, don't forget to remind him.

Remind him to call up members of your family, too; if he has trouble remembering his own mother's birthday, it's hardly logical to expect him to remember his mother-in-law's.

And what if he forgets your own, or your anniversary? Well, by now, you must know him pretty well. If you're the easily hurt type, and you're sure he isn't going to remember, just do what you do with everybody else—remind him. What's the matter with that? But remind him before, not after—after smacks of martyrdom.

Then there is a form of aphasia that husbands are prone to develop. For lack of an official title, I guess I could call it Aphasia of the Immediate Future, or, in layman's terms, the Hey, Honey, What's on for Tonight, I Keep Forgetting syndrome. Its origin is easy enough to understand: Your husband's office schedule is very crowded. At eight-thirty in the morning, he cannot think in terms of what's going to go on in the evening because he can't project himself far enough into the future to believe there's even going to be an evening.

Buy your husband a little leather date book, tell him day by day (or once a week) what to put down in it, and make sure he has it on him at all times. Hopefully, he will learn to regard it as one of his essential pocket items—the kind of thing like car keys, wallet, and handkerchief that he'll feel naked leaving the house without. Then, if he still continues to forget where he's at, you might consider the possibility that you've been making too many middle-of-the week dates for such a busy man—but I'll go into that in more detail later on.

Let's get on to something cheerier, shall we? Surely, after all that feeding, housekeeping, personal maintenance, health maintenance, and trouble-shooting, there must be one or two little loving services having nothing to do with home machinery that your husband could perform for you? There are— but one or two is about it; he doesn't have time for more, and to expect more is unrealistic and unfair. I'm still talking about in and around the house, remember, and the house is supposed to be your bag. He has a right . . . nasty way of putting it, but, anyway . . . he has a right to take for granted what you do for him, whereas what he does for you is of a more voluntary nature. Am I beginning to sound like a fifth-century Japanese wife? I assure you I'm not anything of the sort. On the contrary, there are a lot of things I've never learned to do (too stupid) or I simply can't do (too puny), and now, without further delay and with considerable ill-concealed joy, I'm going to list as many of them as I can. What my husband does for me is:

1. Anything I literally and physically cannot get accomplished without my strapping son who is away at school, or the handyman who, nice as he is, isn't always available: kitchen light bulb changing, hanging heavy mirrors, storing porch furniture, buying and putting up the Christmas tree, moving pianos and taking heavy or unwieldy equipment to be fixed. Lamps, stereo turntables, and a two-wheeler bike in need of training wheels all fall into this category. If we had storm windows to be put up or ceilings to be painted, I don't think I'd tackle those either.

On the other hand, I know a lady who loves to put up storm windows and considers it her pleasure and her duty to drag home the Christmas tree. She's smaller than I am, too, but she comes from Minnesota. Maybe that makes a difference.

2. As I said before, my husband also does anything I am too stupid to do for myself. I must qualify that word stupid, though, because for me, there are two kinds of stupid: pretend stupid and really stupid. Pretend stupid are the things I could probably master if I set my mind to it, but I don't or won't: lighting the concealed oven pilot, assembling unassembled Christmas toys on Christmas Eve, and putting air-conditioning filters back—I don't mind washing them, but I always seem to put them back inside out or upside down or all bunched up or in the totally wrong place—picture hanging, and many others too numerous or too embarrassing to mention.

Fortunately, Hank doesn't mind doing any of these things for me. If he did mind, I guess I could master them—and I'd bloody well have to. After all, pretending to be stupid is a rather common feminine indulgence, and I'm with Martin Luther: Too many indulgences is not a good idea.

As for really stupid, I can only think of one shining example: Reading and understanding the instructions for new household appliances. I'm perfectly capable of deciding which appliance I want, but once it's arrived, it'll sit there unused until hell freezes over unless Hank explains every idiot-simple step to me first. If there's a maid in the house, I get him to explain it to her, too, because even though I finally understand it myself, I am unable to communicate mechanical know-how.

3. Then there are the things I don't know how to do, not because I'm necessarily stupid, but because as a woman, I am simply uninformed. Take cars, for instance. What do I know about cars? Less than nothing. Only yesterday, a crooked gas station attendant sold me a brand-new fan belt to replace the brand new fan belt my husband bought last week. Most women know less than nothing about cars and when it comes to buying one, they should be allowed to state their color preference and that's all. (My Minnesota tree-dragging friend, on the other hand, knows a lot about cars, and when her family needs a new one, she makes the final decision because she does most of the driving in the family. That seem only fair—a tree-dragging chauffeur should get her pick of trees and vehicles.)

Other mechanical contrivances I know nothing about and wouldn't attempt to purchase are hot water heaters, furnaces, electric tools and lawn mowers and, last but not least, air conditioners. I can hardly add as it is, so I'm not in any position to discuss heavy duty versus 220 wiring, or how many BTU's to the square inch with a couple of fast-talking hoods in the air-conditioning racket. They'd probably sell me one without a fan belt. (My collection of bêtes noires is growing. Fan belts have been added to shirts.)

I also know nothing about roofing, plumbing, house painting, sump pumps, tile fields, and septic tanks. My husband takes care of these things, too.

This is getting to be a longer list than I thought. But then it isn't your list, it's mine. Yours may be entirely different, or

husbandry

longer, or shorter, and I can't make any pronouncements about what you ought to be doing because I don't even know who you are. That's why I used my list, I do at least know who I am and I also know that our household, with the vast assistance of a multifaceted, good-humored husband, seems to survive.

There is one more aspect of running a house, and a home, and much as I'd like to avoid it, I don't think I dare. It's a chore, obligation, responsibility, belonging to both you and your husband; it's the single greatest irritant in a marriage, and I know of no one, male or female, who enjoys coping with it. It is, in short . . . Finances.

finances

Consider your close friends—couples you've known for some time, and know well enough to be familiar (as familiar as an outsider ever gets, anyway) with the way these people feel about money. There are various combinations: spendthrift wife and thrifty husband, spendthrift husband and thrifty wife, two spendthrifts, forever in debt, two thrifties, smugly never. But varied as their distinct "money" characteristics may be, even more varied are their methods of dealing with money itself. Some husbands pay all the bills and their wives have no idea what's coming off, or going on. Sometimes it's the other way around—also, and so on. I could go on like this forever, but I suppose I have to lay my head on the block sometime. Here is what I think:

1. Unless either you or your husband is a hopelessly irresponsible nut, neither one of you should be totally in charge because what the other one doesn't know may get you both in trouble. (Your husband sees a lean year coming up, doesn't tell you, you go out and buy a color TV.) Besides, you and your husband live together, have children together, you might as well figure out how you're going to pay for all that together.

Many women who have been overprotected by their husbands are pitifully unaware of the simplest financial arrangements and I have seen tragic situations arise when these poor ladies are widowed.

2. I do not think, however, that all your *money* should be together—just your over-all knowledge. For one thing, each

of you is entitled to some privacy and some independence. You don't want to know how much his birthday present to you cost and he doesn't want you to know. And for another thing, there is the possibility that one of you is an inveterate though well-intentioned forgetter who rips checks out of your mutual checkbook but never writes anything on the stubs. (I know several people who do that. One of them used to be me.) I remember the days when I tried very hard to explain to you that calling up the bank to find out how much money you had in your account really wasn't the way to get an accurate balance. And then there was the story my father told of the woman who said she and her husband had a joint account. She wrote out the checks and he signed them.

bank
accounts

What I recommend is two and maybe three accounts. Your husband should have an account in which he puts his salary, any other money of his own, and out of which he pays and takes care of mortgages, loans, taxes, insurance, school bills, camp bills, vacations, car purchases—the big, serious stuff. Out of which he also gives you a previously agreed-upon monthly household maintenance allowance, pays for his presents to you, and draws cash for himself during the day and for entertainment for both of you at night.

Some women prefer to be given allowances because they like the limitation of knowing what they can spend on themselves and what can be spent on the household. Others would rather not be bound, and I think both ways can work well, provided the arrangements are realistic for you and your husband and the figures reviewed from time to time as living standards and costs change. I, for example, have never been given an allowance, and I suspect that I have probably spent less than I would if I had had one. Dick, who is extremely generous in such matters, would have given me more than I needed. On the other hand, I have known women who have had to be geniuses at juggling figures. Afraid to be frank with their husbands about how much they were spending on the household bills, they would use money taken from their clothes allowances to cover the discrepancy. This way lies trouble. If financial arrangements are so rigid that the wife is fearful of being honest, something is seriously wrong.

husbandry

You should have an account in which you put the allowance your husband gives you, any money of your own, out of which you pay all monthly household expenses—food, clothes, cleaners, small doctors' bills (any doctor over six feet will just have to wait) —pay for presents to your husband and draw cash for during-the-day entertainment for you and the kids.

As any fool can see, you're going to get stuck with most of the paper work because you're paying the monthly stuff, but you have more time to get it done in. And if you tackle it religiously at the beginning of the month, it becomes a mindless sort of task you can polish off while you're engaged in other mindless activities like watching television with the children or talking to a boring friend on the phone. Even when you're talking to an interesting friend on the phone, you can at least be opening the bills and throwing out the junk mail. If you have a terribly busy month, you can always ask your husband to help balance your checkbook and write out the envelopes you're going to stuff with checks—these are the two time-consuming elements, especially the balancing.

For years, I have put the canceled checks back in the checkbook with Scotch tape. Then, if a question should arise as to whether or not a bill has been paid, all the evidence is in one place. Besides, you have to keep the checks for three years anyway, and this way, they don't take up any more room than the checkbook.

You probably already know this, but get in the habit of marking the date on which you paid each bill and save all of them—September in one manila folder, October in another, etc. At the end of a year, put the whole year's supply in a large manila envelope and start all over again with the files. At the end of about three years, it's safe to throw out everything that doesn't have to do with taxes, but if you're following my system, these things aren't your problem anyway, they're your husband's.

It's wise, too, to keep all receipted bills for works of art, furniture, cars—anything that might be sold one day. And it's vital to keep bills for any improvements you may have made to your home.

Keeping day-to-day records for tax purposes is wonderfully

helpful to your husband when tax time comes around. Often, tax examiners will accept notes from a diary as evidence of tax-exempt business expenses. I've kept a diary for years—purposely too small for personal comments but large enough to put down where we went, what we did, whom we saw. It's also enough to recall happy occasions, new friends met on travels, or the name of a particularly good restaurant you might want to recommend to a friend.

I've discovered that a small portable checkbook is terribly handy. If you have one of those, you'll never forget to write in the stubs, even if you're the type who usually does.

I prefer to carry a few blank checks in my wallet. But be careful not to lose them because bank computers read the numbers on the check rather than the signature, and it's relatively easy to forge a check. The bank is responsible in this case, but if you should lose a blank check, report it to the bank. When I use a check. I make a note of the details and transfer the information to my checkbook at home.

If all of this sounds like foul drudgery, I can offer you a consolation tidbit: By paying the monthly bills yourself, you'll be able to keep track of what you're spending. Maybe that sounds like no consolation, but your husband will be delighted.

A third account is optional, but if you have one, it's a joint savings account into which you put large hunks of money for walloping big expenditures like taxes, or Rolls Royces, or emergency operations. This is a thrifty couple's account, the rest of us mortals aren't quite that far-sighted.

credit cards

I don't think it's optional—I think it's a "must." And while we're on the subject of finances and other disasters, I'd like to say a few words about the credit card economy in which we live. Credit cards are fine if they're used to avoid carrying a lot of cash and/or to help keep an accurate record of how and where you have spent your money. However, when credit cards are used as an ever-expanding form of installment buying—for cars, vacations, elaborate stereo or photographic equipment, for instance—it is all too easy to spend more than you need and can afford. Credit is thrust upon us from all directions—via television, newspapers, magazines, and even unsolicited mail. It may be healthy for the economy of the country, but I think it's immoral to urge people to borrow money to do all kinds of delightful things that they can't afford to pay for.

Now that I've gotten that off my chest, I think we ought to consider the question of life insurance. It has generally been assumed that husbands should take out life insurance on their own lives, but I think it's equally important for them to take out insurance on their wives' lives. This could be particularly necessary when there are small children who must be cared for in the tragic event of a young mother's death. Besides the loss of his wife, there is the very real loss of the one who has, quite literally, kept the house. Some men, finding themselves in this difficult situation, and unable to afford (or possibly even to find) a paid live-in housekeeper, have undoubtedly remarried—but often the wrong woman, I'm sure—in order to have someone to look after the children. An insurance policy on his wife's life could make it possible for him to take the time he needs to sort out his life again.

insurance

The entire question of insurance should be gone into with the help and advice of experts. Complete coverage in the area of health insurance is, I think, essential to have in these days of crippling medical bills. If it's at all possible, it's not only thoughtful, but wise to arrange coverage for regular household help as well. This would, of course, be in addition to the Workmen's Compensation policy required by law.

It's a good idea to rent a safe-deposit box from your bank in which to keep all valuable papers—marriage certificates, life insurance policies, mortgage receipts, certificates of ownership, copies of wills, stocks, and bonds. You and your husband should both have access to the box, and it's wise to keep lists of its contents in his office and your home.

safe-deposit boxes

Most people hate to think about making out wills, and they tend to push all thoughts of mortality out of their minds. Yet, when death occurs unexpectedly, families can be plunged into desperate straits because no one has planned for the future. It is really imperative that husbands and wives make their wills soon after marriage and remember to revise them as children appear on the scene. Each spouse should discuss the subject fully with a lawyer who has had experience in the field, and then the two wills should be coordinated to prepare, for example, for guardianship of the

wills

121

husbandry

children in the unlikely event that both parents should die in a common disaster.

Well, with one system or another, most people manage somehow to make it from one year to the next. For those of you who don't, those of you who live in perpetual panic, I'd like to suggest the luxury, highly economical in the long run, of an accountant. He will be your governess, he'll dish out your allowances in meager little morsels, grumbling as he does so. He'll even take it upon his miserable Scrooge self to tell you when you can or cannot take a vacation. Furthermore, he will send you a rather sizable bill for these loathsome ministrations. *But,* and oh, it's a huge but—he will do all that hideous tax work for you, he will see that you have enough money to pay the taxes, he will, bless his little adding machine of a heart, keep you out of trouble. Cheap at the price!

husbands and other people

As we all know, keeping the home machinery running smoothly is one of the minor aspects of marriage. Thank God for that—I certainly don't want to spend my life thinking about the relationship between me and the air-conditioner or my husband and the sump pump. I'd much rather think about me and my husband, or my husband and the children, or both of us and our friends, or both of us and the community we live in. Assuming you feel the same way, the rest of this chapter is going to be devoted to people, beginning with . . . you.

you and your husband

This seems like a logical place to start because you two came first. Then came all those other bodies—children, friends, business acquaintances—interrupting your privacy, taking imperceptible little nibbles out of your apple until there's nothing left but the core. Well, that's to be expected, I guess. Unless you live in a vacuum, people are bound to nibble your apple, but if you occasionally feel that the world is, indeed, too much with us, you're right.

leisure interests

Leisure time is what you have on your hands when both of you manage to escape the rest of the world. How you spend it, and whether you spend it together or separately, all depends on what your interests are.

Mutual interests present no problem. If you and your husband both like photography, pre-Columbian art, Peace Roses—whatever it is, that's wonderful, and especially wonderful if you can manage to scrape up the time and the money for it.

What about the things your husband loves, but you don't understand; are you supposed to keep up with those interests? Antique clocks, for instance. Well, if you don't understand about antique clocks by now, you probably never will, but that won't bother your husband. The only thing that will bother your husband is if you bother him while he's working on his clocks! Buy him the best new book on the subject and then leave him at the dining-room table to mantle and dismantle to his heart's content. If he's still there in the morning, you and the children should have breakfast in the kitchen and don't make any smart remarks. In other words, if you can't keep up with it, indulge it.

Pro football is another instance. There are millions of men in America who would rather watch the Super Bowl Game than eat, sleep, or drink. Houses could burn, little babies could drown, planes could fall in the back yard while these guys sit glued to their TV sets. Meanwhile, millions of wives have nothing to do all that long Sunday afternoon. If you're one of them (and I'm not—I love all that pushing and shoving and mucking around in the mud), what should you do? You can sit companionably in the room with your mesmerized mate, knitting and thinking about your Christmas list or paying the bills. You can sit in another room, knitting and thinking about your Christmas list or paying the bills. Best of all, you can take the kids to a movie you want to see yourself which indulges you, the kids (the girl kids, the boys will be home with their father) and your husband all at once—a smashing solution.

There is one final category of interests—I've saved the stickiest for the last. This, I firmly believe, is the kind of interest which you should not keep up with because, being human, you will only be grudging and unpleasant about it anyhow.

An example: My husband loves opera, and I'm sure he's better off going to the Met alone or with another opera nut, rather than with me. In case you need convincing, let me tell you about me at the opera. For the first few scenes, I squirm, cough, and cross and uncross my legs a lot. I call this my patient stage. Next, I try to read the libretto so I can find out why that girl who's all dressed up like a man is pretending to want to marry another girl who is really a man dressed up like a bird. The libretto doesn't tell me why, because, even though it is in two languages, they are both illegible in the dark. By the time I've begun to figure it out, the transvestites and the bird people have been replaced by a quartet of fat old men. I don't know what they're singing about either. I call this my anxious stage. Next, I fall asleep. This is my sleeping stage—short-lived because my husband doesn't like me to do that.

Now we come to my compulsive spastic period, when I have absolutely *got* to sit on my feet. I uncross my legs. I kick my shoes off. I stand up, storklike, for one second, whip the other leg under me and sit down on it. Then, lightning quick, I bob up again and stuff the other leg under me. I am now several inches taller in my seat, which must be perplexing for the people in back of me, but I am happy for at least five minutes before both legs go to sleep and I have to put them back on the floor. Now I am several inches shorter again, but not as short as I am in the next stage when I search for my shoes under the seat in front of me while the people in back of me hope maybe I left while they weren't looking. Which is exactly what I wish I had done.

If you take a look at what I've had to say about leisure time, my treasonous convictions are clear: I am against the practice of "togetherness." The very word itself is disgusting —treacly verbal camouflage to describe an activity that not everybody wants to do. When my husband and I decide to go out to lunch alone, it's because we want to be together, not because we think we should be, and somewhere lurking in that word "togetherness" is an implied "should." Similarly, when my husband and I and the kids go to the hockey game, it's simply because we all love hockey. As a matter of fact, anybody, including me or my husband, who doesn't feel like hockey that night doesn't go; why should one person's occasional "apartness" signify the total dissolution of the family unit, or, as in the case of me and the opera, the dissolution of the marriage?

One more observation, and then I'm through. When the whole family takes down the Christmas tree ornaments, packs up the lights, drags the tree out the back door and vacuums up the tinsel, some people call that togetherness, too. That's not what I call it. I call it a dirty, boring, obligatory nuisance that we're all doing together because it's quicker that way.

Okay, back to the subject of you and your husband. If you accept the premise that mutual interests are lovely, but dissimilar interests, enjoyed guiltlessly and separately, are equally pleasant, what do you do if you're not interested in your husband's interests and you don't have any specific interests of your own? In order to become a more fascinating and well-rounded person, should you go out and look for some? I say absolutely not! Women with children are busy, busy, busy all day every day, and if by any chance we don't happen to have any outside interests, we shouldn't start manufacturing them at this point in our lives. If we haven't got them already, it's probably because we don't need them or don't have the time for them, and there's not much point in spending the time to find something we then won't have time to do. Forget it. Read a good book. Read a bad book. Or don't read any book. Relax! And don't be put down by women you meet at parties who tell you all about their intellectual pursuits. Bully for them, but it has nothing to do with you.

Sports and competitive games: If you're better at golf or tennis or bridge than your husband, should you avoid playing with him? I don't really know. My husband and I hate golf and we're too feeble to play tennis. When we play Scrabble or backgammon, he always beats me, which I hate because I'm a highly competitive person and he isn't—so it's really too bad the situations aren't reversed. Come to think of it, that must be the answer—whether we're talking about golf, tennis or Scrabble. What kind of personality does your husband have? If he's going to get all shook up over losing (or if you are), don't play with him. If it doesn't make any difference to either of you, forge ahead.

I suppose I ought to say something about golf widows— they must constitute a good third of the female population. Unfortunately, there isn't much to say. With men who love golf, it isn't just a love, it's a mania. You can rail against it or accept it cheerfully, but you can't prevent it and it's a waste of time to try. Fishing and hunting widows have an identical

125

husbandry

problem to contend with—the only difference being that hunters and fishers have to go somewhere else to do it. In other words, a vacation without you. And why not, if that's what he wants. Furthermore—and this is a little more unorthodox—I don't think there's anything wrong with your taking a vacation without him, either, as long as he doesn't mind.

*vacations for the two of you*My favorite form of leisure time, though, is to get away, *with* my husband, out of the house, out of the city, and maybe out of the country. It gives me the feeling that we're restoring the apple—maybe only temporarily, but at least no further inroads are being made in it. Naturally, a vacation with both of you away is twice as complicated to arrange and twice as expensive as separate vacations, but it is also twice as much fun. And at the risk of sounding bossy, I think we all ought to do it at least once a year.

There are men, luckily not too many of them, who genuinely loathe vacations; to be away from the scene of the action makes them nervous and resentful. If you are married to this kind of man and you force him to take a vacation, he may look upon you with loathing and resentment. Well, not really, but he certainly won't thank you for it and you certainly won't have any fun. Better luck next year! Most husbands, mine included, are more rational and more malleable. When your husband says he's afraid to leave because there's so much work, you might point out to him that if executives rationed their vacation time on that basis, they'd find themselves working twenty-four hours a day, three hundred and sixty-five days a year until they retired. Or dropped dead of a heart attack. He will probably admit, grudgingly at first, but with increasing enthusiasm, that yes, he really is very tired and that the company will survive without him for a few weeks. Mission accomplished.

Now obviously, unless your husband is a top-level executive, he can't just march into his office and announce that he's leaving tomorrow; you may have to wait until his allotted two or three weeks roll around. That's okay—it gives you some time to plan, and anticipating your escape is almost as much fun as making it. As a matter of fact, if you don't anticipate rather carefully, it can turn out to be *more* fun than the escape, and there's nothing so demoralizing as an

husbandry

unsuccessful vacation. So what kind of vacation do you want? Does your husband want the same kind? Do you both want to get out from under everything? Then you want . . .

Exhaustion Vacation #1: This means you go to one place and stay there, so you'd better make sure it's the right place. Never mind travel agents, because unless you're very rich and want to go to the Miami Hilton for $120 a day, they can't help you. Furthermore, they probably don't want to help you. (Years ago, I was going to Puerto Rico and asked a travel agent to get me on the cheapest tourist flight available. He said, "Whaddya want to go on a flight like that for? It's got nothing but Puerto Ricans on the plane.")

Your friends are the ones who want to help you and they can. If, for instance, you love hot weather and fishing, find some couple who've just come back from that kind of vacation and ask them the following questions:

Where did they stay and how much did it cost?

Where are the good restaurants? *Are* there any good restaurants?

Will you need to rent a car to get around?

Is the fishing really any good?

Is the weather reliable, and what kind of clothes do you need?

Then, well in advance, get your husband to make the plane, room, car reservations, etc., because men are better at that kind of thing. You can organize your wardrobe, his wardrobe, and the functioning of the household during your absence. That in itself will take you at least six weeks.

Pack your suitcases the way the Japanese arrange flowers: Keep removing a third of what you think you'll need until you're down to practically nothing. Most of the clothing should be drip-dry because the laundry will either take too long, cost too much, or ruin your clothes. Bad pressing can ruin clothes, too, and get them all out of shape. In these days of crease-resistant and no-iron fabrics, it shouldn't be too difficult to avoid sending clothes out to be pressed. Husbands' suits and wool dresses often respond wonderfully to a combination of a good steaming and hanging out in the bathroom.

Take books, traveler's checks, credit cards and a blank check. Under *no* circumstances do you take children. If your husband is an expert fisherman and doesn't want to rent inferior equipment, he might want to take his own, but my theory is that the less encumbered you are, the better.

If you have a choice of American Plan—that's the one that includes meals in your room rate—or some other plan, take the other plan. American Plan may sound cheaper, maybe it *is* cheaper, but it's no fun. You'll be eating the same food in the same place looking at the same people every day at the same time, which is exactly what you left home to get away from. Pretty soon, you'll start skipping meals or eating them somewhere else, and you'll feel guilty about the money you're wasting. There is a Modified American Plan that is worth considering. Usually this offers breakfast and either lunch or dinner, leaving you free to go out for a meal without feeling guilty about not using something you've paid for. It may not be very classy of me, but what I love is a good efficiency motel where you can make your own breakfast and lunch, fix your own drinks and then, having saved a fortune all day, splurge every night on dinner at a different restaurant.

One final word about this Exhaustion Vacation: In spite of your friends' recommendations, things can go wrong. Their idea of a good motel might not be yours. Or the management may have changed. The weather, especially in Florida, can most certainly change. Hank and I have just come back from a nifty spot that was supposed to have fabulous bonefishing —what it had was a lot of inedible fish with a fabulous number of bones. Never mind, remember the purpose of this vacation—to relax. If the fishing is terrible or Florida is cold or there isn't any snow in Aspen, sleep late, read your books or go to a movie. Even dreadful, tacky movies are fun on a vacation. And best of all, you will actually get the chance to talk to your husband without being interrupted or overheard; you can talk about the future, about politics, about why you were so neurotic at that party last February. You can even indulge yourself in the luxury of *not* talking. You can get to know each other again—and a little better. Highly therapeutic and very cozy and satisfying, no matter what the weather is doing.

Many think of a vacation in terms of a resort with sun and beaches and all kinds (or at least a few kinds) of sports. But this is not for me. My idea of a vacation is to go somewhere

—either to a place I've already been and love or to somewhere new, preferably a city where I will get to meet some of the natives and be asked to their homes. I want to go sightseeing, museum-hopping, and restaurant-crawling. I want to live in the marvelous luxurious hotels and not know what I'm having for dinner. If there's theater for me to see too, then I'm really in heaven. I may not rest at all, but I'll come home fully rested and relaxed.

Exhaustion Vacation #2: Years ago, my husband said to me, "Listen dear, you've just had a big flop musical, you're exhausted, and you need a change. Let's go away. Let's go to Europe." (There's a switch for you, the husband telling the wife that *she's* tired and *she* ought to get away.)

So we went. The trouble was, I didn't want to go to Europe. I'd already seen Europe. You know that joke about the kid who says, "Ma, I have nothing to do," and the mother says, "Why don't you go to the library and read a book," and the kid says, "I've read a book." Yeah, well, I'd seen Europe when I was nineteen. My parents sent me on one of those chaperoned, coeducational junkets where you were catapulted through nine countries in thirty-five days, or thirty-five countries in nine days, I forget which, and considering what I actually saw, it doesn't make much difference. All you do on trips like that is pack and unpack and get on and off buses and trains. Once in a while, your chaperone loses the baggage claims and the train tickets, which provides you with a little leisure time to spend in the station, but mostly you are literally running through museums or washing out the wet nylon blouse that you've worn every day since you left the U.S.

What I found out during that trip was that I hate packing and unpacking, and I absolutely detest most museums. Hit me, Ma, go ahead and hit me, but it's true. Museums hurt my feet, I'd rather look at people than paintings, and I'd rather read a book than anything else. I also found out what countries I didn't want to go back to—all of them except Italy, which I loved.

Anyway, there I was, thirteen years later; my husband had never been to Europe, and he didn't seem to want to take my word for it that Italy was the only place worth visiting. Peculiar chap, my husband. He really loved running through all those countries and their museums, and while he was doing all that running around, I was packing and unpacking and washing and drying and crying because I was tired and wanted to stay in one place—Italy—and read a book, or mourn my big flop musical.

In retrospect, several things come clear to me. First of all, my husband was perfectly justified in wanting to see Europe the way we did because it was *his* first time. How else could he find out which countries he didn't like and which ones he wanted to return to? Second of all, I was *not* justified in moping around—not at that price!—and it was a tribute to Hank's benevolence and persistent good humor that he didn't dump me forever in the Milan airport. Last of all, I was obviously not in the mood to embark on that kind of trip and should have realized it before we decided to go.

cruises

There are a few other kinds of vacations that Mary has not gone into. First of all, there are cruises. Few people today have either the time or the money for world cruises, but there are still lots of small, comfortable ships that offer shorter cruises to almost anywhere. If you dislike the mechanics of travel, especially in countries where you don't speak the language, a cruise holiday will eliminate the drudgery for you. I have always been a little apprehensive about finding congenial shipmates, but if two or three couples can arrange to go off together, this worry, too, can be dispelled. If you're on your own, don't get involved too soon with people you've just met. Detaching yourself can get very sticky.

If you happen to be in a position to take a longish holiday and if you have friends who can join you, there are other possibilities, too. For example, there's the whole world of freighters. Friends who have traveled on them tell me that, for those who like the sea and who are happy with books and the simple life, a voyage on a freighter that has room for only twelve passengers (the one they loved was Norwegian) is the greatest vacation in the world. Often the accommodations are more luxurious than on the average passenger ship because they are designed to carry the top brass of the company. Our friends also reported that the food and service on their particular ship were superb, but this bears some investigation since standards differ from line to line. Six couples who could spare the time might take such a trip and feel they were the owners of a yacht.

In recent years, a new kind of trip has become very popular, and it is one that particularly appeals to me. It's the tour that caters to any one of a wide variety of special interests ranging from the arts to sports. In some cases, the trip is arranged by a nonprofit institution for the purpose of raising money. This is done by charging a tax-deductible membership fee in addition to the cost of the trip. Here the advantage is twofold: Not only are you helping to support something you care about, but the group is accompanied by a professional who explains what you are seeing and helps you broaden your own knowledge in the field, thereby making your holiday a most exciting experience.

special-interest tours

Mary has avoided the whole subject of tipping. I don't blame her. Still, in hotels, restaurants, and other public places, it is a fact of life. Perhaps it would be different if there were one set of rules that you could apply everywhere, but there isn't. Some years ago, Dick and I were shocked to learn that the 15 percent service charge added to the bill of our London hotel did not go to the staff, so that we had to tip as though it didn't exist. (It turned out that it was the hotel's way of raising rates without seeming to do so.) This is not true, however, on the continent of Europe, where the service charge really means what it says. However, you are still expected to give "a little something extra." Americans are famous for overtipping abroad, and the natives wish they wouldn't, but it takes a lot of courage to stand up to the sullen stare of a French porter or taxi driver who knows he's been overtipped, but who also knows he can probably embarrass you into giving him more.

tipping

There are loads of excellent travel books packed with valuable information, so we're not going to write one here. But I would like to pass on some suggestions that I've found helpful in traveling.

vacation quickies

If you're making a trip that includes several places—especially if you're going out of the country—consult a good travel agent, and let him advise you and make the arrangements. You'll save lots of time and trouble.

Remember to take necessary medicine and glasses *and* their prescriptions. Window-cleaning spray cleans eyeglasses beautifully. I put it in a plastic bottle with a spray top. (It also does a great job on patent leather.)

Foreign-language phrase books are more useful than dictionaries.

Plastic bags in various sizes are a great help in packing. I use them for shoes, bags, laundry and for miscellaneous small things. (Don't put them over patent leatherlike plastic, however, because they stick to it.)

Tuck a canvas bag that will fold flat, or a shopping bag or two into your suitcase. They will come in very handy for the extras you are bringing home.

Pads, pencils, ball-point pens, rubber bands, a flashlight, and electric plugs made to convert your appliances for use abroad are invaluable.

A lightweight throw is nice to have. Mine fits into a case so that I can also use it as a pillow while traveling.

A small umbrella and several plastic hoods are musts.

If you mark all your luggage with stripes of bright-colored masking tape, you and porters will be able to find it quickly. When you get home, make any necessary repairs to your suitcases before putting them away.

Keep your cosmetic case packed with the items you always need—a sewing kit, assorted pins, transparent tape, a travel mirror, manicure things, ear plugs, tissues, etc. As for the cosmetics themselves, which might become rancid if left too long, write out a list to remind yourself of the things you are currently using and will want to take with you. Keep the list in the bag.

Pack your dresses on flat plastic hangers. It speeds up the packing and unpacking process *and,* best of all, insures you the needed number of hangers wherever you go.

At home, abroad, wherever you are, soda water removes almost all stains, and it can't hurt anything—but use it immediately!

That's about it for vacations, and for the subject of you and your husband alone—until next year, at any rate. In the meantime, there are other people in his life.

If the sociology books are to be believed, two drastic mutations have taken place in modern man: One, he is losing his masculine image, and two, he is a lousy father figure. Women are running the world and children are running amok. Well,

*husbands
and
children*

husbandry

the situation can't be quite that bad, but it does seem that fathers aren't what they used to be. But what was it they used to be? Let's analyze it.

Three centuries ago, a father hung around the cabin and the stockade all day, hammering and hatcheting and jawing with his son. If he saw his son goofing off on the job, he would say something like, "Wield thine hatchet, Tobias, or I'll give thee something to remember." And Tobias did—no fool he.

At night, a father hung around the cabin while his wife whipped up a mess of sturdy porridge, and after dinner was over, he read *A Pilgrim's Progress* aloud for the edification of everyone in general and his virginal daughter in particular. If he saw his daughter nodding off in the middle of a chapter, he would say something like, "Open thine eyes, Chastity, now is not the time to dream of thy neighbor's son." And Chastity did—she was no fool either. That man today would be considered a superior father figure.

But what is there about a seventeenth-century pilgrim that makes a better father figure than a successful twentieth-century vice-president? Is hammering more admirable than IBMing? Not necessarily. Is lecturing a daughter about virtue the most constructive thing a man can do with his evening? Probably not. Is being around constantly better than being out of the house from eight-thirty in the morning until eight-thirty at night? Positively yes. Because you can't be a figure of authority and respect if you're not present. The best father I know is a writer—not *because* he's a writer necessarily, but maybe because he's home all day long. His children are intelligent, happy, responsible, and slightly more in awe of their father than most children. They do what he tells them almost all of the time. For what it's worth, that's more than most of us can say, but then, all fathers can't be writers. So what's to be done about the problem? Anything? Well, a little, maybe.

A father can lay down and enforce major policies. He doesn't have to be home all day to make it clear who gets the car, or who is allowed to ride the bike where, or who is old enough to use the power saw, or light matches. In return, you can support and uphold the policies whenever possible. If you don't agree with one of them, take it up with your husband privately or you'll undermine everything he's trying to accomplish. There are an awful lot of women around who *say* they want their husbands to be strong fathers but, whether deliberately or unconsciously I'm not sure, they keep grabbing the reins away. If one of your children breaks a major policy rule during the day, try not to let that cheery bit of news be the first pronouncement out of your mouth when your husband comes home at night. At least let him have a drink before you sock him with it or he'll get twice as mad as he should—at the child *and* at you.

Mothers are the ones who make minor house rules about the unimportant issues and employ their own disciplinary tactics to enforce them. This is right and proper and I'm sure Pilgrim mothers had their rules. But fathers don't even have to know about what they are and they certainly shouldn't have to hear about them when they're broken. To come home after a long day and hear a recital of infantile peccadillos like who crayoned on the wall is enough to turn a man off fatherhood altogether. Only if one particular child is the consistent troublemaker (an accumulation of small sins that seem to add up to a significant rebellion) should his father have to hear about it. Again, not when the child is around. A serious rebellion requires serious consideration; your husband might be able to shed some light on the problem if you give him some quiet time to think about it.

If your husband has some minor house rules of his own concerning the children, try to respect those, too, even if they seem unimportant to you. Hank, for instance, has a thing about kids hopping up and down from the table during dinner and asking to be excused when they're finished. I happen to know that they hop up and down to take the dishes to the kitchen, which makes life easier for me and the housekeeper, and they forget to ask to be excused because they're in a rush to get to stacks of homework. But it's such a little request, and he makes so few.

Then there are one or two positive actions your husband can take in order to solidify the phantom father figure. He can show up on Fathers' Day, or sing in the Christmas Assembly, or go to the performance of the school play in which his child has three lines. The trouble with all of these things is that they often take place in the daytime and it's

husbandry

hard for him to get there. (I sometimes wonder if schools are under the impression that fathers have nothing to do. They schedule events so peculiarly.) Furthermore, I'm not convinced it's absolutely necessary for him to get there, especially if he dreads the idea. My father never sang in the Christmas Assembly and look how nicely he turned out. Showing up at school is just another way for a father to indicate interest in his child, but if the child doesn't already have that feeling, showing up at school won't give it to him. It's just a bonus.

If you have several children, you could try to arrange a way for your husband to spend some time with each one, individually. Otherwise, he might tend to think of them as The Children and The Children won't appreciate that very much.

And now that I've finished with all those constructive suggestions, would you like to know what I *really* think? What I really think is that all this palaver about the vanishing father figure is overrated and oversold. If fathers were all that terrible, children would be all that terrible, and I don't believe they are. That fathers can't be around very much is regrettable because their children miss them, but a kid with a nice father who loves his wife and loves him—even if he only sees him one hour in the day—that kid'll probably turn out all right.

husbands and friends

Once upon a time, when your marriage was just beginning, there were friends. Your husband's friends, and your friends. Then, through a natural winnowing-out process, you stopped seeing some of your friends because your husband didn't like them, and he stopped seeing some of his for the same reason. Fair is fair. The friends who remained, some of his, some of yours, and some you collected and treasured together became Good Friends, and they are, aside from your children, the most precious commodity in your lives. These are the people who can be asked to stay for dinner at the last minute, the couple who gets along with each of you and both of you so well that none of you cares who's talking to whom—everybody seems equally entrancing. Sometimes you even take vacations with these friends. You can confide in them and know they'll never tell. If you ever had an emergency, real or imagined, at three o'clock in the morning, they'd be right over. And you'd do the same for them.

Friends like these are rare, of course. You only have about eight of them, but these eight are so satisfactory that you don't feel the need of more. And so you never see anybody else—just these eight. The rest of the time, you are home alone with your husband. You never see people you don't like, you never go to parties, and you never give any, either. Life is beautiful. . . .

But life is not like that. I'll start over.

In the beginning, there were your husband's friends and your friends. Some of your husband's friends dropped by the wayside, but some of them still have to be reckoned with because your husband continues to like them even though you don't. As mistress of the date book, you could take unfair advantage of your position, but as a considerate wife, you'd better invite these people over once in a while. Who knows —you might even get to like them.

What about the people you absolutely can't bear? Or the people your husband absolutely can't bear? Exactly how considerate do you have to be of each other? In this case, not at all. The situation calls for honesty and the power of mutual veto. Life is too short for either one of you to have to spend time with people who make you that miserable. Your husband can see his friends at lunch or when you're visiting your mother. You can see yours at lunch or when he's away on a business trip.

There are times when two husbands are old and close friends and the wives don't get along, and in order not to destroy the men's friendship, the wife has to put a good face on it—and do it cheerfully.

And then there are the couples *both* of you dislike but being obtuse types, they keep trying to get you over for dinner. Once they've succeeded, you're in for not one but two bad evenings because, even though you don't like them, the rules of the game say you have to pay them back. Keep a supply of ready excuses tucked away in the back of your head. You never know who's going to be on the other end of the phone!

For instance, you can say you have to check with your husband, and then, after a suitable time lapse, you can call back to say he has a business meeting, or you have a P-TA meeting, or your usual baby-sitter isn't available, or you have theater tickets. How about announcing flat out that your husband never goes anywhere during the week?

Pretty good, huh! Pretty ingenious. Sure. But then Mrs. Dogged rings up to invite you for a Saturday six weeks in advance. There's a joke in our family about that (I think it was originally Groucho's). It goes like this, "Six weeks from Saturday? Oh, I wish we could, darn it, but we have to go to a funeral."

You can handle Mrs. Dogged in one of two ways. You can accept for the time being and call up at the last minute with a plausible excuse. You'll be believed the first time, but if you do it again, you won't be, and you won't be asked again. I don't really approve of this tactic—you are not only hurting the Doggeds' feelings in a painfully obvious fashion, but you are also inconveniencing a hostess. On the other hand, if you happen to know that the Doggeds' party is huge, you can perhaps use this "make and break" ploy—at least she won't feel like Stella Dallas. Or you can simply accept, and go, and not invite them back. This is the most tactful and, curiously enough, the most successful; when people disregard the rules of the game, the game is usually over.

social planning

Although you're the one who customarily makes the plans, it's friendly to consult your husband about most dates even if you're fairly sure he'll approve. Maybe he's tired, maybe he just doesn't feel like seeing whoever they are, maybe he'd planned to stay late at the office. This applies particularly to newly acquired friends, or semi-friends (the people you find pleasant but only want to see occasionally) ; with your very good friends, you can go ahead with the plans on the assumption that your husband will want to see them as much as you do. If you're wrong, they are the people who understand perfectly if you break the date at the last minute.

In general, keep an eye on the number of middle-of-the-week dates you make. Whereas husbands suffer from Aphasia of the Immediate Future, wives often suffer from Aphasia of the Distant Future. After politely checking with your husband about a date for three weeks from now—it seems forever away to both of you—you blithely make a few other dates, for the days before and after the first date. When three weeks from now finally arrives, you are booked for

Monday through Friday, you're exhausted, and you don't want to go anywhere.

big parties

I loathe big parties. I really do. But in my part of the country, nobody will admit to liking them; to admit to liking them is so out it's in. But if nobody likes them, how come people keep giving them and people keep going? Beats me. If you have a lot of friends and want to play the game of having people back, you will have to give a few big parties. There are simply not enough nights to see them all in twos and fours. Maybe life is just one hideous social obligation after another; that's a depressing thought and I don't buy it for a minute. I think people who keep giving and going to parties love them—it's just not chic to say so. (It's also not chic to say you *like* living in New York City any more. DR is the only one who'll admit to that one; the rest of us all talk about how we wish we could move to the country but even those of us who could, don't. What evil force is detaining us, do you suppose?)

Anyway, back to the parties. Cocktail parties are my least favorite but they present no problem: I simply never go. The beauty of it is that both Hank, who isn't mad for them either, and I have believable, built-in excuses: He can't leave the office that early, and I have to be home with the children at their dinner hour. If you feel the way we do, I'm sure you've used the same dodges. If you love cocktail parties, you don't need to use them. If you love them and your husband doesn't, you should go, making the appropriate excuse for him, and vice versa. I'm sure, in this emancipated society of ours, no one will think it's peculiar. At least I hope not.

Big dinner parties, or after-dinner parties (of all the functions I do have to attend, they're my least favorite because I'm half asleep before I get there), are much harder to avoid; you have to show your face in public once in a while or people will begin to think there's something funny going on. ("Where are the Smiths? Anybody seen the Smiths lately? Nervous breakdown? Marriage breakdown? Business breakdown?") And, callous as it sounds, a certain amount of social intercourse is good for your husband's career.

So, here are a few quick tips on partygoing:

tips on partygoing

If the host and hostess are notorious for inviting you for seven-thirty and feeding you at eleven, eat a little something before you go, or be *very* careful about how much you drink.

If you know ahead of time who's going to be there, refresh your memory and your husband's about first names, careers, how many children. Wives have a better head for social trivia—they deal with it all day long—and husbands are likely to remember vague impressions only.

When you first come into the room, take a quick look around while you and your husband are still standing together. If either of you spots someone whose name escapes you, now is the time to fill the other one in. Otherwise, you'll find yourself sneaking off to a friend saying, "Quick! What's Marvin Smith's wife's first name?" If you inexplicably draw a blank on some couple whose names you know you should remember, you'll have to resort to that highly transparent evasion, "You know my husband, Hank, don't you?" If the other couple says, "No," you're in a lot of hot water—there's nothing to do but say lamely, "Well, this is Hank," but the other couple should know better. The "you-know-so-and-so" evasion has become a ritualistic device by now.

As for the person, whom you haven't seen in five years, who comes up to you and says, "You don't remember me, do you?" with a tone of belligerent triumph, give it to him good. Say, "No, I'm sorry, I don't." He deserves it.

Finally, there is the couple you haven't seen in a long time and you wish you could remember their names but you can't. Here I'm all for honesty: "I'm terribly sorry, but I've forgotten . . ." They'll fill in the rest, and they won't mind at all. It happens to everybody, and the older we get, the more it happens. As a matter of fact, I have a feeling it's one of the reasons I hate parties. Aphasia of the Immediate Present.

Once you and your husband have dispensed with the memory game, don't stick to each other like glue. If you just want to talk to your husband, it's quieter at home and the food is quicker. Be adventurous, take off on your own, and reconvene every once in a while to make sure you're both happy and to compare notes on all the fascinating new people you've met. Maybe one of you has met a marvelous couple, potential Good Friends. The other of you should meet them and see if he or she agrees.

If one of you is tired or bored and wants out and the other

is having a swell time, I see no reason why the tired one shouldn't split as long as this is amenable to both. It won't create comment unless you have a reputation for fighting, or playing around, or both.

When both of you decide to go, for heaven's sake, go. Wives are notoriously bad about this; they stand around gabbing for fifteen minutes, saying last-minute things while husbands get sick of waiting and make themselves another drink. Then the wives say, "But I thought we were going home?" and they make *themselves* another drink. Pretty soon it's four in the morning and you started to leave at twelve.

At a small dinner party, even when you both desperately want to leave, you have to be subtle about it, especially if it's early and you're going to be the first couple to go. Eyebrow-raising is a possibility, throat-clearing is another, but be careful—a hostess is sensitive to those signals and is likely to consider them much more insulting than the more obvious, "Gee, I hate to drag you away, honey, but I have to get up awfully early in the morning," which at least implies that you know her and trust her enough to be honest instead of tricky.

If you want to leave a Good Friend's party early, just whisper "good-bye" and "thank you" to the hostess and sneak out the door. She may not know why you're leaving, but she doesn't have to—you can tell her why the next morning on the phone. And you won't be breaking up her party.

family traditions

I'd like to add a word about traditional parties. Husbands and wives create some and inherit others. Knowing that any lonely person is lonelier at Christmas, Dick and I started years ago to invite friends who were alone or away from home to spend Christmas Eve with us. Over the years, the parties grew because everyone who had ever been a guest was welcome and there were, of course, newcomers each year. Eventually we found ourselves giving two parties—a dinner for family and close friends with more friends coming in later. For two months before Christmas, life became unbearably pressured, and by the time Christmas itself came, we were so worn out that we couldn't enjoy it. So, reluctantly, two years ago we broke the tradition.

Traditions are lovely until they become traps and their

real meaning is lost in the struggle to keep them going. For years, Dick and I were expected at my mother's for dinner every Friday night; she was carrying on a custom her own parents had started years before. Almost every Friday, it seemed to us, there was something else we wanted to do. There was no way to arrange it. If we didn't go to Mother's, we felt guilty, and if we did go, we felt resentful. It took a good deal of doing, but I was finally able to persuade her to discontinue these rigidly routine family get-togethers by convincing her that we wanted to see her because we really wanted to be with her—not only because it was Friday and we had to.

Fortunately, some traditions are as precious as they are unavoidable. It is only when they take root for no reason—like *always* spending New Year's Eve with the Macys or Fourth of July with the Gimbels—that they should be examined and weeded out. It's the only way to preserve the meaning of the ones you really hold dear.

Since DR and I are devoting a stupendously long chapter to the subject of entertaining in your own home, I don't have to go into that now, but before I'm done with friends, I want to tell you about one couple I know. Fearlessly unfettered by the standard strictures of society, they have made a rule for themselves and stuck to it: Under no circumstances will they ever allow anyone they don't like across the threshold of their home. This is an admirable, sensible, and enviable rule —for a writer. Yes, I'm talking about the same writer who hangs in there at home, respected and obeyed by his children; he's a truly emancipated soul. The rest of us poor devils can't afford to make rules like that; it's a luxury reserved for the self-employed.

Okay, if we can't, we can't, but what we can do is cut down on the number of people we see out of habit, those semi-good friends we don't really know very well and never, no matter how many years go by, seem to get to know any better. There's a sort of sound barrier of friendship; your Good Friends are behind it with you, and even though you *will* have to see people you don't like, and you *will* have to go to parties and give them, if you reserve most of your remaining time for the Good Friends, life can be, if not altogether beautiful, at least semi-beautiful.

There are men who get through their entire lives without contributing anything more substantial than money to their communities. I'm not knocking them; maybe that's all they have time for, and, besides, money is pretty substantial stuff. Community-minded wives spend long hours scheming to get their mitts on it for one good cause or another, and the man who voluntarily writes out a fat check gets my vote even if he never lifts a finger in any other direction.

Men who *do* get themselves involved in community affairs usually do so out of one of three motives: self-interest, which —in spite of the fact that the end in terms of charity is supposed to justify the means—is revolting; *enlightened* self-interest, which is not revolting; and sheer altruism, which for a busy executive verges on sainthood.

Let's get the revolting one out of the way first. The man who heads a charity committee or runs for local office because he thinks it will further his career, or get his name around, or put him in touch with the right people is (a) crazy and (b) nobody I want to know. Why I don't want to know him is obvious—you don't want to know him, either. He is crazy because he won't get away with it. No busy executive has time to function as anything more than a figurehead for a charity drive, and the one thing a charity doesn't need is a figurehead, male or female, who gets his name in the papers but never writes letters, never makes phone calls, and never shows up at meetings. When the busy executive finally makes his appearance on the night of the Big Event, resplendent in his dinner jacket, everybody there will know what he didn't do and why he said he'd do it. For shame!

The busy executive who dabbles in local politics will run into worse problems. First he has to get himself elected, which takes time, and then he has to do a decent job, which also takes time. No good.

In other words, a man cannot further his career or better his social standing by community climbing into the public eye. Maybe he can get his wife to help him, though. She actually does have the time to write letters and make phone calls, and women are even getting elected to office these days. She can also get her daughter into the right dancing school, which will ultimately lead to a debut at the right charity ball. But I don't want to know her either.

Where husbands are concerned, I think you're wrong. Unadmirable as it is, community climbing frequently does exactly what the man wants. It works in that it gets him into the group he wants to join and meanwhile the charity benefits. Lots of the busiest men not only find time but make time to work very hard as chairmen of committees. True, it's only after they've reached the top, but then they probably wouldn't be asked to serve as chairmen unless they'd "made it." When they get kicked upstairs to become chairmen of the board, they get to be made Honorary Chairmen, and then they really are figureheads.

Now for the enlightened self-interest: These are the activities that benefit the man in the long run because they benefit the community he lives in. For instance:

1.   Attendance at P-TA meetings, even if intermittent, makes the school better. A better school provides a better education for his child.

2.   Attendance at zoning meetings will acquaint him with the latest developments in his town. If the latest development is the threat of a hideous development, he'll know enough to vote against it. If the latest development is a threat, made by conservative citizens, to restrict the zoning laws to five-acre zones because an influx of minority citizens is expected, he'll know enough to vote against the conservatives. (I hope.)

3.   If he lives in a city and his block is having a community clean-up, he could grab a broom and go to work. You meet a lot of nice people that way, and a clean block is pleasanter than a dirty block. (There's a gem of a statement for you!) And so forth and so on. There are a million other things a man can do for his community. I don't know what they all are (they vary from place to place), but your husband can find out if he wants to, and help out if he wants to. I really do mean wants to; maybe he's tired (*maybe?!*) and would rather write out a check. As I said before, that's all right with me and I'm sure it's all right with the community.

Activities of sheer altruism verge on sainthood because they have nothing to do with any form of self-interest whatsoever. They won't do your husband the faintest good—he's casting his bread upon the waters, knowing that the loaves will wash up a hundred miles away or not until twenty years from now. This is more than all right with me; in fact, I'd love to meet your husband!

Giving blood, reading for the blind, working in a settlement house in the evening or on a Saturday, teaching in a street academy—it's not so difficult for you to do these things; as a nonworking mother, you are busy but you can arrange your own schedule. But if your husband does these things, you must be married to an awfully nice guy.

Your husband's career concerns him for half the hours in the day (it's supposed to go on from nine to five, but almost always uses up more time than that), and for two thirds of the days of his life. And we're not just talking about time, we're talking about the guts of the man, of any man. When the job goes wrong, the world goes wrong—for you, too. When it goes right, it sometimes goes too right, and you're left out. Even then, right is still preferable, so I'll start with the positive thinking—and at the beginning.

A company is interested in hiring your husband. So interested, in fact, that they want to meet *you*. What a bloody nerve, you think. What business are you of theirs? What have you got to do with it? Quite a lot, actually. The cautious company wants to make sure you're going to fit in—maybe you're a lunatic, how do they know? After all, hiring an executive is serious business involving a considerable investment of money and time. The executive is supposed to do a good job in the office, but he's also supposed to acquit himself gracefully at social functions, where the seeds of many big deals germinate. It will not do for an executive's wife to be a nut or a nonconformist. If you are a nut or a nonconformist and you are possessed of the insight to recognize it, you'd better have an Important Talk with your husband right now to determine whether or not you can change, and whether or not you want to. If you can and you do, here is how you cope with the executive wife interview:

If you're not sure what to wear, dress conservatively—the proverbial little black dress. Executives' wives rarely go in for high style.

Have one less drink than you usually do, treat the inspectors the way you would any ordinary new people—be friendly, feminine, and humorous until the conversation gets around to business. Then SHUT UP.

If the interview is taking place at dinner, after dinner is usually when the business talk starts. After dinner is when you can make a graceful excuse about the children or something and run along home.

In general, try to relax and, above all, *be yourself* unless you want to spend the next twenty years playing a part. In conclusion, I want to say this: I'd never heard of the Executive Wife Interview until quite recently. It struck me as being the most repugnant, outrageous invasion of privacy ever invented by man. Then, funnily enough, only two months later, I had the occasion to star in one. And you know what? The dinner was good, the inspectors were terribly nice, and I had a lovely time. So there!

your relations with business people

Sooner or later, you're going to have to entertain the boss and his wife. Don't panic. If the whole idea sends you into a paroxysm of terror, you and your husband can get theater tickets and take them out to dinner, thereby avoiding the trauma of exposing your tawdry little home and your raggle-taggle little children to their discriminating eyes. But there's no need, really. Once, long ago, the boss was an underling, too. He, too, had what he thought was a tawdry house full of raggle-taggle children. Somewhere, lurking still within the Brooks Brothers suit, is the bygone soul of a serf. So take a chance. Be intrepid. Invite the august serf and his wife to dinner.

The other side of the coin is, of course, your entertaining people who work for your husband—something that can certainly add warmth and an extra dimension to what might otherwise be a cut-and-dried relationship. Basically you treat it like any other party and keep it informal.

As for potential clients: Be subtle! If you want to give your husband a clever boost, talk about how much he loves his work rather than how good he is at it. The latter won't necessarily be believed, you see, but usually if someone loves what he's doing, he *is* good at it—just like kids in school.

If you're inviting potential clients over for dinner, try to put together the same kind of evening as you would for the boss—interesting. If you can manage to convince yourself that they are not potential clients, just potential friends (which is perhaps what they'll turn out to be in the long run), you'll be more relaxed and so will they.

Once in a while, you may find yourself talking to a potential client at a party while your husband is on the other side of the room, unaware of his presence. Don't get your hostess to arrange an introduction or try to maneuver one yourself. Instead, clue your husband in and let him worry about it.

If your husband is an executive, he has a secretary. What should your relationship be with her? Obviously, polite and friendly. I, personally, have a problem in this department. The first week, I say, "Hello, this is Mrs. Guettel, is Mr. Guettel there, please?" Next, it's "Hello, this is Mrs. G. Is Himself there, by any chance?" Then I descend to "Hi, love, it's me. Is Hank around?" The total disintegration of dignity! What's the secretary supposed to say, "No, love, Hank's in the men's room right now"? I'm putting her in an awkward position because, like so many other people these days, I'm terribly anxious to atone for and single-handedly correct the inequities of society. That's nice and democratic, but I'm not going to correct them by being clubbily and inappropriately informal with the secretary.

Speaking of the phone, there are a few rules about that, too:

1. Don't call the office nine times a day; don't call at all, if you can help it.

2. At home, if you have only one phone, don't tie it up, and don't let the kids tie it up for hours at a time.

3. When your husband either receives or has to make business calls at home, keep the kids out of the room and quiet. Don't stand around kibbitzing yourself, either; it'll make him nervous and self-conscious.

Unless specifically invited, stay out of your husband's office. It's all right to pick him up at the end of the day when you're both going out somewhere together, but none of that impromptu dropping in to show him your new hat.

business trips

Be willing and available for business evenings and trips. When wives are included in a convention, there's usually a reason for it—maybe your husband is up for a promotion he doesn't even know about and you're in for another executive interview that *you* didn't know about. Or maybe it's just to see how well all you wives get along with each other. Who knows? In any case, conventions are not the drag they used to be. Wives aren't compelled to attend boring sales meetings; some companies arrange for special activities for wives alone, and anyway, why pass up a free opportunity to get out of the house and travel?

For Dick, business trips have usually meant that he would be "on the road" for a period of several weeks while the show was being tried out before its New York opening. When our children were small and still at home, I used to divide my time between them and Dick—spending the middle of the week with the girls and going, usually to Boston, for the weekend. It wasn't until after Mary and Linda were married that I was able to stay with Dick the entire time he was away.

His days were filled with conferences and rehearsals and, of course, at night he would go to the theater to see how the show was playing and whether the cuts and changes worked or not. My job was to count the laundry, get his suits pressed, and be available.

Although business trips in the theater world are very different from those in the business world, they have one thing in common: Wives must keep out of the way. And if no entertainment has been planned for them, it's up to them to find their own ways of occupying their time. Being in one place for several weeks has great advantages, especially when the place is Boston. I was never at a loss for things to do. One year, I took Italian lessons from the Berlitz School across the street from the hotel. Another time, Recording for the Blind loaned me a tape recorder and gave me some books they wanted recorded. And then there was the time I took along my sewing machine and made myself a dress.

Most business trips, however, are shorter, and many wives who need a break in their routine welcome a chance to have a few days of reading, or even wasting time. And, of course, there are always museums and art galleries. I found antiquing in a city like Boston was both fun and rewarding because, in those days, it was still possible to find charming little things that I would buy and put away for Christmas gifts. Dick's shows often opened in spring, which meant that we would find ourselves in Boston in February—a bit early for Christmas shopping, but I was able to choose things at leisure instead of under pressure.

Whatever you do, don't make your husband feel he is neglecting you. Remember it's his business trip and you can be a big help or a big worry.

Some husbands want to leave their work behind them when they come home at night. I don't mean paper work—that's out of their control, unfortunately—I mean they don't want to talk or think about their jobs. Others, usually the very enthusiastic ones or the ones with worries, want to be patted on the back or encouraged. Not always easy to do, because the average wife knows very little about the machinations of big business and isn't in a position to discuss them, let alone guide or advise. Perhaps in the area of personnel decisions (the irascible boss, the neurotic coworker, the lazy secretary) her innate common sense and an objective point of view might come in handy, *if requested*. Otherwise, the most constructive contribution she can make is to listen to him if he wants to talk, and to retain what little information he passes on. If her mind is half on what her husband is saying and half on dinner, he'll soon conclude that it's a waste of time to tell her anything at all.

broadening horizons

As your husband's career advances, should you try to broaden his horizons? On paper, it sounds good—all work and no horizon-broadening—but it isn't as easy as it sounds. You can't just say, "Up, up, Harold, it's a nice Saturday morning and we're going to go horizon-broadening at the Museum of Modern Art." Why can't you? Because Harold probably won't go. If his career in electronics has been advancing, it's because he loves his work and is good at it and he was planning to go to the office Saturday morning. Also Sunday morning. Maybe he just wants to hack around, or dismantle clocks—an interest he already has.

What you can do, however, is broaden his horizons in

terms of people. If you agree with me that your social life cannot be confined to your eight Good Friends, that you *will* have to give and go to parties, and lastly, that you can stop seeing the people in your life whom you see purely out of habit, why then can't you collect new people? Older people, younger people, bachelor or widowed, black, white, or Zen —it doesn't matter as long as they're different from the types you see all the time, with different interests, different careers, even different speech patterns. People are just as horizon-broadening as museums—possibly more so.

living with success

Sometimes, a very successful husband makes for a very unhappy wife. He's busy and she's left out. He's out to dinner with business associates; she's left at home with the kids. When he *is* home, he's late for dinner, or dinner is interrupted by important phone calls; after dinner, he has paper work to do or he's too tired to do anything but fall into bed.

It's a bleak picture. I've seen enough of it myself to know what it feels like, but in our house, we're lucky. Aside from occasional snarling over the phone at dinner time, or an occasional wail that goes, "Oh, come on, now—you have to go out again *tonight?*" my frustration is kept to a minimum because as a part-time working wife, I'm pretty busy myself. If I weren't and if I complained more, it would net me nothing but an irritated husband. He loves his job, but he'd have to do it whether he loved it or not and if it takes x amount of time, that's the amount of time it takes. Ask yourself, "Who would I rather be? Who would I rather be married to?" It puts things in perspective.

For wives who are not working, the biggest problem is being lonely. Having dinner with the children night after night may keep you busy, but this can pall on even the most appreciative of mothers. So don't have dinner night after night with the children. Dr. Spock would be the first to reassure you that it's not necessary. And anyway, if your husband weren't habitually at the office of an evening, you'd be going out together some of the time, wouldn't you? There is nothing wrong with going out without him. Go to friends' houses for dinner, go to the theater or a concert, or to the movies. Invite some friends over for dinner, go visit your parents, or take a night course in something you haven't time to pursue in the daytime.

Most of all, count your blessings. Your husband is successful, you have no money worries (or shouldn't have), your future is secure, one day he'll be retired and then you'll have him all to yourself. In the meantime, his world is going right and he is happy. Everybody should have your problems! Everybody should but everybody doesn't.

. . . *and without it*

The unspeakable has happened, the world's gone wrong, your husband has lost his job. Heavy, heavy over thine head hangs a multitude of burdens, both practical and emotional: What can you do to help your husband, what do you tell the kids, what do you tell the outside world, what do you do about money, and, of course, what do you do about your poor panicky self?

Last things first. Get a grip on your poor panicky self. If you disintegrate now when your husband really needs you, you're no kind of wife! Better start worrying about him.

His biggest worry right now is you. Assure him that you're not worried, that you know everything will work out, maybe it's all for the best, etc. These are all ridiculous lies, of course, but it's essential for you to act confident even though you aren't.

Next, when the initial shock has worn off, both of you should sit down and be cold-bloodedly honest with each other in appraising his chances for the future. For one thing, do you know *why* he lost his job? Was it merely a political shift —one of those miserable things he had nothing to do with? If so, this sudden revelation will tend to make you question your values and those of the society you live in. You're quite right to question them, but maybe you should have questioned them earlier. At this point, halfway through your lives, you're stuck with them, and condemning society won't solve your immediate problem. On with the self-examination.

Did your husband make a monstrous goof—a one-shot mistake that won't be repeated once he gets another job (and of course he will!), or is it a question of his ability in general? Maybe he's in the wrong company or even the wrong field. If it's the latter, you two have a lot of talking and analyzing to do, and some scary decisions to make. They must be made and the talking must be done, but be tactful. He's very insecure and very vulnerable right now and any self-disparaging remarks about how he's only fit to be a mail clerk are not to be taken seriously. He's testing you to see if you agree.

Now, about what to tell the kids. Tell them the pertinent facts: Daddy's out of a job, Daddy is going to find a new job, and in the meantime, we have to not spend any more money than we have to. Yes, it's worrying. (They'll notice that you look worried anyway so you might as well admit it or they'll think it's something worse. What's worse? Well, a fatal disease or a divorce is worse although you may not think so at first.) But things will be okay, and it's happened to an awful lot of other people and they all survived it.

This sort of thing is often marvelous for kids. I'm not recommending that your husband get himself fired or anything, but kids like to feel needed, helpful in a crisis. They want to feel part of grown-up life. I used to wish my parents would lose their money so I could prove I loved them anyway, but I never got the chance.

You handle the outside world the same way you handle the children: "Craig is out of a job, Craig is looking for another job, we're flat broke, but what the hell, come on over on Saturday and we'll eat spaghetti and you'll cheer us up."

Do not pretend. You won't fool anyone. It's much classier and much, *much* more appealing to tell the truth. Your friends want to help and they can, if you let them, by listening to you, making suggestions, and reminding you that it's happened before. (Just what you told the kids, of course.) One of your friends might even be able to steer your husband in the direction of a new job, but none of these things will happen if you pridefully keep it all a horrid, humiliating secret.

emergency financing

All those bills, what do you do with them? You can eat them, toss them over your shoulder, or play cute games like mailing empty envelopes: "How silly, I forgot to put the check in, I'll mail it right away" or putting the check to the phone company in the envelope to the cleaners and vice versa. I don't advise this, however. It's tacky.

And another thing, you will find you have an almost uncontrollable tendency to be very rude to the bill collectors when they call up. Well, control it because it's not their fault and if they're rude it's because you're making them nervous. (Small merchants get especially nervous. Big stores are remarkably tolerant if you explain that you can't pay it all now, but will send them a partial payment. You do have to send it, though, or they'll lose patience.)

My own feeling about bills is that you should first pay the people who might really need it—the small stores, the people who deal in services, because big stores are not only better able to wait for their money, but their mark-up allows for it. Furthermore, their top credit rating is thirty to sixty days so your rating won't be affected whether you pay in two or fifty-nine days. This reminds me of a favorite anecdote Oscar Hammerstein II loved to tell about his grandfather, Oscar the First. Many years ago, when the first Oscar was building the Manhattan Opera House, he got several estimates for the cost of installing elevators in the building. The highest estimate was that submitted by the largest and best-known elevator company, and William Hammerstein, Oscar's son (father of our Oscar), was astonished when his father told him that that was the one he had accepted. When William asked why, his father said, "Well, since we're not going to pay them anyway, I figure they can stand the loss better than the others."

Cut down immediately on luxuries—sell the extra car, sell or rent the summer place, stop going out to dinner or look for inexpensive places, don't send all your rugs and draperies to be cleaned in the spring, cut down on part-time help, borrow and exchange children's clothes. This is the every-little-bit theory, which is not only true but is the one single *active* step you can take while your husband is waiting for the phone to ring. The feeling that you're doing something will make you feel better.

Borrowing will make you feel worse, but you may have to do it anyway. However, if you only need to borrow in order to maintain your old standard of living, don't borrow— change your standard of living.

If you're going to borrow, there are two ways to do it. You can borrow officially—from banks, on insurance, you can get a second mortgage on your house, you can borrow on private school tuition, or if you have a smart kid, see about a scholarship.

152

Borrowing unofficially from friends involves no interest, but more conscience. Obviously you should pick on people who can afford it and be honest about telling them you don't know how soon you can pay them back. It's better to borrow a big hunk from one rich person than bits from several people. The several people are bound to talk among. themselves, and pretty soon it'll begin to sound as though you're on your way to the poorhouse.

One last observation about borrowing: The classic pattern is to resent the people you borrow from. (This is the main reason most people hate to lend money.) With parents especially, your resentment comes from loss of pride, and fear of dependence. But if your parents are willing, and they're usually more than willing, something rather wonderful can come out of it: You discover that your pride is still intact and that you are just as independent as ever. What you are saying, in effect, to your family is, "Okay, so we're vulnerable. If you want to take advantage of our indebtedness by pushing us around, you can. But we trust you and think you won't." P.S., they won't—unless they're stinkers, and if they're stinkers, you knew it long ago and shouldn't be borrowing from them in the first place.

I think I've told you just about all I know about husbands. Oh, I suppose I know a few other little things like: If you have a fight with your husband, don't have it in public; don't tell your mother about it because she'll get all upset; don't even tell your best friend. When you and your husband have made up, you'll resent her knowing. Don't tell other people because they'll blow it up out of all proportion and spread it all over town—that's one. Another is, don't discuss your sex life with other people, it's none of their business. But you know these things anyway. They're not very original and hardly worth repeating.

I can remind you to accept the man the way he is, whatever he is, because you won't change him significantly no matter how hard you try. I can urge you to be ruthless about time alone with him—you simply must have it no matter what you have to do to get it. I can, most passionately of all, urge you to talk to each other about anything, everything, and, freely, about yourselves. I guess you know these things, too.

153

husbandry

So here I am, several thousand words later, still sitting in my hot seat. As a last attempt to be of service, would you like me to try to define a husband? A husband is a person to live with, not for, to keep you company, to lighten your miseries, to heighten your highs, to make you laugh. A husband is for fun.

And what is a wife? The same thing.

THE
CARE AND FEEDING
OF GUESTS

All of us entertain our family and friends—informally and formally, often or occasionally. Entertaining is an important part of life, and it should be a pleasant one. For most of us, the era of the four-course seated dinner and the formal tea—complete with silver tea service and lace banquet cloth —has passed. Even the few people who would still like and can afford to entertain in the grand manner are hard-pressed to find the staff to handle it. So everyone is in pretty much the same boat. True, if you have the money, you can hire lots of come-in help, rent whatever you want in the way of special equipment, and even have the party catered (although catered food is seldom very imaginative). But the usefulness of these services depends as much on their being available in your neighborhood as it does on what you have to spend, so fewer people give large formal parties. That's why it's the smaller, more casual day-to-day kind of entertaining that I am most interested in. Besides, when you don't have to struggle through the vast amount of detail involved in a big bash, it's the easiest and the most fun for you.

The primary purpose of entertaining is to have fun, and nobody has ever passed a law that restricts the fun to the guests. The best company evenings are those at which the host and hostess have a good time. In fact, a party at which the host and hostess don't have a good time is almost invariably a bad party. Asking friends for dinner or a party isn't, or shouldn't be, a formidable chore: It's a pleasant part of life. That is why it's sad that so many would-be hostesses—charming, bright, and logical wives and mothers—are terrified whenever they are faced with party planning or "important" guests for dinner.

What makes a party successful? People, people, people. I

can't emphasize that too strongly. It's lovely to have good
food and to sit in attractive, comfortable surroundings, but
unless you start with people who will be interested in meeting each other and talking together, it can be a deadly
evening.

When it's a party built around a special occasion, your
guest list will be shaped by the event itself. It may also start
with a particular friend or couple, in which case the choice
of other guests will, and should, be influenced by the "guest
of honor's" preferences.

The one special guest with whom almost everyone has to
cope eventually is "the boss"—and his wife, who probably
seems even scarier . . . for two reasons: one, women are
usually more afraid of other women than they are of men;
and two, the boss's wife is often a totally unknown quantity.
Anticipating "the Evening," the poor hostess really suffers,
and she shouldn't. Actually, there is no special list of "do's"
and "don't's" for business entertaining. But because you
want everything to be particularly right, you can set all sorts
of impossible goals when, again, the thing to remember is
that what you find easiest you will do best, and people
(bosses included) will enjoy most. Nobody is impressed for
long by extravagance for extravagance's sake—least of all
the man who knows better than anyone else what you can
really afford. But you *can* make his evening enjoyable by
giving special thought to the people you invite with him.
(Caution: Even if you know the boss is a bridge buff, don't
set up an evening of cards before you know his game and the
stakes he plays for.) Your husband will be your best adviser
on this, and he may even know some of the boss's likes and
dislikes in the food department.

Other business acquaintances present fewer problems. You
treat Harold, your husband's opposite number from the Chicago office, like any other guest when he's in town and has a
free evening. If he has friends in your part of the world, or if
there are company people he particularly likes, making a
small party of it is a very nice thing to do. On the other
hand, if he is an old friend who makes the trip often, he
might have more fun just sitting, talking, and having dinner
with the two of you. Whatever you do (and this goes for all
guests of honor, business or otherwise), if you call it a party

for Harold, make it one genuinely planned for him, one that takes into account the things and people he really enjoys. Don't use him and the evening to pay off obligations. That way nobody has fun, and if Harold resents it, he's right. Also, don't be like a friend of mine who tells two or three friends (each separately) that he or she is the guest of honor. Sooner or later notes get compared, and there's only one sure loser. To me, the phrase "guest of honor" belongs to another era—unless you're entertaining royalty or giving a political cocktail party ("Mr. and Mrs. Smith invite you to meet Congressman X"). "Having a party for Harold" is a much less stuffy way of putting it.

In big organizations where transfers are frequent, company people are often your first friends in a new community. But don't let this trap you into the "company party" habit. You'll meet other people, too, and when you meet couples you like, make it a point to phone and invite them to your house—don't wait for them to make the first call. New community or not, try to keep your guest list mixed, a blend of non-company people with local company friends. As Dick and I learned years ago on the Coast when Hollywood was a one-industry town, one of the surest ways to produce a truly dull party is to limit it to couples whose husbands are all in the same business. Whether they're lawyers or doctors or brokers, show business or movie moguls, the result is always the same. Even in Hollywood, with the room full of gorgeous women, the men would congregate in a tight little knot at one end of the room to talk pictures while their wives were left at the other to compare notes on the same things women everywhere compare notes on when left to themselves—children and help. So avoid the company party like the plague it is. Mixing different interests and age groups, as well as new friends and old, makes for a better party.

what kind of party

However, most party plans originate simply because you'd like to have friends over. Fine. But what sort of party should it be: large or small? early or late? brunch or lunch? dinner or supper? Entertaining is not like remodeling and decorating; you don't need a professional's help to tell you how to plan a party. Through trying out different kinds of parties, you and your husband will discover the ones that you enjoy most. And they are the right ones for you.

Having six or eight friends in for drinks can be very pleasant. When there are newcomers or visitors in town, it's a nice relaxed way of introducing them to the community. And it is also a good way for a hostess to entertain until she feels comfortable about more ambitious parties.

Although large cocktail parties are a favorite form of entertaining for many people, for me, they have a kind of frenetic quality that I dislike. All of us are harassed and pressed for time these days, and I suspect that many people use huge cocktail parties as much to write off obligations as to see their friends. It is certainly more flattering to be asked to friends' houses with just a few people and, for me, infinitely more enjoyable.

However, since almost everyone has to give a large party at some point, I'd like to recommend an after-dinner party as a possible alternative to the cocktail party. For one thing, it's a party that stands on its own as opposed to the cocktail party, where everyone is on his way from or to something else. Guests who are invited to a party "after nine-thirty" will probably expect to spend the evening and will be generally more relaxed. The food can be even simpler to prepare and serve than cocktail canapés. Plan to serve it around ten-thirty or eleven, as people will already have had their dinner and won't be hungry too early. Cold ham, salad, cheese, coffee and cake won't win you a prize for originality but it's certainly easy to do. Put everything out on the dining table, use an automatic coffee maker that will keep the coffee hot, and let the guests serve themselves.

Having friends in before some special occasion—like a club dance or the opening of an exhibit at the museum—is another easy way to entertain. A party before another event has the advantage of being self-limiting as far as time is concerned. You don't have to worry about bored guests (they won't be there that long and they start with something in common) or soggy stragglers. If you're concerned about whom or how many to invite, a party before or after a benefit or a meeting can include only those directly involved without risking hurt feelings. And you can be pleasantly sure that an hour or two at your house helped to make the evening more fun for everybody.

The best times we have had in our own house have been

at small lunches and dinners. Eight has always seemed to me the ideal number—large enough to include some variety among the guests, and small enough to give everyone a chance to get to know someone a little better.

*choosing
a date*

The choice of a date is important. Obviously, you'll try to steer clear of a conflict with a major community event. And the evening of a predictably unpleasant session at the dentist or the day you've promised to work all afternoon at the school book fair is a bad idea. But the most important part of the art of timing is to allow enough hours for preparation so you won't end up feeling harassed. The trick is to remember that there is more to a party than food. There is help to get, the house to clean, equipment to check, wine and liquor to order, and silver to polish. There are tables to set and flowers (if you plan to have them) to arrange. (You might save both minutes and money on large arrangements by doing backgrounds of leaves in advance—magnolias or rhododendron are great—and adding a few fresh flowers like carnations, peonies, dahlias, or a spray or two of flowers on the day of the party itself.)

*party
help*

Do you need part-time help? How much and what kind do you want? For a large or small party, the answer will depend not only on your needs, what you can get, and what you can afford, but on what will give you the most comfort. For my money, the best extra help is the lady who comes in to do the things you hate to do. That might mean someone to clean and polish and vacuum, shine silver, fix flowers, and get everything ready the day before the party. It might mean someone to chop, mince, mix, wash greens and help you get a head start on the food. Or it could be a baby-sitter to take the kids off your hands so you can chop-mix-mince, or have a leisurely bath and dressing time before your guests arrive. You may want a man to handle drinks so that both you and your husband will be free to greet people and make introductions. You might want a maid to serve the dinner and clear the table. Or someone behind the scenes in the kitchen to keep an eye on the food, help with last-minute preparations, and wash up after dinner. Your regular cleaning woman could fit in very well here. If you really hate cooking, you might even want someone to come in and take all that off your hands. (This presupposes getting together in advance with the cook on such basics as menu, cost, payment, marketing, and clean-up arrangements.)

If you haven't built up your own list of favorite come-in people, friends can often recommend men and women they've found good and reliable. Club personnel are also often happy to help at private parties on their days off. Be clear in advance about uniforms (part-time help usually provide their own) and hours, and find out, too, how he, she, or they prefer to be paid. If it is someone who has never worked for you before, on the day of the party allow extra time—even though it means paying for an additional hour or so—to go through *exactly* what you expect him or her to do. Take it step by step, perhaps two or three times—you can't be too explicit, as a friend of mine can testify ever since the time she asked a new waitress to serve the salmon "with parsley in the mouth"; so she did—hers.

serving arrangements

If it is a matter of serving, explain just what is to be brought in, and remember that an untrained waitress may need to be told to serve from the left and take away from the right. There are two schools of thought about whether or not to start with the hostess. I happen to think a hostess should help herself first out of simple consideration for her guests. When serving starts with her, they aren't left worrying about whether to take one chop or two or making that first cut into a quiche or a mold of ice cream. I've been to parties where the waitress serves all the women first and then leapfrogs back to serve the men—a very disconcerting system. Clockwise is better. I also believe it is thoughtful to have things passed twice, with the hostess taking a bit on her plate the second time to reassure people who might be shy about helping themselves again. And since good food should be enjoyed at its best, it is absurd to allow dishes to get cold and sauces to congeal while waiting until everyone has been served; it's no longer considered rude to start while everything is hot.

Perhaps because I am married to a man who doesn't care about starring as a carver . . . That's one way to put it. The honest-to-God truth is that he'd probably slice off a finger if he tried! . . . I prefer to have meats sliced in the kitchen. Electric knives can really do a marvelous job. And when it comes to things like chicken breasts, baked potatoes, or chocolate eclairs, I always plan to have extra pieces because nobody really likes to take the last one, and in a household of any size, the food is never wasted. Besides, those "extras" can save your life when an unexpected guest materializes at the last minute.

Once you've cleared the day with the people you'll need for help, you can send out invitations. For a small group—up to eight or ten—telephoned invitations are easiest and perfectly acceptable. But you should be sure to reach the person you are actually inviting. Phone messages can get confused, and that way lie social disasters like having guests arrive on the wrong night or not at all.

telephone invitations

For more than ten, casual written invitations are safer, and a written response is most thoughtful. A telephoned reply is all right, however, providing, again, that you speak directly to your host or hostess.

written invitations

Make your invitation specific as to time, place, and dress. In written invitations, avoid such phrases as "Come to a party" or "Come to the Joneses' "—they don't tell your guests what to expect in the way of food, dress, or time. If your name is Smith, you can say, "Come to the Joneses' " and avoid giving the party altogether. When you really mean cocktails (no buffet), it's a good idea to suggest how long you expect the party to last—5 to 7 or 6 to 8, gives guests a clue about what dinner plans they should make. "Cocktails and buffet" can mean anything from olives, salted nuts and dried-up sandwiches to a gloriously elaborate smorgasbord, so it might help to indicate that food will be served by saying, "Cocktails and Buffet from 7 on" without suggesting when the party should end. Some people seem to enjoy long cocktail hours (and I do mean hours) before dinner. But for those who don't (like me), it is thoughtful when you're having a large group for dinner to include both the cocktail and the dinner time on the invitation. If the hostess herself prefers the "long hour," "Cocktails 7:30; dinner 9:00" leaves her guests the option of arriving a little late without upsetting anyone's plans.

Having set her times, the hostess should stick to them. There will be occasions when things go awry in the kitchen or when guests are unavoidably late without being able to give you warning. But keeping your other guests waiting for the late arrivals is unfair, and it's very hard on the food!

*timing
invitations*

The more important the party, the earlier your invitations should be sent—especially during a holiday season. Otherwise, three weeks' advance notice is considered about right. For informal get-togethers, the timing depends on how socially active your community is and how well you know the people you are inviting. On special nights like New Year's Eve, Christmas night, or the Saturday nights of the Memorial and Labor Day weekends, most people hope for some special and glorious invitation to come their way. Often they delay making plans until the last minute, and sometimes the nicest evenings can develop as a result. Last year Dick and I, hating to go out on New Year's Eve and disliking the kind of big party that someone is always giving, found ourselves without any plans ten days before the first of the year. Rather apologetically saying, "If by any chance you have no plans for New Year's Eve, would you like to come to dinner?" we called a few old friends (all of whom would know at least some of the others) and guess what? Everyone we invited said, "We'd love to come!" It turned out to be one of the happiest New Year's Eves we've ever spent. We were spared all guilt feelings for having left out so many people we love because obviously we were giving a small party, spontaneously planned, and no one's feelings were hurt. So if, at holiday time, you start feeling sorry for yourself and you're convinced that all kinds of gay parties are taking place to which you have not been invited, pick up the phone and see what you can do about getting together your own spur-of-the-moment party.

*menu
planning:
first
courses*

Now that you know who is coming and what kind of party it is going to be, think about the food and wine you'll serve. Most first courses fit into one of three classifications: soup, fish, or vegetable—any of which can be served hot or cold. Quiches, smoked salmon, and prosciutto with melon also make good beginnings. The best choice for you on any particular evening depends on the season and, again, a great deal on what you've planned to follow.

*balancing
your
menu*

The color and texture of the whole meal is important to keep in mind at every stage of planning. It's a matter of looks, taste, and good nutrition, too, because, coincidentally, a menu that is appealing to the eye and the palate almost

the care and feeding of guests

always rates higher in food value than one that isn't. A dinner that starts with vichyssoise, goes on to fricasseed chicken, rice, and creamed onions, and finishes with vanilla ice cream may be perfectly cooked and seasoned. But all those creamy white things won't look very appetizing, and their blandness adds to the boredom. If you start with a quiche, it would be a mistake to end with an apricot tart—too many pastries. And a rich main course calls for a fresh light dessert like oranges in red wine or water ice with fruit. A balance between light and rich, crisp and smooth, sweet and tart enhances a meal's interest—a point you should keep in mind when you substitute one thing for another in a menu you've found successful. In general, the new dish should be similar to the one it is replacing. A clear turtle soup can substitute for bouillon, or beef Stroganoff for veal Marengo without further changes. But a switch from cold leeks vinaigrette to hot leeks hollandaise would require a main course substitution of simple roast chicken for chicken curry.

I tend to think of the dinner as a whole rather than emphasize any one course. But if you remember that a guest particularly enjoys a special dish—and if it isn't too exotic, like tripe or snails—it's especially thoughtful to serve it and plan the rest of the meal accordingly. Keeping a book with your guests' names and the menus you have served can help you to avoid repeating the same dish unintentionally. I have such a book, but I must confess I only occasionally manage to discipline myself to use it!

presenting food The way food looks matters enormously. By which I don't mean you should major in French glazes, truffle stars, or carrot curls (the bloom is also off the radish rose). None of these is worth the time it takes, and they all give me the uneasy feeling that the food has been handled too much. I think it is nice to know what you're eating, not puzzle about what is quivering under the jelly or hiding under the sauce. But I do think cold poached bass looks infinitely more tempting surrounded by tomatoes or shrimp and served with a green sauce than it does with a plain mayonnaise. Lemon water ice is immediately more attractive with black bing cherries. Chopped parsley or chives sprinkled on a bland-colored dish is certainly a help. And crisp parsley or watercress is indispensable to me for garnishing a platter. But don't overdo it: Your guests shouldn't have to cut grass to get at the food.

combining courses

Whether or not you combine one course with another is a matter of taste, literally. Cheese with salad? Certainly. Salad with the main course? Quite all right. But usually not on the same plate. Salad on a separate plate served at the same time as boeuf bourguignon is quite a different matter from having the two fight it out on the same piece of china because hot roasts and stews are not compatible with oil and vinegar. Wine with salad? Better not, because salad dressing and wine can never be friends. In some parts of the country, it is customary to serve the salad as a first course, and then it is easy to hold the wine for the main dish. Personally, I prefer to have salad and cheese as a separate course just before the dessert.

preparing food: city services

Cooking for me, perhaps because I don't have to do it all the time, is great fun; I find it both relaxing and creative. And there are many men who enjoy cooking as a hobby. If you are lucky enough to be married to one of them, encourage him and glory in it. Don't ask him to cook for himself or the children as a chore. But when you're having guests perhaps you and he can collaborate on the dinner.

However, even if neither of you likes to cook, the actual preparation of food for dinner guests shouldn't be a problem for anyone who lives in a big city, even if you want something other than the commercially prepared things offered in large markets. There are gourmet food shops, pastry shops, restaurants that prepare food to take out, and telephone services from which you can order coq au vin or beef Stroganoff for two or ten to be delivered at dinner time. Many markets are equipped to cook roasts or poultry for you. All kinds of help are available—at a price—from the part-time two-handed variety to fully staffed catering services. You can have a skilled cook come in to do soup to dessert, or you can do it all yourself: It depends on your needs, your likes, and your budget.

suburban suggestions

In the suburbs, such services are hard to find. Frequently, there is a Women's Exchange where cakes or pies will answer your dessert needs—and that is about it. However, considering suburban wives' problems for this section of the book gave me an idea for a service that would help them and could even turn into a very successful business. Not only would it answer the needs of women who haven't the time or don't like to cook, but so many women fall into one or the other of these two categories that there would be instant customers for anyone who provided such a service.

In every community, there are women who love to cook and *are* good at it. The chances are that one of them could be persuaded to prepare party dishes or even entire meals in her house for you to serve in yours. Mothers of teen-agers, for instance, might very well find they have time to cook (and add to the family income) while their children are in school. The trick is to find the women who cook. An ad in the local paper might be productive, or the Women's Exchange might provide names of possibilities.

Another solution might be a professional chef whose style of cooking you like. You might pay him (or her) to work in your kitchen for a whole day every month, or however often your needs and budget allow. Let him cook up a storm (very low in calories), then package, label, and stack everything in the freezer. Decide in advance on the dishes and amounts you want, and make sure you have room to store them. Before "the day," see to it that all ingredients and packaging materials are ready, and that the equipment he'll need is in good working order. Keep a list of foods as you store them, and note the number of servings. Then sit back and think of all the times you'll be grateful for your visiting chef. After you get to know him, perhaps he will even let you hang around and learn some of his tricks. (Possible sources for candidates might be graduates of local cooking schools or, again, responses to newspaper ads.)

Failing all else, do the cooking yourself on a day you set aside to do nothing else. You'll be handsomely repaid the next time you have guests or feel too tired to cook for the family.

One wine is enough for anything but a very formal dinner, but make sure there is enough of it. Two bottles should serve four wine lovers generously. Whether red, white, or rosé, ideally it should be one you and your husband have tried before and liked. Many husbands enjoy buying wines and liquors and tending bar, and most wives are delighted to

selecting a wine

have them do it. When in doubt, ask advice from a good wine merchant (not necessarily the liquor store man on the corner, unless he really does know something about wines). If you're going to serve wine regularly, it is worth the investment in time and effort to locate a specialist who can answer questions and steer you to good buys as they come along. (Incidentally, if there'll be eight or more for dinner, ask whether the wine you've chosen comes in magnums. Not all wines do, and not all liquor stores stock them, but the big bottles look very festive and experts agree that wine bottled this way actually is likely to taste better since it ages more slowly.)

Whether or not to decant wine before serving it is purely a matter of choice. If you have especially pretty decanters, you may enjoy using them, but they aren't required equipment. If it's a vintage wine, you will probably want to serve it in its original bottle. The important thing is not to disturb the sediment which gradually settles to the bottom of the bottle and which you certainly don't want to pour into anyone's glass. All wines should be stored in a cool place near the floor and never near radiators or in the kitchen. Red wines improve with "breathing" and should be uncorked an hour or so before serving and left to stand in a cool place, but they should never be chilled. White wines on the other hand, should be chilled and opened just before pouring. But don't put any wine in the freezer for a quick cooling—it kills the flavor.

ordering liquor
Ordering other kinds of liquor isn't very complicated. The basic ones are Scotch, a blended rye, bourbon, gin, and vodka. Don't forget to order soda and soft drinks. If you are not sure about quantity, your liquor store man will help. You will also need dry vermouth for martinis (if you are going to use it by the drop, get a half bottle), dry sherry, and/or an aperitif like Dubonnet for people who prefer something light. Being one of these myself, right here I would like to enter a passionate plea on their behalf. Fortified wines, which include vermouths, aperitifs, sherries, ports, and madeira, do turn to vinegar just like their untreated relatives, but they do it more slowly. And while they may be left open and taste quite fine for some time, after weeks or months of sitting around, they change color and

166

taste vile. I've been poured mahogany-colored dry vermouth (in its ideal state, it is almost colorless) in the homes of some of the most particular hostesses I know. Literally, it's a very bitter experience. So I beg you, when it's your house, look and taste before you serve.

serving drinks

If you are having drinks passed or served by a bartender or a waitress, you can set up your temporary bar in the pantry, if you have one, or a corner of the kitchen. But very few kitchens are roomy enough to accommodate all the food preparations for a large party plus a constant stream of people bustling in and out to make drinks. So on a big evening when you expect guests to ask for their drinks, the bar should be in a place that is easy to get at. Almost any place that's not center stage in the living room would be fine: in a convenient corner of the living room, at the end of an entrance hall (when we had our Christmas Eve party, which was always a large one, we had the bar there because the rooms opening around it made circulating easy) or in a room to which you'd like to attract people. Don't, however, tuck it away at the far end of a narrow room unless you want to stop traffic entirely. (Sober thought: Some bartenders seem to feel that their skill is judged by the strength of the drinks they pour; unless you want a really reeling party, speak firmly to your man ahead of time.)

hors d'oeuvres

Whatever you serve with drinks should be planned with your dinner in mind. Obviously, if you're having seafood for dinner, you won't serve shrimp with drinks. Forget about hot canapés because without constant attention, they have an unappealing way of turning up lukewarm and greasy. Variety is important, especially to a guest who's not wild about cheeses or who can't eat seafood. But that needn't mean lots of fussy canapés or too many unusual things. And I hope it won't mean chopped egg decorations that settle on the guests' clothes and the hostess's furniture. The simpler the choice, the better. We like smoked salmon, homemade pâté, and stuffed eggs. And we always have a platter of raw vegetables—carrots, zucchini, cauliflower, celery, and cherry tomatoes—sprinkled with seasoned salt—because they are nice for nibbling and low in calories. I find it works best to put the various kinds of hors d'oeuvres on separate dishes because it's easier to pass them. The dishes can be placed on a convenient table where guests may help themselves or, if you prefer, the hors d'oeuvres may be offered by the host, hostess, or children if they're old enough. And be sure to plan in advance who shall clear the remains of the pre-dinner drinks and hors d'oeuvres before the guests return to the living room after dinner.

While we're on the subject of hors d'oeuvres, I want to complain lustily about catered canapés from the local delicatessen—the mingy blobs of pressed caviar on damp toast, the dry and salty smoked salmon on damp toast, and the single anchovy surrounded by a delicate latticework of cream cheese on—what else—damp toast. Catered hors d'oeuvres cost too much, fool nobody, and taste repulsive.

small dinners without help: menus

For a small party when you aren't having anyone come in to serve, think things through extra carefully (informality and lack of planning are not synonymous). Make your menu a relatively foolproof one. For two or three couples, a good rule of thumb, I think, is to serve approximately what you serve your own family. I'm assuming you don't settle for hamburgers or TV dinners every night. For one thing, you're completely at ease making the dishes your family enjoys; you *know* how they're going to turn out. And anything you do well enough to inspire family applause and calls for encores might very well become your personal *specialité*. In any case be sure to plan the kind of menu that will permit you to do most of the work ahead of time so that you won't have to spend too much time away from your guests. For me, the pleasure of doing something very special for my guests is well worth any amount of time I can spare, providing the work can be done in advance. Baking bread, making pâté or pastry at home instead of using the bought kind are some of the things that I find particularly appealing.

Having chosen your main course, you might add a first course—an extra you wouldn't ordinarily serve on a night when your guest list is limited to your husband and kids. You could also serve a board of assorted cheeses with the salad or finish with a special dessert. All this is a far cry from the fancy kind of food hostesses once felt obliged to prepare when they were having guests.

serving plans

With your basic menu decided, concentrate on keeping things simple. At a small party, serving the first course with the drinks is pleasantly informal—especially if the hostess is doing her own cooking. And it works particularly well with pâté, a quiche, varied hors d'oeuvres, or a generous platter of shrimp or crab fingers with a delicious sauce. Dinner then starts with the main course, and the hostess is saved one change of plates at the table.

Otherwise, I think it goes smoothest if you have the first course on the table when the guests are seated. Then, when it's finished, the hostess (perhaps with the help of a close friend or a daughter) can clear away and the guests move to the buffet to serve themselves to the main course. I'm ruthless about breaking one old-fashioned rule—the one that says all men must hang back until all the women have served themselves. This only leads to lonely waits and chilled food. It's more fun and more civilized to integrate the line, although it is sometimes a job to get traditionalist males to relax and go along.

Again, the hostess clears away (I'm hoping she has someone—a woman or a capable child—waiting in the kitchen to wash up), and the guests help themselves to dessert, either at the buffet or from one of those small foldaway serving carts that can be wheeled right up to each table. Again, I repeat, planning is the key. It's a tremendous help to have your kitchen as tidied up as possible and to have the sink and dishwasher empty before you sit down to dinner so that there will be room for everything when you clear the table. It is almost always best to decline, with thanks, the well-meaning offers of guests who volunteer to clear away on the spur of the moment. Too many people, no matter how good-hearted, spell chaos in anyone's kitchen. And pity the poor guests left stranded at the table with no one to talk to. Children, on the other hand, can be a tremendous help—provided they're old enough to be reasonably careful and interested enough to try to do the job right. My niece Judy has brought up a staff who serve, clear, and do the cleanup beautifully, thank you. It's not a chore, it's a job, she pays them for it, and they are really very good. Besides, they are nice to have around.

checking equipment — The next step in getting ready for your party, whether it is large or small, is to check on china, glasses, linens, flatware, and serving dishes to make sure you have enough and the right kinds for your menu and number of guests. The right

the care and feeding of guests

kind is very important. Things like rice, fish, and pastas do best in shallow dishes. In deep ones, rice and pastas get gummy, and fish is likely to break when you have to dig for it. Stews and casseroles, on the other hand, do better in deep, ovenproof dishes because they're easier to serve from and the sauce keeps the meat moist. Don't plan on using any one piece or set more than once during a meal—there won't be time to wash them in between. Baskets are helpful in all sorts of ways: for potato chips, crackers, bread, baked potatoes, wine.

You can borrow from friends or rent supplies to fill in the gaps on your own shelves; rates for party supplies are quite reasonable on everything from oyster forks to outsized coffee urns. Unless you give big parties often, I think renting makes more sense than buying or trying to squeak by with a scrounged assortment of plates and glasses. However, you might well decide to invest in extra flatware (there's some marvelous looking inexpensive stainless steel around these days) or dinner plates like the quite plain Japanese ones that cost no more to buy than they would to rent a couple of times.

plastic glasses and paper napkins

Personally, although I realize that for huge parties they may be the only solution, I don't like plastic glasses. Most of them are insulated against the cold and drinks don't seem to taste good in them.

In the matter of napkins, I know that many people object to the paper ones, but at a really big, informal party I don't see why they shouldn't be used. Be sure they're large enough and made of the heavy quality paper that looks and feels almost like cloth. Paper napkins come in such pretty colors and patterns that you can often make a decorative point with them.

table settings

Before a big party, I can be found prowling through the house stealing things from other rooms—boxes, ornaments, bits of china—to make my tables prettier. Having matching sets of everything is not only not necessary, it can be very dull. Plain and patterned china can be mixed, and if you happen to have two odd lots of three or four plates, you can alternate them around a table.

When it comes to glasses, I like the simplest of stemware, and I like all of it to match. Clear thin glass really does seem

170

to improve the taste of wine. To allow the bouquet to collect for greater enjoyment of the wine, the glass should only be partly filled. If it is red, the wine should be poured to one half capacity. If you want to have more than one kind of glass, choose the smallest glass for the whites, the largest for reds, and a slender tulip-shaped one for champagne.

I don't believe flowers are necessary, though miniature arrangements in brandy snifters or tiny bowls can look delightful. Big arrangements take up too much room on small tables; they are also expensive and take special time and trouble to do well. With imagination, you can do very nicely without them. Candle holders are no longer automatically silver. You can use pewter, china, glass, or even colored votive candles.

But when it comes to table decorations, I learned the hard way not to get *too* creative. Years ago when Billy Rose, the producer, was married to Fanny Brice, he brought her to lunch at our house in Beverly Hills. Inspired by the fact that Billy had a revue called *Corned Beef and Roses* touring the country, I rushed out and bought a nice big chunk of corned beef, surrounded it with roses on a silver platter, and used it as a centerpiece on the table. We went in to lunch, and for what seemed like ages, no one said a thing. It was as though raw meat and flowers were an every day table decoration. Finally, Dick's collaborator, Larry Hart, did a double take and said, "What's *that?*" I could have kissed him. I answered, "Corned beef and roses," and got my laugh. But the fun was lost in the effort. And I wouldn't try that hard again.

If it's at all possible, I seat people at tables of six or eight even for a buffet (we've found that bridge tables with round tops added do nicely for six) . It is a lot easier than juggling all the equipment you need, and men loathe balancing plates on their laps. (If large tables are impossible, do give them individual tables to put their plates on.) For women, place cards eliminate the worry of where to sit or whether men will join them. I set the tables with silver, napkins, salt and pepper, cigarettes, ashtrays, and, depending upon the menu, glasses and wine. If it's a buffet and you're offering a choice, you may want to place red and white wines and glasses on the serving table. But when you are serving only one wine, I think one goblet that can be used for either red or white is fine. The wine can be left in a coaster or basket and passed or poured by the host.

lighting

As for lighting, nothing is quite so flattering as candle-light. However, at a very big party with lots of tables, candles may not provide enough light, in which case, try to combine candles and artificial light for a soft, not too dim, effect. Pure mystery (what's this? who's he?) and clinical glare are equally undesirable.

seating plans

Lighting, the way the food is presented, the way your table looks—all these are important. But because I think your impression of having had a good or a not-so-good time at a party depends so much upon the people you sit with at dinner, I pay special attention to seating plans and—if there are more than eight of us—to place cards. If you're stuck with boring neighbors, the evening is a torture no matter how great the food. I'm the first one to admit that no hostess can make all her guests happy on both sides 100 percent of the time. But she can go a long way toward pleas-ing a lot of them by actually picturing them talking to one another, by pairing talkers and listeners (two listening lis-teners side by side don't do much for the action), and by separating too-good friends and practiced antagonists— if she is unlucky enough to have a pair on her list for the same evening. Pencil, paper, and a written diagram are essential, no matter how good your memory, because one displaced person can throw the whole design off, and it is always awkward for guests to be forced to stand and wait while you make a new mental picture. Incidentally, if you have eight or twelve at the table, either you or your husband will have to give up your traditional place at its head or foot. From a practical point of view, the only real essential is that when a hostess has people to serve the food, she should sit facing the pantry or kitchen door so that she can signal what's needed. When she's doing the serving herself, she should, of course, sit conveniently near the kitchen so she can slip in and out as unobstrusively as possible.

after-dinner arrangements

At our house, at the end of the meal we have coffee served at the table because when guests are happily involved in talk, it seems too bad to disturb them. But many people like to have coffee in the living room, which may well be the most considerate if you have people waiting to clear, clean up, and get home. On the question of men and women separating after dinner, I suppose I stand on the dim side of the generation gap. I was brought up in the tradition of ladies withdrawing—usually to the hostess's bedroom—while the men remained at the table or adjourned to the living room or the den for brandy and cigars . . . and to tell dirty jokes. From the point of view of "man" or "woman" talk, I don't think there's any reason for ritual withdrawing today, and it would be silly to make a point of it. On the other hand, women usually like to fix their make-up and hair . . . and talk about children and baby-sitters . . . sometime during the evening, and it is often pleasant and easy to do it just after dinner. Whatever works best for you and your guests is exactly the thing you should do.

Well, we don't do that in my house. People know perfectly well where to find the bathroom if they want it, we all tell our dirty jokes, or whatever, in mixed company, and besides, the bedroom is full of coats and the ladies wouldn't be able to sit down in there. And we don't have a den. We do, but there's a child in it.

What happens after dinner? Should there be games, dancing, entertainment? Generally, I don't think so. Once upon a time we were great-game fans, and we had lots of clever friends who loved them and were good at them. And I do think an evening of charades and puzzles can be marvelous when you have the right people. But it does take an enormous amount of advance work on the hostess's part. And somehow, today this kind of entertainment seems terribly contrived—rather as if you were afraid that your guests will be bored and have nothing to say to each other. At those "wild Hollywood parties," screening a film after dinner was almost standard procedure (before you made caustic comments, you had to be very sure that the man next to you was not the producer's father). This, I think, was because people *were* bored; it was such a homogeneous, inbred group that people really had run out of things to say to each other. I think all that has changed now; everywhere, on whatever coast, parties mix all sorts of people with different talents, income levels, backgrounds, opinions, and ages. And without the benefit of games or screenings, talk is better than ever.

At our house, there is music sometimes when Dick or one of our friends feels like sitting down at the piano. But we never press it. Pressing is very bad for pianos. And we never have it as "background"; Dick, like many composers, finds it too distracting because automatically, if it's music, he stops and listens.

I find records as "background" distracting, too. And although they invariably raise the decibel count in the room, giving the hostess the impression that her party is a success, all they are actually doing is raising the decibel count in the room.

host and hostess roles

People make the party; it's true. And pretty tables, good food, and good talk all help a great deal. But without a host and hostess who care and work at it, none of it goes together. It is not enough to sink into a chair and chat with one or two friends once guests have arrived and been provided with food, drink, and people to serve them. Without seeming to fuss or hover, a thoughtful host and hostess will always be aware of a guest who might like a drink or needs to be drawn into a group or a conversation in danger of stalling that might be turned on again with a change of cast. If the party is large, you won't be able to spend a great deal of time with each of your guests, but you should get around, circulate, see them all, and let them know you are glad they came.

emergency meals

Up to now all the suggestions I've made have been for planned guests, but there's no reason why you can't be ready to rustle up a really good meal at any time for unexpected guests as well. Even emergencies can be prepared for in advance so that the contents of your freezer plus your stock of canned goods and staples can provide an unlimited variety of menus. It takes thought and organization, but it pays off handsomely when you turn a potential disaster into a triumph.

It's a simple matter always to have enough canned or frozen food on hand that needs only to be reheated or quickly thawed and checked for seasoning. (Soups and sauces tend to need more seasoning after they have been frozen; and to recover their original velvet texture, be sure to put them through the blender after they have been thawed.) Whenever we prepare a dish that freezes well, I make enough for two meals and freeze half. Apart from

174

the care and feeding of guests

everything else, it's a great timesaver because the work involved in preparing twice as much—and washing up the equipment—is very little more than you would be doing for the smaller amount. We do this not only with dishes in the casserole family, but with roasts of all kinds. Most roasts are delicious served cold, and some can be used for curries or hash or salads. We also try always to have a variety of soups in the freezer so that a first course is readily available.

Desserts are almost the easiest of all. Commercial ice cream, water ice, and sherbets can be packed into molds of different sizes and when they are unmolded and surrounded by some fruit of a contrasting color, they completely lose their "bought" look and take on the appearance of a custom-made dish. Sometimes I sprinkle a little ground Italian expresso coffee on lemon ice. It's crunchy and for some reason tastes like a combination of coffee and chocolate. Soufflés can go directly from the freezer to the oven, and a chocolate roll doesn't require much time to thaw, nor does a cheesecake (either the bought or the homemade kind). Freezing actually improves unbaked pastry dough, so I like to have a tart shell or two ready for baking and filling. I try, too, to keep emergency supplies in the freezer against the day when I run out of bread or butter, eggs or meat. (When freezing eggs, freeze the whites and yolks separately and be sure to write the amounts of each on the container. The whites take a long time to thaw and should be at room temperature to beat them to their maximum volume.) When freezing uncooked meats it's easier to stock small parts that will thaw quickly. Chicken breasts, small steaks, and veal scallops have proved to be the most useful for us. A bag of shrimp is marvelous to have in reserve because shrimp are so versatile.

When you have a little time on your hands, freeze a few timesavers: lemon juice frozen in cubes, tarragon butter for use on steaks or chops, chopped parsley, chives, or any of the chopped and measured ingredients you need to make a favorite sauce. In addition to the items you have deliberately planned to freeze, be sure to leave space in your freezer for leftovers. Such things as whipped cream and hollandaise sauce can be successfully frozen (a cube or two of hollandaise can add immeasurably to a vegetable or even to an-

the care and feeding of guests

other sauce). Often there'll be a bit of cream left in a container. Freeze and label it; it might be all you'll need for a sauce someday. If one of your emergencies is caused by running out of food midway through a buffet party, bring out an extra dessert and remember for the next party that it isn't wildly extravagant these days to have more food than you think you can possibly use because nothing need be wasted.

To ruin an important part of your dinner at the last minute, whether it be by burning, curdling, or dropping it on the kitchen floor, is a calamity of major proportions but not irreparable if you have more than one first course, main course, and dessert in your freezer that need only to be reheated or quickly thawed.

The greatest catastrophe I've saved for the last. Suppose something should happen to your stove and/or your refrigerator-freezer? This *could* be the moment to accept defeat and take your guests out to dinner. On the other hand, you might be the kind of person who rises to the occasion and comes up with something superb when faced with a challenge of these dimensions. If you are, you'll surely be able to think of various menus for which you can be prepared in advance. The food will have to come from cans, jars, or boxes, so get out the can opener.

Start with a beautiful pâté—right out of a tin, of course— served with Melba toast, then open the canned cooked ham, corned beef, pot roast, turkey, or chicken that you were far-sighted enough to have bought in advance and serve one or more of them with two kinds of mustard. You can have a choice of vegetable salads even if you hadn't planned to serve one and there is no lettuce among your stores. The fat white asparagus that grow in jars or tins are delicious with a vinaigrette sauce, as are canned mushrooms, hearts of palm, artichoke hearts (or bottoms), and tomatoes cut in quarters. These can be combined or used singly. Surely you always have some cheese in the house for a snack or a mouse, assorted crackers, and, for dessert, how about sprinkling a little liqueur and some almond slivers on canned tangerine sections or white peaches? There are even some excellent Italian cakes that keep indefinitely in their plastic containers without benefit of refrigeration.

the care and feeding of guests

You probably already own an electric coffee maker so you'll be able to serve something hot, and if you don't have an electric frying pan, I suggest buying one as a further contribution to your peace of mind. There is also a refillable butane gas burner that sits on a stand and is designed to support almost any pot—a wonderful thing to have if the electric current fails. (If you have one of these, there's no limit to what you can heat up—hash, stew, or Stroganoff, all of them available in jars or cans.)

Even without disasters, all women who like to cook want to develop their own tricks and specialties. Some of the combinations we use might appeal to you, and even if they don't, your imagination will probably suggest lots of other ideas.

soup tricks

We serve many different kinds of soup at our house— clear, jellied or creamed, bland or spicy, hot or cold. Sometimes when we're serving a hot soup of the hearty variety buffet style, I like to ladle it from a handsome tureen. Somehow it seems to make the soup taste better. And on a hot day, it's lovely to see well-chilled soup poured from a pretty glass pitcher.

Greek lemon soup is high on my list of favorites. It's delicious and very easy to do. Canned chicken broth, lemon juice, rice, and a whole egg with some extra egg whites beaten into it at the last moment makes the soup incredibly light and frothy. Commercially prepared borscht comes in jars and it can be improved immeasurably by adding some chopped cucumbers, onion, hard-cooked egg, lemon juice, and masses of dill (fresh is best, but frozen or dried will do). Finish it off with a dash of sour cream and serve it either hot or cold. Black bean soup needn't be homemade to be good. Dilute it with some beef consommé, add sherry and some lump crabmeat. Or if that's too heavy, try adding the sherry and crabmeat to canned chicken gumbo. (The black bean and chicken gumbo soups are served hot.)

The Chinese use ginger in many of their dishes, and we have found its unexpected flavor gives a subtle and delightful accent to otherwise conventional foods. A pinch of ground ginger, for instance, makes good chicken soup even better. (Ginger root, thinly sliced, does lovely things to some sauces and, like truffles, it can be kept indefinitely in the refrigerator if it is covered with Madeira or sherry wine.)

the care and feeding of guests

Artichokes, hearts of palm, asparagus, and leeks make rather unusual first courses. All of them may be served hot with hollandaise sauce or cold with vinaigrette. Fresh asparagus early in the season are particularly good but, as I've said, I'm also partial to the fat white ones that come in jars. There are also lovely green, artichoke hearts and asparagus among the frozen foods and, of course, they have the advantage of being available the year round.

Possibly the most spectacular first course is one that not only doesn't require any cooking skill, but one that you can always have on your shelves ready to serve to unexpected guests. Call it hors d'oeuvres, antipasto, or anything you like —the combinations are infinite. (You'll need a fair number of small dishes that have some depth for things with sauces, so be sure to give a little thought in advance to the choice you'll be using.) Many kinds of fish come in tins or jars, and they usually don't need refrigeration until they have been opened. Smoked salmon, sardines, herring (several varieties), tuna, mussels, potted shrimp, and mackerel in white wine are yours for the asking. Then there's the family of pickled or marinated vegetables like mushrooms and artichoke hearts and bottoms. To this mélange, you might like to add some black olives, sliced salami, stuffed eggs or those marvelous little quail eggs that come in tins, and a bit of pâté. I'm not suggesting that you serve all the things I've mentioned. Make up your own list from your favorites and from what is available in your part of the country.

On a night when you and your husband are home alone and you don't want to spend much time in the kitchen, try paillards of beef, veal, or chicken. Pound thin slices of beef, scallops of veal, or half chicken breasts until the meat is about one quarter of an inch thick, and broil them quickly on a ridged grill that has been preheated and lightly greased. Turn them once and put a dollop of lemon- or tarragon-flavored butter on top of each serving. Season to taste and serve immediately on hot plates. (Heating plates is too often overlooked and results in a chilly reception for food that has been prepared with loving care!)

I stole an idea for fixing vegetables from one of New York's best restaurants and whenever we serve it friends are both puzzled and delighted. It's a purée of several kinds of

the care and feeding of guests

cooked vegetables. Blending carrots, peas, string beans, and broccoli brings out a whole new flavor. The texture should resemble that of mashed potatoes and the color is mostly green. Of course you might get very creative about this dish and see what happens when you use beets, cauliflower, and lima beans. Who knows, you could be responsible for developing a new range of colors as well as a new flavor!

salad ideas

In the last year or two, I have done some experimenting with salads that don't use any member of the lettuce family. Here again, imagination plus the likes and dislikes of your family will guide you. For starters we use bite-sized pieces of beef (leftover pot roast or boiled beef is great for this purpose) or chunks of white tuna or duck. The meat or fish is marinated for an hour or two in a dressing of oil, vinegar, seasonings, and herbs. Then we add some or all of the following: artichoke hearts or bottoms, cherry tomatoes or tomatoes peeled, seeded, and cut in quarters, hard-cooked eggs (quartered), pitted black olives, raw sliced mushrooms (or some of the more exotic foreign canned ones), and some rings of the lovely red onion. Raw zucchini, celery, hearts of palm, or endive can be used as substitutions or additions.

different desserts

Ever since Dione Lucas taught me how to make a chocolate roll, it has been a great favorite at our house. Recently I changed the basic recipe by melting the chocolate with very strong coffee instead of water, giving a mocha flavor to the roll. And instead of using jelly to fill a roll of sponge cake, I like to spread the cake with an apricot purée. Chill the roll in the refrigerator until time to serve it, and then dust the top with powdered sugar.

Canned white peaches are as good to look at as they are to eat if you serve them with a raspberry sauce. Use frozen raspberries strained through a fine cheesecloth and add a little kirsch. The sauce is a beautiful, shiny red, and it's marvelous poured over strawberries, too. Make it in advance and store it in the freezer. Assorted canned fruits attractively arranged in an ovenproof dish taste delicious when heated with a little sherry and served with a cold custard sauce.

Most guests are quite willing to wait for a soufflé. All the preparation can be done days ahead of time and the soufflé can be stored in the freezer until you're ready to bake it. I seldom serve it when we are more than six because it's a bit tricky to time the guests at dinner—lots of good talk and slow eating can turn the soufflé into a disaster. (To get around this, you can have a cheese soufflé as a first course so that timing doesn't become a problem.)

In the Appendix you will find a list of things I've found useful in stocking my cupboards and freezer. I've also included some menu suggestions—maybe you'll find them helpful as taking-off points.

The dinner menus, also in the Appendix, will work just as well for lunch, and some of the lunch menus (with the first course eliminated) can double as menus for late supper parties. Substitutions can always be made, of course, keeping in mind the balancing of color, flavor, and texture.

having a bunch of people over for dinner

There are three kinds of entertaining: formal, informal, and what I call Having a Bunch of People Over. Now, Having a Bunch of People Over is, I suppose, a form of informal entertaining, but if you're the kind of person who has a fit at the thought of any kind of entertaining at all, it's better for the nerves if you can trick yourself by calling it something else. I am that kind of person.

When, if ever, is the right time to have a bunch of about sixteen or twenty people over for dinner? When is the right time? When you and your husband have run into at least three of your favorite couples, all of whom act surprised when you tell them how old your children are now; now is the time to see them again or you will lose them altogether.

Sit down with your husband and make a nice list which includes the three surprised couples, a couple of other couples who also belong in this category, and about four people you think you ought to have. Include the boss and his wife, who will enjoy being around the younger set, and the other two might be a dull pair who had you to dinner a year ago. You have to have them back sometime and now is as good a time as any.

How many people do you have now? Fourteen? Wrong! Sixteen. You forgot to count you and your husband. This is a bad mistake, leading to not enough food, not enough silver, and a last-minute conviction that you are losing your mind.

the care and feeding of guests

All right, sixteen it is. The remaining four should be new people.

At least six times a year, you probably go to a dinner party where you meet a marvelous couple; they like you and your husband, you like them, and all four of you go through that familiar dance of promising to call each other up and get together for dinner, and then nobody does anything because nobody remembers anybody's name two months later. What's worse is that even as you are going through the motions of your familiar dance, you already have a sinking feeling, *déjà vu* perhaps, that nobody is going to do anything. There is a very simple solution to this problem, however. If, as soon as you get home, you write down the names of these people, what they do (John Doe, lawyer, Margery Doe, teaches at Head Start), and where they live so you can look them up in the phone book, you *will* remember them two months later, and they'll be delighted to come to your party.

Maybe you've run across an interesting unattached lady. Add her to the list. If you can't think of an unattached man to go with her, never mind—invite her anyway, because most unmarried, widowed, or divorced women would rather be asked without an escort than not be asked at all.

You now have a list of nineteen or twenty people. The very next morning before panic has a chance to set in and far enough in advance to deceive yourself into thinking it's never going to happen at all (about three weeks), start calling up your friends and inviting them to your party. Phone calls are perfectly acceptable, but if you prefer written invitations, go right ahead and send them; you won't get your answers as quickly that way, though, and since anything written seems more formal than a phone call, you might frighten yourself needlessly.

Once the nineteen or twenty friends have accepted, you are trapped. You can always pray for a serious family illness (hopefully your own) or a fire in the house, but those are last-minute excuses and you can't use them yet anyway. Besides, you still have loads of time left in which to get organized.

getting organized

Check your basic equipment *now*, because if you wait until the last minute, you may find yourself lacking something too heavy to lug home. You will need the following:

the care and feeding of guests

two big ovenproof casseroles, or one big ovenproof casserole and one huge serving platter, a large salad bowl, a forty-cup electric coffee percolator, a couple of bread baskets, four sets of serving spoons and forks, two dozen dinner plates, two dozen salad plates, two dozen dessert plates, two dozen coffee cups (some of them can be demitasse), two dozen wine glasses, two dozen drinking glasses (most people drink things on the rocks these days, so old-fashioned glasses are the best, but you might have a few martini glasses and highball glasses just in case), forks and spoons, *large* paper dinner napkins (the expensive, soft kind), small paper cocktail napkins, paper guest towels, a mammoth double boiler for heating up mammoth amounts of something or other, and a nest of little tables. (Most of your guests will fit themselves around your coffee table or eat on their laps, but collapsible tray tables are a handy investment, and you can store them in a closet when you're not using them.)

Oh, by the way, when I say two dozen of something, I don't necessarily mean two *matching* dozen of something. If you find you have only thirteen "good" dinner plates left, go out and buy a dozen plain white Japanese ones as my mother suggests. Or borrow some plates from a friend. Your guests are not going to care what they're eating from, in fact they probably won't even notice. By the same token, they also won't mind using paper napkins, they won't mind your not having any flowers around if you decide not to bother, and they won't mind putting their coats on your bed. (On a rainy night, you can hang up some of the really wet ones on a shower rod.)

If you have a small child who is going to get in your way on the day or night of the party, now is the time to hire a baby-sitter to keep him occupied. Better yet, ship him off to a friend's house for the night and use *his* bed for the coats.

food

Unless you just happen to have a nice dinner for twenty in your freezer or a reliable cook who will come in on the day of the party to produce a culinary masterpiece without any help from you, the food department is your next big headache. Don't worry, just keep it very simple. For instance:

1. Hors d'oeuvres—no last-minute hot ones. As my mother says, they'll be cold and greasy and, besides that, you'll be too

busy when the guests arrive to run in and out of the kitchen.

2. The main course—a nice, big casserole of something (prepared the day before) that will stay warm in your oven until you're good and ready to put it on the buffet table. Menu suggestions come later, but for now I want to issue one stern warning: Avoid serving anything that needs to be cut. People simply cannot manage tricky knife work when their plates are balanced on their laps, and no matter how many coffee tables and tray tables you provide, there will still be a few people who have to do the balancing act. At other peoples' houses, my solution is to hunch over on the floor, but I happen to be particularly limber and not everybody is.

As for the rest of the main course, some kind of pasta, salad, and cheese, and wine to go with it. Oh, and bread or rolls if you want, but I've been to lots of houses where the hostess didn't bother and I never missed them.

3. Dessert—another warning: nothing sloppy or juicy, unless you plan to serve it in soup bowls. Actually, just some brownies, or cake, or some home-baked cookies (from your local bakery) will do nicely. Most people seem to be on diets these days, and I've discovered that unless you literally force them to get up and serve themselves, they seem to forget all about dessert.

4. Coffee.

That's it for food—a primitive plan, I admit, but the more primitive the better, because if you're the nervous type, you don't want to cope with lots of little side dishes and sauces and dribbly extras that no one really cares about anyway. And now that you have your basic equipment and your menu organized, there are still two weeks left during which you can go back to pretending that you're not Having a Bunch of People Over, or praying for the disaster.

THE DAY BEFORE

preparation

1. Buy all the food and make the casserole.

2. Start making extra ice, or, if you think you'll need more than you can make, order some.

the care and feeding of guests

3. Clear off one entire kitchen counter, polish the silver, and run all the dishes, glasses, and serving platters through the dishwasher. (Even if you do have twenty dinner plates, the top ten will be clean because you use them all the time, but the bottom ten will be dusty.)

4. Have you looked at your bar lately? It probably has two half bottles of gin, an almost empty bottle of very ancient sweet vermouth, three or four bottle caps, sticky bar tools, and several dead bottles of soda. Pour the contents of one gin bottle into the other one, and throw out the empty one. The same goes for Scotch, bourbon, vodka, etc. You can merrily combine different brands of the same thing—no one will know.

Throw out the vermouth and the soda bottles and caps. In fact, wash the whole bar, order whatever liquor and wine you'll need, and when it comes, put the liquor on the bar and the wine in the kitchen, on its side. You probably don't have room on the bar for all that liquor *and* twenty glasses; set up a card table nearby for the glasses, the ice, and the clean bar tools.

Now that you've accomplished all this, you should be in a marvelous mood. The worst is over; you might even allow yourself a sneaky little sense of joyful anticipation.

THE DAY OF: MORNING . . .

1. Clean the living room and put cigarettes and matches around. (When the children come home from school, keep them out of the living room. In fact, send them right to their own rooms to straighten them out; otherwise, some curious guest might wander in there and be shocked.)

2. Wash your hair, or get it done, and decide what you're going to wear. Make sure whatever it is is clean and if it needs ironing, do it now, not at five-thirty in the afternoon when the second wave of panic has set in.

For me, the party clothes decision comes down to a matter of picking a top to go with some pants. My compliments to those of you who can figure out how to run around the kitchen and living room in a diaphanous hostess gown with-

the care and feeding of guests

out either spilling something on yourself or tripping. Besides, for a floor-sitter like me, pants are the most comfortable.

3. Fill the salt and pepper shakers, replace candle stubs.

If you're planning to use your dining room table for the buffet, pretend you're a guest and walk through the mechanics of getting your food before you arrange the silver and china. ("Let's see now, I come in here, I get the napkin and silver and a plate next, then the hot thing and the pasta, and then the salad and cheese, and over here is the wine . . .") This is an important instruction because if you haven't routined the choreography ahead of time, your guests are going to end up putting beef on the dessert plates, salad on the dinner plates, and so on.

By the way, unless you have an extraordinarily long dining room table, you'll find that by the time you've spread out twenty forks, knives, and spoons in a gleaming row, you have no room for anything else. I struggled with this dilemma for years and finally solved it by wrapping each person's silver allotment in his expensive paper napkin.

The final morning activity is to clean up the bathroom the guests are going to use and put out the paper guest towels. If you happen to have some embroidered trousseau hand towels, leave them in the linen closet; guests never seem to use them, and if you don't put out paper ones, the guests will dry their hands on their clothes or surreptitiously use the back of the bath towel. How do I know all this? Because I find myself doing it in other peoples' houses. If the guests' bathroom is ordinarily your childrens' bathroom, don't let them use it when they come home from school; they'll dirty it up again. Let them use your bathroom; you'll have to clean it up at the last minute anyway.

. . . AFTERNOON

1. Wash the salad and put it in plastic bags in the fridge, make the salad dressing and the hors d'oeuvres, take the cheese out of the fridge to soften, put the white wine (if that is what you are serving) in the fridge, set up the forty-cup perc, and get rid of your small child.

2. Two hours before the party, take a bath, clean up the bathroom, and get yourself looking lovely.

3. One hour before, put out the ice and water and double check everything; then get your husband to double check the bar because he's probably the one who will be making most of the drinks. He'll ask you about the martini mixer (which you forgot) and about the lemon twists (which you also forgot).

4. Fifteen minutes before, put out the hors d'oeuvres, make yourself a weak drink—preferably in a glass that doesn't look like anyone else's, so that you don't spend half the night saying, "Where did I put my drink?" If you live in an apartment house, warn your elevator man about the twenty people who are coming in a minute. Otherwise, he'll keep ringing you up on the house phone.

HAPPENING

If you have teen-age children, let them take the coats. If not, show your guests where to put their own coats, convey their drink orders to your husband, and introduce everybody to everybody. This is the agonizing part, but it only lasts about fifteen minutes. Tell your guests to feel free to replenish their own drinks if you don't get to them first. Guests seem to like doing it, and it'll save you a lot of trouble.

Assuming that your guests are reasonably prompt, allow forty-five minutes for drinking. Well, maybe an hour, but any longer than that makes for hungriness, grumpiness, and sogginess. Your schedule for getting dinner on the table should go roughly like this:

1. An hour before you plan to eat, put the casserole in a low, preheated oven. Heat the water for the pasta in a large pot. If you're serving red wine, open it now—it's supposed to breathe or something.

2. Fifteen minutes before dinner, toss the salad with the dressing and put it and the cheese on the table. Turn on the

the care and feeding of guests

coffee machine, put the wine near the wine glasses, and the bread in the oven.

3. Seven minutes before, put the pasta in the boiling water (never mind the instructions on the box—they always tell you to cook it too long) and melt the butter you're going to pour over it.

4. Five minutes before, tell your husband to announce dinner while you light candles and put the food on the table. (It takes at least five minutes to get people to move from one room to another.)

Synchronize your watches, everybody! I admire your efficiency, but I'd be a nervous wreck by now.

Let your husband show everybody where the food is and help them serve themselves while you and the children run around the living room picking up the hors d'oeuvres plates, the cocktail napkins, and the empty drink glasses, which you will run through the dishwasher *now* so that they'll be ready for after-dinner use. (Don't run the cocktail napkins through the dishwasher.) Open the living room windows; it's very smoky in there. If you've washed the ashtrays—and you should have—don't forget to bring them right back or people will use their empty dinner plates.

Speaking of empty dinner plates, a good way to get rid of them is to ask your guests if you can get them some more food. If they say no thank you, it was delicious but they're stuffed, whip their plates away and put them in the dishwasher. Eventually, you'll get the main course over with and then you'll have to begin the uphill struggle to entice everybody back into the dining room for the dessert and coffee. Actually, I find it easier to bring the dessert and coffee to them; by now, everybody is relaxed and comfortable and has staked out his own chair or corner of the floor; nobody really wants to move. I, on the other hand, am by this time so full of euphoric energy because the worst part of the evening is over, that I'd be happy to do all the fetching and carrying for the entire Eighth Army. If a couple of good friends want to help me load the dishwasher, fine, but I discourage whole

the care and feeding of guests

hordes of people trooping into the kitchen—it's too messy and disorganized.

The rest of the evening is pure gravy; there's nothing to do but make drinks and empty ashtrays, both of which provide you with a marvelous opportunity to talk to everybody in the room and enjoy what you've been dreading for three weeks. You are also provided with a good excuse to get away from a conversation that's going on too long. "I'll be right back as soon as I've made Helen another drink."

This leads to a pet theory of mine, having to do with the subject of outside help. I happen to think that when you're just Having a Bunch of People Over for dinner, visible outside help is a mistake. The minute a uniformed person shows up in your living room, you have somehow injected a formal note into your nice, informal group. People will now expect fancier food; they may even wonder why you're using paper napkins! And most important of all, they'll no longer feel free to help themselves to another drink, or to more food, which means that they can't circulate as freely around the room. You can't circulate as freely either, because if someone else is emptying the ashtrays, you haven't any excuse to get up. Of course, maybe this is just my own weirdo point of view, but I really like running around at my own parties. Maybe it's my way of saying, "Listen, I don't want anybody else to work for you tonight; this is my party, and you're my friends, and *I* want to work for you." All I know is that I feel the need to create for my guests the same atmosphere, or approximately the same atmosphere, in which we ordinarily live, and that doesn't include uniformed ashtray emptiers and drink makers. (About ten years ago, I gave a fancy party with catered food and a bundle of red-coated waiters dashing around. I was absolutely miserable all night. Among other things, I couldn't figure out what to do with my hands—and it was the only bad party I *know* I've given.)

The kind of help I like at a dinner party is the aforementioned baby-sitter or someone who stays completely out of sight and helps you to get things ready in the kitchen and/or to help clean up. Ideally, this someone is your usual cleaning woman who knows her way around and knows how you like to do things; you don't want to start in with a total stranger who will be more trouble than she's worth.

the care and feeding of guests

The only other thing I want to tell you about my kind of dinner party is how to get rid of guests when it's very late and about four or five of them don't seem to want to go home. Here's what you do; it's a cinch. You say, "George, how about another drink?" George, even without a watch, is subliminally aware of the hour and, in nine cases out of ten, will refuse on the grounds that it's getting late; he'll suggest to his wife that she find her coat and, suddenly, the other late-stayers will start doing the same thing. This little gambit has only failed me once, when a garrulous old lady who didn't even drink requested another ginger ale, but don't try it before eleven-thirty—it won't work. Or you can follow the old Chinese custom of turning a broom upside down. Or yell "Fire!" Conversely, if you want your guests to stay and are afraid that they will get up and leave when you offer them another drink, you don't offer. You just take George's empty glass away from him, ask him what was in it, and fix it before he has a chance to demur.

Well, I guess that's about it for Having a Bunch of Sixteen or Twenty People Over for Dinner. It's never as bad as you think. In fact, it often turns out to be more fun than going to other people's houses.

As you've undoubtedly gathered by now, I don't go in for very elaborate menus at these large gatherings, but here are a few suggestions for casseroles that can be cooked ahead of time, or even cooked and frozen ahead of time: beef Bourguignon (*fancy nomenclature for beef stew cooked in red wine*), veal Marengo (*brown veal stew with tomatoes and mushrooms*), stuffed cabbage, and Swedish meatballs.

The recipes for all of these casseroles can be found in any good cookbook . . . just follow the book slavishly and everything will come out all right. As for what to put with them —I usually serve pasta or rice, salad, cheese and crackers, bread, a bought dessert, and coffee later. If I get good and bored with the same old noodles, I sometimes throw in a bunch of caraway seeds or some chopped scallions; when I'm tired of ordinary rice, I switch to herb rice (comes in a nice package) or wheat pilaf (also comes in a nice package); and when I'm tired of mixed green salad, I make raw spinach and bacon salad instead.

I also have a few suggestions for cold main courses (the

the care and feeding of guests

pasta, salad, cheese, crackers, etc., will go equally well with them) : steak tartare (*this is obviously a cinch to prepare but not everybody likes raw meat so you'd better have something like a cold, sliced turkey for the people who don't*), cold mustard chicken (*delicious but rather messy to eat . . . you have to use your fingers . . . serve only to people with relaxed, picnic mentality*), braised beef in jelly, and tarragon chicken (boned) in jelly.

Now those last two sound pretty imposing but if I can do them, *anybody* can do them. They take time . . . quite a lot of it, but it's all the day before; on the day of the party, you barely have time to think. (The other thing they take is faith because you will be convinced that the jelly won't gel. It will, though—gelatin is darling, reliable stuff, you can positively count on it.)

Having ten or twelve people over for brunch requires practically no advance preparation; you can dream it up on Wednesday and bring it off on Sunday. As a matter of fact, Sunday is the best and the only day for it, because your whole family is together.

I suppose, if you want to, you can give a brunch and exclude the children, but since they usually exclude themselves and their guests as soon as they've eaten anyway, brunch is one of the few times when you can successfully combine all ages in a nice, relaxed fashion.

You can serve a lot of fancy extras if you're feeling energetic, but the basic menu includes Bloody Mary ingredients (or whiskey sour or bullshot ingredients), eggs, bacon, English muffins, an assortment of jams and jellies, fruit, coffee, and either chocolate milk, cocoa, or Cokes for the children.

Here again, the buffet system is the easiest and the equipment you need is minimal. I can only think of one really vital item: either a Salton hot tray, or a couple of dishes in which the food can be kept hot—because there is nothing worse than cold eggs. I am not a chafing dish enthusiast; if you are, this is the perfect occasion for one, but I don't happen to like cooking in front of people—it embarrasses me —and whenever I try to keep something warm in a chafing dish, it ends up overcooked because I have never learned to regulate a can of Sterno—the stuff seems to have a malevolent mind of its own.

Well, anyway, back to business. As long as you have all the food in the house (remember, it's Sunday), you don't have to begin doing anything until eleven o'clock for a twelve-thirty brunch.

At eleven, straighten up the house a little and throw out the sections of the Sunday paper you're not going to read. ("The Industrial Revolution in Yucatan—an advertisement," the classified ads, and probably the real-estate section.)

At eleven-thirty, make the bacon, which will stay warm in the oven, split the muffins, take the butter out of the fridge to soften, measure the coffee, get out the ice, squeeze the lemons and oranges if you're having whiskey sours, or chill the tomato juice or beef bouillon. Then ask your husband to organize the bar while you organize the table.

Unless you're a brilliant omelet maker, scrambled eggs are the simplest kind to make for a lot of people. Obviously, you can't cook them until the last minute, but you can at least break them into a bowl. I always add one tablespoon of water for every three eggs instead of milk. The eggs will be lighter and fluffier. By the way, I always count on three eggs per person; I don't know what it is about scrambled eggs, but there is never enough, even when they *don't* stick to the pan. They won't if you use the pans only for eggs and never wash them. Wipe them out with paper towels and scour with a little salt. Smarty!

At twelve twenty-five, sit down and look at the headlines of the Sunday paper—it's the last chance you'll get for several hours.

From twelve-thirty to one, drinking. Half an hour is probably long enough because all of you, guests included, are hungry, having skimped on breakfast to save room for brunch.

From one to two, everybody eats and everybody helps you clean up, because it's that kind of informal thing.

From two on, the children usually go somewhere else, quite of their own volition, and you and your friends can sit around and watch the Jets, or play bridge, or talk. One or two of your guests might even fall asleep; if so, it's a compliment, not an insult.

last-minute people

And now we come to my very favorite form of entertain-

the care and feeding of guests

ing. Sit up and take notice, because this is one of the rare indications of the much-touted Generation Gap that doesn't often exist between me and my mother: I love last-minute guests, and my mother hates them. It's not that she's inhospitable; it's just that her household is organized well in advance, as it has to be. Mine isn't and doesn't, and a good thing, too, because I have a feeling it never will be—my mind just doesn't work that way.

Last-minute guests are people who've been invited for drinks only, but suddenly you hear yourself saying, "Listen, we're having hash, but please stay," or friends who call you up to say hello at five-thirty and you hear yourself saying, "Listen, we're having hash, but what are you doing for dinner? Nothing? Come on over, *right now*, don't change, just come!"

When the person at the other end of the phone says, "Okay, we'd love to, but can we bring something?" you say, without a qualm, "Sure, bring dessert, or bring some lettuce, we may not have quite enough, or if you want your usual martini, bring gin, we're out of it."

Maybe the best way to explain the difference between these people and everybody else is this: When other people come for dinner, you tell yourself that they won't mind if dinner isn't very good—and you're right, they won't. But when these people come for dinner (with the head of lettuce or the gin), *you* don't mind if it isn't very good. Now that may sound like pure semantics, but it isn't, it's a subtle but gigantic difference in mental attitude.

For these people, you don't bother to take your husband's bathrobe off the hook in the bathroom; these people sit in your kitchen with a drink while you fold diapers or make salad dressing; if they arrive while you're giving the baby a bath, they sit around in the living room amusing your other children or reading the evening paper until you show up. And if, because it's a weekday night, you're tired at eleven o'clock, you don't have to ask them if they'd like another drink; you simply announce that you're sleepy and would love them to stay for another drink with your husband, but you're going to bed. Or if your husband is the tired one, he can go to bed. Or you can both go to bed, having fearlessly and affectionately pushed them out the door.

192

Whether you know it or not, these are the people you really love best in the world. You are not only willing but delighted to entrust them with a view of your non-company, non-public existence. In my book, trust makes love—or is it the other way around? Or maybe both?

entertaining away from home

Today, with regular help so hard to find, entertaining away from home—both socially and for business reasons—is becoming more and more popular, and taking guests to a club or a restaurant can be pleasantly special or impersonally commercial. Ideally, the place you choose should be one where you are known and can be assured of attentive service. (Clubs offer a more personal welcome and atmosphere than public restaurants, even though the food is less likely to be four star.) In any case, it is a good idea to have your husband call in advance, make a reservation, and talk with someone in charge about your plans for the evening. Reserve a table and settle on a method of payment; having him sign the check and having the restaurant bill him is the most graceful, if it can be arranged. If possible, have the waiter's tip added to the bill, but your husband should take care of the captain as you leave. It is considerate, too, for the host to take care of tipping the checkroom attendant.

Whether or not you order the meal in advance is a matter of timing, place, and your inclination. Ordering for your guests may make it possible to have special dishes not listed on that day's menu; it also saves time if you are on your way to the theater or a party after dinner. On the other hand, for many people, part of the treat of going to a restaurant is being able to order the things they like best. Many restaurants have *prix fixe* dinners that offer a good choice of dishes.

Whenever you can, ask your friends to join you at your house for cocktails before going out for dinner. However, for people who live in the suburbs, that isn't always possible. At a dinner for six or more at a restaurant, you should make a seating plan as you would at home. Remember to give your guests the seats with the best view of the room. If there's a floor show or entertainment, you can always turn your own chair around when the time comes.

Even when the guests decide what they want, the host should be the one to take the orders and relay them to the maitre d'. It is also the host who asks for the wine steward, examines the card, and makes the selection or selections. (Since you will want more than one bottle if there are more than four people, he can order red, white, or both so that everyone may have whatever goes best with the dinner he has ordered.)

When you're entertaining guests at a restaurant before the theater, be sure the captain knows what time you must leave. And remember that transportation can be a problem, especially in New York City, where cabs are hard to catch at theater hours. If you care as much as we do about getting to the theater on time, it's wise to provide transportation for your guests from the restaurant to the theater, and it's thoughtful, too, if you're having a supper party after the theater, to arrange for your guests to be picked up at the theater and taken to the restaurant. (If it's an early curtain, many people find it pleasanter to eat after the performance, when there's no need to rush.) In smaller cities, where parking is easier than it is in New York, most people drive their own cars and the host can give the tickets to his guests so that no one holds up anybody else. Dick and I have an agreement on the subject of theater tickets—I am to ask him whether he has them as we leave our apartment for the theater. So far he always has, but the day I forget to ask, I'm sure, will be the day he forgets to put them in his pocket.

*house
guests:
where and
when*

The most personal kind of entertaining there is involves the care and feeding of house guests. Making them feel at home and seeing to their comfort and pleasure is probably the biggest challenge a hostess ever faces. And also the most fun. It all depends on the time, the place, and the guests.

We rarely have overnight guests in our New York apartment because our lives there are so busy it's impossible to give them all the time and attention we'd like. The infrequent guests we do have in the city are usually very good friends from abroad who understand and know we're delighted to give them a reasonably comfortable room with a bath and breakfast, keys, and use of the phone. We love making evening plans with them, but during the day they are pretty much on their own to make dates and business appointments and explore. In a city like New York, there is so much to do that there's no danger of their being bored.

For most of us, the ideal time for house guests is summer,

194

when obligations let up, the pace slows, and life is relaxed. The ideal place is a country or vacation house where the tempo is easy and scheduled activities are at a minimum. The perfect guests? People you feel relaxed with and who feel the same about you. People who have a sixth sense about knowing when to offer help and when to go off on their own and leave you to your chores.

We love having people for the weekend in the country, and our house and life there are planned with guests in mind. We always let guests know that in our house, a weekend means Friday before dinner to Monday after breakfast. Arriving later or leaving earlier is up to the guest. If it's a holiday weekend, we suggest arrival and departure times accordingly. Over the years I've found that, like a party, a pleasant weekend starts with the cast. Not everyone is happy as a house guest. Some people, for example, are simply miserable sleeping away from home. Dick's father was one of them. He loved coming out for lunch and a day in the country. But by evening he was delighted to go back to New York and his own bed. Everyone has friends who are lovely and lively and great fun to have lunch or dinner with, but too kinetic to live with for a whole weekend. There are also city people who are unnerved by country quiet and lack of pressure, sybaritic souls who would be tortured roughing it in anyone's rustic cabin and—better face it—grown-ups who are confused and uncomfortable in the presence of small children. Ask any or all of these to come out for brunch, lunch, or a swim if you're within easy driving distance, but cross them off your list of potential overnight guests.

You'll find you develop weekend ways to suit your house and your household. There is no set formula for success. You want your guests to feel welcome but not smothered, unpressured but not bored. Too many dates in a strange setting leave most people feeling dragged out, so we try not to plan too much. We usually ask local friends in for one lunch or dinner, and we may take house guests out once during a weekend to a restaurant or to a friend's house. But we leave it at that, because we have discovered people like being left free to wander off for a walk or a nap (a treat usually hard to find time for at home), to pick up a book or just to lie in the sun.

the care and feeding of guests

Because more people are worried than thrilled by the unexpected, I try to let guests know roughly what we'll be doing a week or so ahead of time. Women guests feel uncomfortable if they don't know what sort of clothes they'll need (most of us pack too much anyway). Men, though they won't admit it, are even more put off when they find themselves in the wrong clothes. (Did you ever watch a man in black tie at a blue-suited dinner party?). A hostess can do a lot to put guests at ease by letting them know ahead of time what special events are scheduled, by reminding them about sweaters, sports clothes, a long dress, or dinner clothes for a dance. On the weekend itself, the hostess can adapt her own clothes to what her guests have brought with them. It's a simple matter for her to switch from pants to a skirt, or from a long dress to a short one.

What comes first when guests arrive? In our house, it's a drink and a few minutes to breathe. We show them where to find the ice and the fixings, so that from then on they'll feel free to mix their own when they like—even if we're not there to suggest it. Then a chance to go to their rooms and freshen up before dinner. By this I don't mean dressing up; we don't in the country. If they're visiting us for the first time, I point out such things as light switches, the handles that raise and lower the blinds, thermostats and extra blankets. There's nothing more forlorn than being cold in a strange house and not knowing where to find an extra blanket. This is also the time to explain about night lights, family pets (Do they sleep in or out?), and any eccentricities like squeaking stairs or gurgling plumbing your house happens to be blessed with. If you don't always have as much hot water as you'd like, you might suggest the best times for a tub or shower, or tactfully explain that since the children have their baths between five and six, there's likely to be a shortage at that time.

preparing guest rooms

When it comes to guest rooms, a hostess can do a great deal before her guests arrive to insure their comfort. If you have a choice, give them a quiet room (not next to the kids or over the kitchen) and, if possible, a bathroom to themselves. I think you should sleep in your own guest room at least once a year, twice, if you use it winter and summer. That way, you'll *know* that the beds are still firm and the pillows

the care and feeding of guests

lumpless; that screens and shades really fit properly (for some people, one chink of dawn's early light can ruin a beautiful morning) ; that doors close; that drawers slide; that each bed has a good bright light focused for reading. In the bed department, unless you know you'll be using the room for only one guest at a time, I think twin beds are best (two pillows for each guest); most double-bed users can bear to be parted—for a couple of nights anyway—while many single-bed people simply can't sleep with anyone else.

Check closets for space and hangers; there should be three different kinds: heavy for men's coats and jackets, medium weight for women's dresses, and pants hangers, which can be used for skirts, too. See that drawers are empty and clean, and that there are ashtrays, cigarettes, matches, a small alarm clock, and an insect spray. If your guest room doesn't have its own radio, maybe you can borrow one from some other part of the house. I also make sure there's a choice of things to read—current magazines, a few mysteries, perhaps some short stories—nothing too long or weighty. If it's possible, plan to buy an extra newspaper each day when you have weekend guests. One to a couple should keep them happy and, if you like doing the Sunday puzzle, you won't have to forego the pleasure of having your own to work on.

There should be a full-length mirror, as well as one a woman can use for make-up and doing her hair. A combination dressing table-desk will provide drawers for cosmetics, stationery, stamps, pens, and a small mending kit fitted with assorted pins, needles, colored thread, and scissors.

In the bathroom, there should be a shower cap, facial tissues, absorbent cotton, and an extra roll of toilet paper; talcum powder and toilet water are nice to find there, too. In the medicine cabinet should be two glasses, an emery board, an orangewood stick, mouthwash, aspirin, disinfectant, Band-Aids, *and* enough room for the toilet things your guests bring with them.

I do think guests appreciate knowing at the start what the habits of the house are. Are they expected to appear for breakfast at a specific hour? Should they fix their own, or do you like to fix trays so they can eat in their rooms? What time is lunch, and is there a set hour for dinner?

It depends on the household, of course, but I think a

the care and feeding of guests

hostess should let her guests know if she'd like them to make their own beds or help out in other ways. A guest should volunteer to help if the hostess is doing the work herself, but be ready to take "yes" or "no" for an answer without pressing the point. In any case, when your hostess is her own staff, I think you should take special care to leave your room reasonably tidy; if you don't, it's just that much more work for her after you've gone.

guests'
obligations

On the subject of guests and tipping, what can I tell you? Whether you do or you don't depends on the household custom (not the easiest thing in the world to find out about) and your own feelings. Without question, guests mean extra work for servants and tips do make them happier to do it. On the other hand, gauging how much and to whom is a ticklish and embarrassing business. Ordinarily, you don't tip if you're family or if you've only spent one night, but you certainly should if someone has done something special for you like pressing things or washing out some laundry. In an average household with casual help (at best a live-in housekeeper), it would be a good thing for the employer to add something to the week's pay for the extra work involved when there are guests; the hostess should explain this to her guests.

I don't think a guest owes his hostess candy or flowers. On the other hand, I know very few ladies who are offended by presents. The nicest gift has a personal touch—a book you think she'd enjoy, or a box that's her favorite color, or even a silly toy. Or it might be something you've overheard her say she wished she had. However, some gifts are more gifted than others. Large offerings of perishable food can be pretty dismaying to a hostess who has planned her weekend meals. Don't bring nine boxes of assorted cakes and pies; she may not be feeding an army, and her freezer may be full. On the other hand, she might be delighted by the right cake or cheese or wine to complete her menu (phone first, and ask).

"Thank you" notes have always been known as "bread-and-butter" letters—an apt, if not ept, description—and I think guests should always write them. It's not important to come up with a whole new way of saying "thank you." Just saying it is always appreciated.

weekend
guests

If I'm planning to invite a childless couple or single peo-

the care and feeding of guests

ple to my house for the weekend, I make sure they know what they're getting themselves into. Finicky sleepers or people who don't know and like my children are going to have a terrible time and so will I. When it comes right down to it, the ideal childless guests are the Last-Minute People I rhapsodically described before; if they love an impromptu meal and ratty confusion on a Thursday night, they'll love a weekend with us, too. The only extra consideration I show them is to persuade my kids not to barge into their bedroom at six in the morning, but that's about it for special treatment.

Couples with children are a much more complicated proposition. In the first place, are our children the same ages as theirs and do they like each other? If the answer to either question is no, I think carefully before I issue the invitation. Otherwise, I'm probably going to spend most of the weekend troubleshooting and worrying. By Sunday, because I'm defensive and embarrassed and so are the other parents, I may find I've jeopardized the adult friendship for the sake of four (or six) ill-assorted kids who didn't care about each other in the first place.

One other negative comment: People, with or without children, are discouraged from bringing their dogs and cats —assuming that they're polite enough to ask me whether it's okay to bring them, and not just arrive with their mewing, yapping menagerie. If we haven't any pets of our own, and we haven't, it's obviously because we don't want them, aren't equipped for them, and won't know what to do for them. (If you happen to have pets of your own, you'll have no way of ascertaining ahead of time how compatible they'll be with *their* guests, and by Sunday, you may find you've jeopardized an adult friendship because your Dalmatian has eaten an ear off the visiting poodle puppy.)

living accommo- dations
A perfectly lovely couple and their two perfectly lovely children are arriving Friday in time for dinner. Like most people these days, we have no guest room. Where do I put everybody? Very simple. The adults go in our neatest child's room. (I know immediately which room this is, because neatness is a trait that either shows up or doesn't at a very early age. As a matter of fact, I secretly believe it can be predicted like Mendel's sweet peas: Given one neat parent and one messy one, you'll get one meticulous picker-upper,

the care and feeding of guests

two sporadic picker-uppers, and one absolutely incorrigible slob.) I empty out two big bureau drawers, make the beds, make some room in the closet, supply some decent hangers, check the light bulbs, dust around a little, supply some ash-trays, cigarettes, matches, a couple of juicy books, and that's all.

If the two lovely children are used to sharing the same room, they will probably love the novelty of sleeping with our children instead of each other. I pair them off according to age (or if they're older than about seven, maybe according to gender) and prepare myself for an hour's worth of gig-gling and bed-bouncing at night before they go to sleep. Clean sheets, closet space, and drawer space are the only preparations I make for kids.

It's possible, of course, that this model family has a third, and younger, child who can't be left behind with a baby-sitter. In that case, I have to juggle everybody around to pro-vide a single room for him, preferably near his parents, so that if he wakes up during the night, he won't wander around in a panic, looking for the bathroom or a familiar face.

When the family arrives, I show the adults their sleeping quarters, their bathroom, and their towels. Since the bath-room is going to be shared with members of my own family, I use different colored towels for the guests—it prevents confusion. And while I'm in the bathroom, I explain the plumbing peculiarities. ("To stop the toilet from running overtime, jiggle the handle"; "Turn the cold on first because the hot will scald you to death"; or "Let me know when you're going to take a shower, because if someone else is taking a shower at the same time, you'll both freeze.")

For child guests, the arrival procedure is the same, with one addition: Now is the time I tell the visiting small fry about my local house rules of behavior and safety. If they're decent kids, they'll conform to them even if the system isn't the same at home.

weekend food

For Friday night, I plan something that can be made ahead of time and heated up. It's hectic enough when week-end guests arrive without having to worry about last-minute cooking. Even though my own children ordinarily eat with us, I sometimes feed all the children first in the kitchen.

the care and feeding of guests

Because they have guests, they don't object—they actually prefer it, and it allows us and our friends the freedom, very welcome on a Friday, to eat whenever we feel like it.

With the children out of the way, I can then begin to deal with the adult dinner. When the guests ask if they can help, I say no; they won't know where anything is, and it'll be easier to do it myself. But I'll let them sit around the kitchen with drinks, keeping me company while I work. They'll begin to notice things like where the Cokes, ice bucket, and dish towels are, and by the next day, they won't be asking what they can do to help—they'll just do it. **Or they get thirty lashes.** (If they don't, they're not the perfectly lovely couple I thought they were.)

Before we all go to bed, I show the guests where the basic breakfast ingredients and equipment are, just in case one of them gets up before me. With small children, this is not likely, but any guest who gets up with the birds (or because of them) is going to want to have a cup of coffee while he waits for the rest of both families to show up.

For most of you, the actual breakfast will depend on your schedule for the day. If you've planned all kinds of well-organized activities for yourselves and the kids—ice-skating, golf, nature walks (?!) —you'll have to eat at a definite time. I never plan anything, and the guests we have are as unathletic as we are (that's why we like them) so I just hang around in the kitchen from about eight to ten, providing anything and everything within reason that anybody asks for. Should I be more specific? Eggs, bacon, toast, muffins, orange juice, cold cereal, and more coffee. No pancakes. I make lousy pancakes.

Come to think of it, I guess by some people's standards I make lousy lunches, too, because I can never think of anything to serve for lunch. (Eggs would be perfect, but we've just had those three hours before.) As a matter of fact, to be absolutely honest, I really don't serve lunch at all. If I feel very hospitable, I make a gallon of gaspacho the day before, or if it's winter, I open up some cans of black bean soup the minute before, but lunch usually consists of the following:

I put the cold-cut box, peanut butter, jelly, mustard, mayonnaise, pickles, lettuce, tomatoes, fresh fruit, brownies, plates and napkins on the kitchen table.

the care and feeding of guests

I invite everybody to concoct their own sandwiches and help themselves to soup if there is any. If not, they shouldn't. Or they go to the cookie jar where there are no cookies.

If I'm in an especially benevolent mood, or the various members of both families are all over the place and can't be corralled into the kitchen without interrupting their various individual pursuits, I take sandwich orders, make them myself, and *then* invite everybody in to eat. Either way, it's not what you could call gracious living, but I'll tell you one thing it is—it's easy. And maybe before I go any further, I'd better tell you, in case you haven't noticed, that easy is very important to me when I'm having weekend guests. If it isn't easy, it isn't fun, and if it isn't fun, why do it?

You'll be happy to hear, however, that Saturday night dinner actually takes place in the dining room; it consists of something like roast beef, baked potatoes, salad, cheese, dessert, and coffee because, unless I happen to know ahead of time that the guests are adventurous eaters, it's risky to present them with anything bizarre.

Sunday breakfast is exactly like Saturday, except that if anybody wants them, Hank makes pancakes. He makes good ones. The schedule will depend on whether or not you or your guests are churchgoers. If so, or if everybody has gotten up early and lunch is obviously a must, there's always the leftover cold meat from the night before, plus salad and maybe a cheese soufflé. If not, Sunday breakfast can drag along pleasantly until two o'clock in the afternoon, thereby avoiding the problem of lunch altogether.

As far as Sunday supper is concerned, I never worry about it because my guests usually leave in the afternoon in order to beat the traffic. I think they leave to get something to eat. If they stay? Well, there's always spaghetti with meat sauce.

That pretty much covers the food department. For those of you who have higher aspirations and more energy, my system probably sounds, uh, let's see—casual? sloppy? unimaginative? Yes. But then, as I said before, easy.

As for the rest of it:

_____
odds
and ends

1. My adult guests automatically make their own beds; I don't discourage them! My children guests usually do what

the care and feeding of guests

they see my children doing, i.e., making their own beds. I don't discourage that either.

2. When guests want to help me clear the table, load, or empty the dishwasher, get out the ice, or make drinks, I let them.

3. When I'm putting things in the washing machine, I collect the children guests' dirty blue jeans and do them at the same time, so the parents don't have to go home with a bunch of dirty laundry.

4. When there are small visiting children, I don't make plans to go out in the evening with their parents—little kids don't like being abandoned in a strange house with a strange baby-sitter. In fact, I rarely make plans to go out anyway; weekend guests have come to relax at our house, not to be dragged off to someone else's. If seeing other people seems like a good idea, I invite them over *after* dinner, Saturday night.

5. I make it perfectly clear that guests should feel free to go upstairs to sleep whenever they feel like it. And if I feel like it, or Hank and I both do, we extend ourselves the same privilege, having first told the guests what we do about turning out lights and locking doors.

6. At departure time, I double-check for forgotten socks, underwear, toys, and briefcases—it's a colossal bore to return them later.

As you may have noticed, my approach to entertaining is rather different from DR's. Between us, we run the gamut from gracious to what some of you will consider ghastly. That's the whole point. That's precisely what we intended you to notice, because if you have the time and the talent, the energy, the urge, and the equipment to do things DR's way, now you know how she does it. It shouldn't scare you anymore. If, for any number of reasons, you'd rather do it my

way, now you know how I do it. That certainly shouldn't
scare you.

As for the lists and menus and technical information you'll
find on pages 303-15—they're a wealth of immaterial for you to
pick and choose from. Any system that suits you and makes
you comfortable is the system to use. How you feel about
entertaining is important, how you actually go about it is
not. After all, I like being in DR's house and she likes being
in mine. That ought to prove something.

the care and feeding of guests

ABOUT THE
CHILDREN

Child experts are always writing books on how to bring up children. I've noticed that these experts—psychologists, pediatricians, educators, whatever they are—are usually men (naturally they're men, who else has the time?) with very definite opinions about the right and wrong way to go about things.

Well, I'm not an expert. I'm just one more mother with a lot of children (three teen-agers and two little boys), and it's not my function to push psychological, medical, or educational theories at you. But when it comes to living *with* children, as against bringing them *up*, I can at least present you with a series of options; I can point out some of the choices you have available to you; and I can reassure you (as I constantly have to reassure myself) that there's absolutely no right or wrong way to go about anything.

And now, I hope you're sufficiently reassured, because I'm about to tell you, in neat, chronological order, what I think you should do about everything!

newborn babies: hospitals

If given a choice of a five-day trip to the Bahamas or a five-day maternity spree in the hospital, I think I'd take the latter. It's one of the most self-indulgent delights of a woman's life . . . flowers, presents, adoring visitors, and nothing to do all day but lounge around in a new bathrobe, looking lovely. It's the sixth day that's the trap, when you come home feeling as though you'd been on a five-day mountain-climbing expedition because there have been too many visitors, there are still thirty-five thank you notes which the visitors didn't give you a chance to write, and you are just plain depressed. Doctors will tell you you have post-partum depression and it will probably cure itself in a few weeks. Actually, you can cure most of it yourself, by being ruthless about how you spend those five days. In the first place, look out for the visitors. People you haven't seen for months turn up, with or without notice, like seventeen-year locusts. It's flattering, but when your room is packed full of oddly assorted types who don't know each other, who range in age from sixteen to sixty-five, and who have nothing in common with each other but you and your event, you'll find yourself perspiring nervously under your scratchy hospital sheets, trying to be a good cruise director. Everybody in the room is happy but you. One way to avoid this is to keep a date book for the visiting hours. When a great-aunt and your best friend want to come at the same time, suggest to the great-aunt that she visit you and the baby at home where you can have a quieter time of it. You can even put it all off on your doctor; he wants you to rest, you're not seeing anyone but your husband and your mother. If your great-aunt won't be put off, you can at least time her arrival to coincide with your grandmother's arrival and tell your best friend to show at a different time. If you have a lot of best friends, you'll have to schedule them rather carefully, too, or they'll all descend in a clump just when you were counting on a few peaceful minutes with your husband, who wants to see you alone—because he likes you and because he's been holding down the fort at home, coping with household details he knows nothing about.

flowers

Everybody sends you flowers. It's as good as being dead and on display in a funeral home. In the rich old days, nurses' aides used to come and change the water, get rid of the dead orange zinnias, and take the whole blooming bower out of your room at night. Now they just sit there, dripping deciduously all over your floor (the flowers, not the aides), until you're forced to take up instant gardening yourself. Not me, thank you very mulch! A few flower arrangements are lovely to have, but if you're sending them to anyone in a hospital, avoid big baskets of large or fragrant flowers. Remembering how little space there is in the average hospital room, I try always to send arrangements of small flowers in a tall goblet so that there is room for a book or clock or radio below the flowers and the flowers themselves are up where the patient can enjoy them. If people are thoughtful enough to ask me ahead of time if I want flowers, I tell them please not to bother. If they insist on sending "something . . . what do you want instead?" I suggest some minor piece of equipment for the baby, like Toddler Two overalls—the kind of thing you always have to go out and buy because most baby presents are totally impractical bits of froth which you stow away in a drawer and forget all about.

If, in spite of all your polite discouragement, you still have too many flowers, ask the floor nurse to take them to the children's ward or anywhere else she thinks they'll be appreciated. Don't, by the way, get rid of your great-aunt's zinnias unless you are sure she's not dropping in on you tomorrow. My last word on flowers is that if you note down the color and type on the back of the card, you'll know what to thank people for. I only recognize about four kinds of flowers—roses, pansies, orchids, and tulips—and if you're like me, just write down something like, "Lovely pink and white things, smell nice, blue rattle tied on," which will be enough of a reminder for you to concoct a vaguely enthusiastic note later on. Don't let it be too much later on; it's rude to the donor and a drag for you. The hospital is the best place to dispose of the note-writing chore; if you've been careful about the guests, you'll have more time there than you will at home.

birth announce-ments

If almost all your friends live in your community, you don't really need to send out formal birth announcements; a notice in the newspaper and notes and/or phone calls to your friends will do. If you've recently moved or you simply want to send out announcements, by all means, go ahead, but be discriminating about the people you send them to. If you send them to anybody and everybody, it'll come across like a bid for a baby present. (Maybe it's my peculiarity, but that's the way I always react when I am notified of the birth of some passing acquaintance's child.) Also, be discriminating about the kind of announcement you send. Adorable, cute ones are irritating—I like the old-fashioned, formal variety, myself.

hospital etiquette

Hospital etiquette is somewhat different now that nobody has private nurses and all hospitals are woefully understaffed. If you plan to serve drinks to your friends, ask the floor nurse where the ice machine is and get it yourself. She'll love you for it. Don't ask the nursery nurse to make an exception and raise the shade early to show off your baby.

She'll hate you for it and will probably refuse anyway. When you leave, tip the maid who does your room ($3.00–$5.00), and give the floor and nursery nurses either cookies, candy, or fruit. I find that most nurses, like most of us, are on diets and they like fruit the best.

baby clothes

As I said before, you're going to get an awful lot of froth: fancy crib sheets, twelve little blankets, organdy pillow cases, shirred French rompers or embroidered Italian dresses. Are you really going to use them? Do you have someone else to iron them? If not, exchange them for the things you do need, or for credit, which you'll need badly when your child is a destitute Toddler Two. Don't save them to give to other new mothers; they won't use them either and when they try to return them, it'll be embarrassing. It's not that I have anything against all these fancy appurtenances, but when you come right down to it, almost nobody gets to see a tiny baby anyhow; he's usually asleep, and when he isn't, he's spitting up on the shirred romper. What you need is a ton of undershirts and rubber pants!

pediatricians

I care deeply about the subject of pediatricians, and I intend to be extremely didactic about it; consider yourself warned. It is imperative for your own sense of well-being, to say nothing of your child's physical well-being, that you find a man or woman in whom you have confidence and whom you definitely like. If this is your first baby, your obstetrician will recommend someone, probably connected with his hospital. If you're moving to a new community, your old pediatrician will give you the names of several men whom he either knows personally or by reputation. But locating the man who is professionally adequate is not the difficult part. It's the *liking* part that can be difficult, because if you find yourself irrevocably tied (so you think) to a doctor you know is good in the strictly professional sense but you just can't stand him, then what do you do? Well I'll tell you what you do: *You find another one.* We're all understandably chicken about firing doctors. Unlike changing markets or laundries, it often involves an awkward personal confrontation with the man himself, and at the very least, you have to call the nurse and ask her to send your child's charts on to the new doctor, which is uncomfortable enough. Nevertheless, you have a right, no, an obligation, to find a man *you* like who likes you and your kids. They say the old "family" doctor has disappeared, but I say you can sometimes literally force your pediatrician into that role by fixing your beady eye on him and asking him questions about the whole child, not just about his immunizations. And if your doctor repeatedly ignores your attempts to establish this kind of rapport, or you don't like his answers, then you have the wrong man for you. ("Madam, your whole child is a mess." "Doctor, you are the wrong man for me. Good-bye.")

Once you have the right man, be considerate of him. Some mothers panic more easily than others. If you're the panicky kind, when it's nine o'clock at night, your child has a temperature of a hundred and one and you're afraid it might go up, call the doctor *then*. Don't wait until it does go up at three in the morning. The best time to get a doctor is at about seven a.m. (they all get up early) before he begins hospital rounds. If you miss him then, he may not get around to calling you until lunchtime, and because he's much too busy for a house visit and he probably can't prescribe over the phone, he'll ask you to bring the baby in. Yes, with a raging fever and the rales and rattles and everything. And you know what? He's absolutely right. His office is equipped, your house is not; his office is near the hospital, if it's that kind of emergency; and, most important of all, if you waited for him to come to your house, you might wait until midnight because that's what doctors' schedules are like these days. So have a little pity and a little patience.

One final thing: Your doctor is going to take a vacation some time and he's also going to take some weekends off, or at least Sundays. He'll leave an associate in charge of his practice. If, after you've gotten to know him, you don't like him, ask your doctor to recommend some other substitute. This, too, is awkward, but do it anyway; it's better than worrying.

small children, aged two to five

If you can live through this period, you can live through anything. Little kids are delectable, horrible, ingratiating, infuriating, invigorating, enervating, beautiful when they sleep—but they practically never sleep. The most descriptive adjective for them is busy—which is what they want to be all the time. So without further fanfare, here are some suggestions for busy-ness.

about the children

There's always television, but I take a dim view of too much of that. There have been plenty of psychologists' surveys on the effects of violence on a child's mind, and I leave the ultimate conclusion there for the experts. What I object to is the catatonic state that kids get into when they watch dull TV, and almost all daytime TV is, God knows, dull. That's about the best thing you can say about it. Furthermore, after my four-year-old son has been home sick for a few days, he begins to say things like, "Good-bye, my darling, I love you" to his older brother, or, "I am so sad; it hurts me in my heart." And I spent two hours this winter convincing him that if he tried to fly off the bed like Superman, he was going to fall down.

Although none of our kids has a set of his own because then you *really* can't control what's going on, we are, I admit, a many-setted family. In the old days, I used to let the sets get broken, one by one, and never get them fixed; nobody questioned it because repair jobs are usually lengthy, unsuccessful, and sometimes involve eviscerating the machine altogether. Lately, however, my husband and I occasionally like to watch it ourselves, and it's hard to control little kids unless you can say sanctimoniously, "Daddy and I never watch it." When I told my child with the sore heart that TV was for dummies, he said he *wanted* to be a dummy, which is not a decision I think he is ready to make for himself.

So what do you do? Well, you can make rules. "Batman and that's it, buddy." And exceptions to the rules for, let's say, Jacques Cousteau. Primarily, of course, a kid will only watch the boob tube if there is nothing else available. If you offer to read him a book, or play a game with him, or take him outside, he actually prefers it. This is a pretty good indication of what children use TV for: to keep them company. (Sometimes this can't be avoided, but it's usually when you're fixing dinner for a million people that your kid, who has finally been told that he may watch TV, announces that he doesn't want to because TV is for dummies). What he's really after is your company; he wants you to keep him busy, and for a few hours a day you'll simply have to give him what he needs.

Aside from giving him your undivided attention, there are compromise measures that'll keep you both happy. Jobs that are very boring for you are very interesting for small children. They love to empty things—wastebaskets, laundry hampers, ashtrays. It helps, too, if you remember to teach them where and when cigarette butts can safely be emptied. Teach them how, and then go about your own chores while they rather sloppily go about theirs. Little boys love to vacuum—they love all noisy machines—and little girls love to straighten up anything that doesn't belong to them. Let them clean out and reorganize your sewing box. They like to dust, too.

If you're desperate on a rainy day, and your child is old enough to be careful, put him in the bathtub with plastic toys, blocks, a pail, and a Krazy Straw and leave him there until his fingers are wrinkled and he wants out. Check up occasionally to make sure he hasn't poured so much water on the floor that it's dripping down to your dining room. Don't worry about his catching cold; he probably won't, but if you're a worrier, fill the sink with warm water, roll up his sleeves, put an apron on him, and let him scrub his own dusty toys instead. That's the kind of thing you'll never get around to, but he'll love it.

Another good rainy-day occupation is dime-store shopping. Let your kid loose with a dollar—it'll take him a good two hours to figure out how to spend it, during which time you can be stocking up on pot-holders, cup hooks, sewing equipment . . . all those little jibby things you've been meaning to get for ages.

at home with a guest

At home, one small guest (and I mean one!) is an afternoon's entertainment. It's hard enough for two little kids to learn how to get along with each other—sharing and turn-taking are not built-in characteristics of the very young. But three is a hideous combination because someone is always being left out. Even with just one guest, stick around for a while to make sure the kids are making out all right and get down the games and equipment they need before you take off for another part of the house. Don't take off for long, either; you never can tell when one of them might start hitting, or hogging, or biting, all of which are nice things to prevent! Actually, hitting and hogging are fairly par for the course, but biting is nastier to deal with. If the other child bites, feel free to speak sharply to him, and maybe put him in another room for a while. If your own child bites, feel free to hit him, speak sharply to him and put him in another room, and feel compelled, no matter how you dread it, to tell the other mother about it. If you don't, her child will anyway, but aside from that, you're going to find her much more understanding than you'd anticipated. Her primary reaction, unless her child has a jagged hole in him somewhere, will be relief that it was your child and not hers who did the biting.

A short visit—a couple of hours in the afternoon with juice and cookies—is better than a too long one, especially if it's a new friend and you're not sure how well the two will get along. If you can see that they're not getting along, call the mother up and suggest that she pick up her child a little earlier. Unless it's terribly inconvenient for her, she'll be glad to accede because she knows just as well as you what may happen if she doesn't: biting, hitting, or hogging!

If you've planned a visit and at the last minute your child has even a minor sniffle, call up the other mother and ask her if she still wants to keep the date. She probably will, but she might be one of those panicky mothers, so it's polite to give her the option.

informal play groups

If your child is too young for nursery school but bored at home alone, try to find a few mothers in the neighborhood with whom you can start an informal play group. Anywhere from four to six children is about right; you can share expenses for snacks and equipment, and take turns with the houses—Monday at yours, Wednesday somewhere else, Friday somewhere else. Move cautiously when you're forming the group, though. You can't expel a difficult customer —mother or child—without creating quite a lot of bad feeling, and unless you're an ex-nursery school teacher, you aren't capable of effecting any major personality changes.

nursery school

If you live in a big city and you want your child to go to private school, you'll find that your choice of nursery school, believe it or not, will depend on the preference of the private school you're going to try to get him into later. If said private school provides a "structured" education, you'll have to dig up a structured nursery school and get your child in there, even if it's five miles out of your way. Ridiculous, but that's how it is these days.

If you don't live in a big city, or you don't care about private school, your job is much simpler. Your choice is dictated by three things: How expensive is the school, how close is it to your home (if it's only a three-hour nursery school, it's a maddening waste of time to spend your whole morning delivering and fetching), and what kind of education—even at the block-building level—does it provide? There's nothing difficult about the first two, and as for the third, take a trip over to the school and see for yourself. If you hit a classroom with twenty children rolling around in the mud and sand, it's a big, permissive school. I don't happen to go for those, but maybe you do. If there are fewer than ten little children playing quietly in separate corners— one corner for housekeeping, one corner for paints, one corner for books—it's a structured school. If you can't quite tell which it is—seven and a half children rolling around in the sand and seven and a half reading quietly— ask questions of the teacher and the principal. Whatever you pick is fine with me; I only have one opinion on the matter: I think it's a mistake to figure that because your home is strict, your child will benefit from a permissive classroom atmosphere, or the other way around. When children are very young, it seems to me they benefit more from consistency of approach than from contrast, which only mixes them up.

Clothes do not matter one bit at nursery school. If you're dying to put your child into gorgeous little suits or dresses, nobody's going to stop you, but they won't last long and they're awfully confining for him or her. Three or four sets of permanent-press polo shirts and overalls, or shirts and jumpers, will do nicely and by the time you're sick of looking at them, your child has outgrown them anyway. (Zipper-front overalls or slacks with elastic in the waist are easier on little boys and their teachers until they can manage buttons, by the way.) And *mark everything, including shoes.*

birthday parties: giving them

Some nursery schools will allow you to give your child his birthday party in school. In fact, they actually give it for you; all you do is supply them with individual cup cakes, horns, balloons, and tiny toys and they cheerfully do all the work. This is an ideal solution if your child is in a big class and you want to avoid having the whole screaming mob at home, or just part of the mob at home, which hurts the feelings of the ones left out.

If you can't give the party at school, or your child has some neighborhood friends he wants to invite, it's my opinion that birthday parties for two-, three-, and four-year-olds should never last longer than an hour and a half (unless you can have an outdoor picnic in the spring or something like that), should never be bigger than about six children, and are much more successful in the morning and for lunch than in the afternoon when the children are tired and so are you.

If the prospect depresses and terrifies you, get a friend or another mother to stay and help.

The latest birthday party innovation is, as everybody knows, the Loot Bag. This isn't quite as crass as the name would imply because you can fill the Loot Bag with fairly tawdry, ten-cent-store loot and a couple of lollipops. The kids really don't care what they get anyway, as long as they all get the same thing and the same amount.

One thing they do care about, though, is losing at games, especially games with prizes. At this age, kids are great competitors but lousy losers, so if you want to avoid scenes, give a prize to everybody or nobody. Even without prizes, musical chairs, that old favorite, strikes me as being the most diabolical invention there is. Some kid starts walking in the wrong direction and feels stupid, some other kid gets bumped and starts crying—it's a mess. If you want a suggestion for a pleasant little pursuit that keeps everyone happy, sprinkle new pennies (or old pennies), or jelly beans around the room and let the kids keep what they find. This is only mildly competitive and everybody has a pretty good time.

If you want a suggestion for winning instant gratitude from your husband, tell him he doesn't have to attend the party!

The average little girl doesn't need more than two real party dresses in her wardrobe. At this age, being seen twice in the same dress is no tragedy. The dresses don't have to be expensive, either. If there's an indulgent grandmother in your family, fine, but most people notice the length of a dress more than the material or the style, as long as it's simple. And if you're caught short at the last minute with a dress that suddenly looks too short, don't worry about it—it'll look

birthday parties: going to them

about the children

kind of cute. If you're caught with a dress that's too long, don't worry about that either. It won't look as cute but who cares?

Clothes for three-to-five-year-old boys are in a transition stage. At any given party, you're likely to see anything from a pale blue linen, one-piece number with red, English, Mary Jane shoes and little white socks to grey flannels, a polo shirt, black oxfords, and long gray socks. Then, too, there's the Eton suit and the Eton shirt. It all depends on what part of the country you come from, how mature your child looks, and what you yourself prefer. The main fact to remember is that little boys hate to look different and especially hate to look like little girls, so beware of the blue linen suit and the red shoes unless you're sure there's going to be another little pseudo-Englishman at the party.

Presents don't have to cost much; a flashlight for a dollar twenty-nine or a bottle of bubble bath is often just as exciting as a ten-dollar educational toy. Obviously, don't choose anything you'd hate your own child to have; it's inconsiderate to the other parents and if it's a noisy gun or Silly Putty, your own child is going to want it too. Books make a great present; I don't know why it doesn't occur to more people to give them—they're easy to carry, they're in the right price range, and they can be exchanged if they're duplicates.

If you want to bother with a birthday card, I suppose you can, but considering the way all children rip packages out of their guests' hands before even the surface amenities like "Hello, Happy Birthday" have been proffered, I think it's hardly worth the effort. Few children can write or read before they're six anyhow, so you might just as well scrawl the appropriate message on the wrapping paper with a magic marker yourself. In all probability nobody, including the mother, will know the difference.

Deliver your child promptly and pick him up promptly; there's nothing more annoying for a mother than having to wait at either end for a delinquent parent. And just before you deliver your child to his destination, remind him that this not his birthday, that he'll be able to play with his friend's new toys (unless his friend is an acquisitive rotter) but he can't have them, and that when he has a birthday, it'll be his turn to collect the goods.

When it comes to health, I think there is such a thing as too many rules—especially in the food department. Unless they are forced in the old-fashioned way to "eat everything put before them," most small children are by nature rather selective and cautious about what they eat. In other words, they hate almost everything and they usually hate anything new that isn't nine tenths sugar. They hate mushy things (tapioca), slimy things (okra, gooey soft-boiled eggs), gristly things (liver), things with things *in* them (baked apple with any of the core left in it by mistake, fish with bones), things with fat *on* them, and, especially, things they can't chew very easily but which grown-ups can (asparagus stalks). Sometimes I think adults forget that children's jaws just aren't as strong as ours and that they really can't grind up what we can grind up.

We all know what they do like; I don't have to list those items, but the point is, should we make them eat what they don't like? Here again, the decision is up to you, but if I'm home alone with a child, I'd much rather ask him what he wants and watch him enjoy a hot dog and chocolate milk, than have to throw out a whole lamb chop, baked potato and a vegetable. If he's eating dinner with all of us, I ask him to try everything, but if he doesn't like it, I don't make much of a fuss about that either. If he's eating out with us at a restaurant or at someone's house, I handle it the same way with one added touch: when I can see that he's come across something he considers revolting, I hiss at him to swallow the mouthful he's already got, to keep his opinions to himself, and to wait till we get home where I can feed him the hot dog and the chocolate milk.

I do have one tip for mothers of fussy eaters or non-eaters: in-between-meal nibbling and guzzling is impossible at nursery school—a small cup of juice and a couple of crackers is about it for refreshments—so plan to feed your child his main meal as soon as he gets home from school, when he's at his hungriest.

Maybe this is all unorthodox, but since I've known children who had to eat everything when they were little and grew up to hate everything they ate, children who only ate hot dogs and are still only eating hot dogs, and children who only ate hot dogs and are now eating calves' brains, I have a feeling that it doesn't matter a tinker's damn what we do anyway.

Some things have changed since Mary and Linda were children. And I realize that right here and now more of my generation gap is about to show. Because I am thinking of days gone by when well-ordered households had cooks and waitresses and even governesses to sit with children at mealtimes when the parents weren't there. For me, good food has always been a source of pleasure and delight. I've enjoyed every aspect of it—its selection, purchase and preparation up to and, in fact, most of all, eating it. I believe this is a direct result of the fact that in my parents' house, food was always delicious—and presented and served attractively. There were no taboos that I recall, no dire warnings of sudden death if I were to eat this or that, but I was expected to eat everything put before me unless I was ill. When we traveled, I was encouraged to be adventurous and try unfamiliar dishes.

All of this is very difficult, if not impossible, for most mothers to manage today. The course of least resistance—and also the main course—is the inevitable hamburger. So there are lots of children running around who will have no truck with anything new and who will, furthermore, assure you that they don't like it before they've tried it. If the child drinks a Coke before lunch and then decides he'll have a bologna sandwich or a pancake, that's it.

Occasionally, all the conditions will be such that a child, even today, enjoys experimenting with food. But that means parents who care, a mother (or someone else in the household) who loves to cook and, quite probably, a child who eats with his parents frequently, both at home and in restaurants. If you're one of *those* parents, you might like to make the effort to let the child in on your kind of food. He'll be very grateful when he's older.

danger   I do think you have to be stern about danger. Any kid of mine who stands up on a window sill, reaches up on a counter or near a stove or iron, stuffs things in light sockets, lights matches under thermometers (or lights matches at all, for that matter), tries to eat aspirin, or dashes into the street after a ball, gets slugged. Hard. Likewise, any kid of mine who bites another kid or deliberately tries to beat up on a baby. I do this *guiltlessly* and immediately; it has a memorable effect. For minor infringements like throwing wet Kleenex out the window, blocks and socks down the toilet, in fact for anything that doesn't maim or literally endanger a life, I don't hit because it doesn't work effectively and is inappropriate and irrelevant punishment.

medicine

I make my drugstore put the name of the child, the name of the prescription, and its expiration date on the bottle. Otherwise, after a few months of winter, I end up with five different shades of pink medicine, at least two of which I accidentally and expensively duplicate later on because I don't know what they are or that I already have them. If I come across a bottle I can't identify, I call the drugstore, give them the number, and ask them to look it up for me.

hospitals

If your child has to have his tonsils out, or needs some other minor operation, many hospitals now have sleeping-in facilities so that you can stay with him if you want to. If you have other children who need you around, or yours isn't that kind of hospital, I'd like to tout you off the private room, which is terribly expensive and in which you will be trapped like an animal for the duration of your child's stay, unless you want the added expense of a special nurse. A semi-private room or a children's ward will be much less lonely and much more fun for your child anyway.

fear

The first time my children got intestinal flu, they all wanted to throw up over my shoulder with their arms around my neck. I guess it's a frightening experience if it's never happened before. So teach them how, and tell them if they can't make it to the bathroom in time, to aim for the nearest wastebasket. Buy a new wastebasket.

Most small kids howl their heads off when they're given immunization shots at the doctor's office. Some kids howl the minute they get inside the door, whether or not they're getting shots, because they remember the last time when they did. Don't worry about it; all that noise is perfectly understandable. Your doctor and the other mothers are quite used to it.

Generally speaking, most childhood fears fall into two categories: children are afraid of the things we tell them to be afraid of—fires, being run over by a car, electric light sockets, etc., and they are afraid of things we tell them they

about the children

shouldn't be afraid of—the dark, thunderstorms, big but friendly dogs. The first category is justifiable and good; the second is usually outgrown.

The only thing I can think of that is neither good nor easily outgrown is a child's fear of death. If you believe in God and you believe in Heaven, your child will, too; his sense of loss will be somewhat offset by your mutual conviction that he will see whomever it is again, some day. If, on the other hand, you are in the unenviable position of not being able to promise Heaven to your children, there are two things to remember: (1) Whether it's the death of a grandparent, or a friend, or a pet, your child's grief will fade eventually—more quickly, in fact, than an adult's. We have a tendency to guard and savor, even torture ourselves with memories. For us, forgetting is disloyalty. For a child, forgetting is, luckily, just forgetting. (2) With a child, fear is primarily what you have to contend with.

If the person was old, and as we all know, even forty seems old to a child, you can explain that all people die when they're very old. "Will I die, too?" "Yes, but not until you are very, very old which is a long, *long* time off." "Will you die?" "Yes, Daddy and I will both die, but not until *we* are very, very old, and I know we look that way now, but we're quite young, really."

When a young person dies? A few years ago, we lost a son. Adam was too little to remember him, but he knows about him—he's seen pictures, heard conversations, realizes his brother was young, not old. "Well, why then?" he asks. "Because he got very sick, too sick for the doctor to be able to fix. But this doesn't happen very often, and it won't happen to you." "Oh," says Adam, "can I watch television now?" . . . which makes me think that a child feels pretty much the same way about dying as the rest of us do: "It happens to other people, but it doesn't happen to me." And this is quite enough for him to know until he gets older and has to work out his own philosophy.

Manners have to be taught. Unfortunately, children don't just pick up such surface niceties as *please* and *thank you*. You have to instruct them. Setting a good example sounds like the ideal, unpressured substitute for instruction, but it doesn't work because they're not paying any attention. When

manners: the simple basics

219

about the children

you're purposefully and pointedly saying "Good morning" to the grocery clerk, they are just as purposefully looking for the Hostess Twinkies. You can go on saying good morning for a solid year; a three-year-old won't even notice.

You can sometimes disguise the instruction by making a game of it, though. ("I'm the grocery clerk and you've just come into the store. What's the first thing you say?" ". . . ." "No, first you say good morning, *then* you ask him where he keeps the Hostess Twinkies. And after he tells you, what do you say next?" ". . . ." "That's RIGHT! You say *thank you!* Go to the head of the class," and so forth.)

You can also explain to him what the word "please" is for: that the use of it makes the difference between a request and an order. A request is pleasant and is more likely to get results. An order is rude, unpleasant, and will get him nowhere. He ought to understand that—because whether we're aware of it or not, we give kids orders all day long: "Get down off that sofa," "Stop kicking the table leg," and they often get *us* nowhere, too.

Kids also have to be taught basic moral values—not to steal or lie and, most important of all, not to be cruel and not to be prejudiced. Parents should search themselves carefully for any vestige of prejudice. Even if they can't uproot it in themselves, they have an obligation to realize that they can warp their children at this early age by passing on any shred of racial or religious prejudice.

table manners

Kids will never learn table manners unless they eat at the table with you. It may be easier on the nerves and less conversationally disruptive to stuff them in the kitchen, but if you don't let them out once in a while, they'll be eating with their fingers forever. Teach them how to cope with all the grown-up utensils, how *not* to interrupt, and how to ask to be excused. One more thing: If you think it's O.K. to pick up chicken legs and lamb chops (and I do), remind your kids to ask permission to do so anyway. They might some day land up as a guest in a house where it's considered primitive, which will be embarrassing for them.

bad language

Last summer, at the beach, Adam was heard to say "Oh, ship!" rather frequently. Several elderly ladies were doing the hearing, not to mention some impressionable three-year-olds. And me. I was there, too, and I told him he absolutely could not say "oh, ship," but he could say "oh, boat." This didn't appeal to him as much because even though he'd only been saying "ship" in the first place, the elderly ladies thought he was saying something else and they were looking shocked—precisely the fun of it all. Little kids really do pick things up, so if there's anyone in your family given to mouthing expletives like "oh, ship," tell them to cool it. If that proves impossible, you'll have to explain the meaning of these words to your small children, and explain that they don't shock you (if they don't), but that they may be offensive to other people, especially old people, grandparents, teachers, and ministers. If you can manage to convey the somewhat lofty principle that bad language in front of people who hate it is inconsiderate and another form of bad manners, so much the better, but you may have to settle for an old-fashioned *don't*. The same rule applies to swearing.

respect for property

Save one "public" room from total destruction. No matter how relaxed or devoted a parent you are, there's got to be one place where the little rotters aren't allowed to jump on the furniture and crayon on the walls or plane off the edges of the table (which one of my own wonderful sons did, years ago). Let them make a muck out of the family room or the den or the dinette, but they should learn to lay off the living room, for instance, because if you have anything good, it's probably in there, and that's also the room the guests are usually in. Teach them that the living room is for grown-ups and grown-up is the way they're expected to behave when they're in there.

guests

Guests in your home fall neatly into two categories: old friends who love children, are interested in seeing yours, even eating with them, reading to them, admiring their cache of new toys, and don't mind being treated like one of the family. Everybody else (old friends who don't like children or see enough of their own at home, V.I.P.s, and big parties full of people, no matter who they are) belongs in the second category and your small children shouldn't hang around for more than about fifteen minutes.

It isn't worth the trouble to get them all dressed up for fifteen minutes and it's kind of unfair to the kids; clean pajamas, bathrobe, and slippers are fine.

Curtsies for girls and bows for boys are pretty much a

about the children

thing of the past, but your kids should know how to shake hands and look at people when they're saying hello. Years ago, just before a big Christmas party, I told my three older children, who were then quite young, that I'd give them each a penny for every person whose hand they shook while saying, "How do you do, Mrs. So-and-So." It worked like a charm and I never had to repeat the bribe because the adult delight was so instantly gratifying for the kids. I guess in some instances, virtue does turn out to be its own reward.

Little children love to pass appetizers. (They also love to eat them; mine will eat things from an hors d'oeuvres plate in the living room that would choke them to death in the kitchen. Even smoked oysters!) First of all, it gives them a great sense of accomplishment when they don't drop the shrimps on the floor. They also begin to enjoy the art of conversation:

"How old are *you,* Jimmy?"

"Fine, thank you," says Jimmy. Ah well, it's a start. And Jimmy is too busy thinking up polite answers to boring, anticipated questions to jump on the furniture. As I said before, according to my rough calculations, it'll be about fifteen hot minutes before he starts that. When he does, get him out. Fast! Look out, here comes another bribe. If you're too busy to do it yourself, bribe an older kid to get rid of the younger kid by reading to it and stuffing it into bed. And yet another bribe (I'm a morally corrupt mother!): Bribe the younger kid. "Hey, Jimmy, Susie's going to take you to bed now, and there's a surprise in your room." (Leg irons. Failing that, a cookie. Never mind brushing the teeth, one night won't hurt.) Do not make the mistake of asking or even allowing your child to make the rounds of the guests. As you know, saying good-night takes an extraordinary length of time when there aren't any guests. Multiply those minutes by the number of guests in the room and you'll realize that you've successfully stopped the conversational flow. Furthermore, you've put an unnecessary strain on your guests and on your child.

If the whole idea of coping, simultaneously, with an im-

about the children

portant party and your small children makes you terribly nervous, I have a few suggestions for you:

1. Put your children in bed before the guests arrive. If they feel deprived, you can always bring in a couple of favorite friends for a brief hello and good-night.

2. Hire a baby-sitter to put your children in bed for you. Not a strange new one, naturally, but a beloved old one who'll seem twice as entrancing as the people in the other room.

manners outside the home

First of all, whenever you and your husband decide that your first child is old enough to tie his own shoes, own and operate electric trains, know his colors, go to the bathroom by himself, and understand about sharing, you're about a year early. This advice, which you undoubtedly won't take (by the time you have a second child, you'll know better), is equally valid for public excursions like going to the circus, to church, to a movie, or to a restaurant.

Even if you do take my advice, you'll find that everything lasts twice as long as it should because in all of these places, kids are required to keep quiet and sit still, which they're terrible at. The attention span of the average small child is rarely longer than about an hour.

Warn your child ahead of time, tell him what to expect. Remind him that people don't shout on buses or in restaurants. Explain to him when and why people applaud at the circus and at the theatre, and why they don't applaud in church. The art of whispering doesn't seem to come naturally to children; let him practice that ahead of time, too.

If your child is visibly squirmy and bored at the circus, or a movie, or a play, don't think of it as wasted money if you decide to leave early. If you make him stay, he may end up hating these things forever and you're going to spend the remainder of the performance trying to silence him anyway.

Churches have been hipping up lately. Actually, they may just be returning to the Suffer Little Children philosophy, but the little children are certainly suffering less than they used to. A reasonable amount of climbing around the pews is fondly tolerated, but if your child seems bent on hiking his way to the altar, shouting boisterously in the middle of prayers, or making any other kind of undue commotion, haul him right up the aisle and out. If people are properly tending to business, they won't notice you and if they do—well, it's happened before and it'll happen again! Amen.

Jean Kerr buys different colored socks for each of her kids. If you have six children and one, therefore, gets stuck for ten years with purple or something, try sewing a different colored thread into the toes of the socks for each child. This won't work too well if the socks last long enough to be passed on to the next child, but that's rare. The same suggestion works on little girls' white cotton gloves.

If your child hates having her hair washed—what child doesn't—teach her to like showers, then put her in the shower with you and wash your hair and her hair all at the same time. Your husband can do this with the boys. If you can't teach them to like showers, I can't help you.

My problem is that I have long hair, and you're not going to teach me to like showers. How about using no-sting shampoo?

Baggies over rubber-soled shoes get them into boots immediately.

Some little kids wet their beds long past time when you think they shouldn't for the pure and simple reason that they are heavy sleepers and literally don't wake up. Pick this kind of kid up before you go to bed, and then put a noisy alarm clock under his bed, set for three in the morning. This saves your having to get up with him. Tell him you're going to do this, though, and why. Otherwise it might come as a nasty shock. If you're visiting friends for the night with this child and he has to share a room, don't ask me what you do!

Whenever possible, do not tell a small child about something nice you've planned for him until five minutes before it's going to happen. As you know, somebody is always getting sick.

By the way, do take some pictures of your second child, and your third, fourth, and seventh. Their feelings are so hurt later on if you don't. I've never done it, but putting your children's voices on tape over the years must be fun, too.

Don't spend a lot of money on your child's phonograph. You'll need a new one next year anyway.

These days, the toy situation in general is enough to drive any mother up the wall. There are one or two reputable manufacturers who make durable wooden toys or safe metal ones, but most toys are made of plastic and made, quite deliberately, to break within a week. After years of crunching little bits of self-destruct cars into the carpet and hammering tin trucks back into shape, I've finally made a rule which the kids reluctantly accept: No plastic toys, no tin toys, and nothing advertised on television.

If you have a lot of kids, use a different color wrapping paper for each child's Christmas presents from the family. Saves writing cards—most of them still can't read anyway. As a matter of fact, kids love to make their own wrapping paper. Give them a roll of white shelf paper, felt-tipped pens, and little boxes of paper stars and dots. It keeps them busy for hours and saves you the trouble of doing it yourself.

Withhold a few Christmas presents for times when they'll be much more appreciated.

Keep a small stock of "things to do" hidden away in a closet for a child who has to stay in bed or in the house. They're handy, too, for those emergency birthday present you haven't time to go out to buy.

To entertain a child who's really sick, make a Jack Horner pie of small presents. Indicate on tags attached to the ribbons when each gift should be opened.

middle-aged children, aged six to twelve: schools

Aside from the Vietnam war, I can't think of a more highly controversial subject than that of schools, schooling, teachers, and education in general. Furthermore, by the time this book comes out, the Vietnam war may be over, or we may be enmeshed in some other military pursuit, but the subject of schools will continue to be highly controversial and in a state of change for a long time to come. Because, as I've already stated, an educator is one of the many things I am not, I am reluctant to voice any high-level educational theories. Come to think of it, I don't have any to voice—like the rest of the country, I am uncertain.

But never mind all that. The fact is that school is the most prominent item on the middle-aged child's calendar, taking up more than half his day, and providing him with his first real brush with the outside world. The way he feels about learning *now* will influence, even determine, his attitudes and behavior in that outside world for the rest of his life, so it's with no small trepidation that I embark on this large, explosive topic—I have such unoriginal, uncontroversial, un-unconventional things to say. I wish I had some beautiful, illuminating thoughts to contribute; instead . . . well, instead, I'll just plunge in.

homework

Keep track, especially in the early years, of what your child is doing in the way of homework—how many subjects he has each night, approximately how much time he's supposed to spend on each one. The most radical teachers of today will admit that in order to promote good "work habits," children, just like adults, need a quiet place and an uninterrupted block of time in which to study, even if the work only consists of reading four pages of *The Cat in the Hat*. I don't mean that all family life has to come to an abrupt halt while he's reading his four pages; he'll just have to get used to little noises, other voices in other rooms, but if you provide him now with his own quiet place, he'll demand it for himself later on.

It's almost too obvious to mention, but never do a child's homework for him. If he asks you to quiz him before a test or to read over a composition for minor mistakes, you ought to find the time for that, and if he asks you to explain some simple matter of spelling or grammar, that's fine, too. But if he comes wandering in to you for help in New Math or fancy phonetics, both of which are just as much of an enigma to you as they are to him, don't monkey with it. You might get it all wrong and it's much better to convince him that he should ask his teacher, who will get it all right.

television

This is the time to make a firm rule about television and stick to it: With very rare exceptions, No TV on School Nights. You'll hear wild screams of anguish to the effect that everybody else does—an exaggeration, of course—and that he's finished all his homework so why can't he? Well, O.K., why can't he? My reasoning goes like this: If his homework is done (right after supper seems to be the best time for homework, by the way—it gives the kids a little time to unwind in before they hit the books again), and it's not yet time for bed, he is indeed entitled to a period of relaxation. But to me, relaxation and television are not only not synonymous; they are, in fact, the very antithesis of each other, because for children, TV is an acknowledged stimulator. (I don't know of any other medium that can claim the distinction of being both stimulating and boring at the same time. Some distinction!)

If you don't happen to agree with me about this, let me point out a couple of other drawbacks before I give up. If your child watches television every night, he'll soon get hooked on weekly programs. There may come the night when he still has homework to do, but he wants to watch the show. He'll end up watching the show and not doing his homework, or watching the show *while* he's doing his homework which is an even more disastrous habit to get into. Pretty soon, he'll start reading books while the television is on, too: the ultimate catastrophe is that he may never start reading books! End of speech.

When our girls were kids, there was no television, but there was radio. It presented many of the same problems. We used to let Mary and Linda pick their own programs, but they were never allowed to get into the habit of having the radio on as background noise. Letting kids choose specific shows they want to watch at times that seem reasonable to parents can help control the situation. Having a second television set helps keep the peace, but I think it should be a "floating" portable set that does not stay in the child's room. It will also then be available when someone is ill in a room with no set or when the major machine breaks down.

school problems

If you sense that your child is having trouble in school—in one particular subject, or with too much homework, do something about it immediately. Don't be afraid. Mothers used to be fiercely defensive and protective of their kids, but the pendulum has swung. Now we're all scared blue about this occult idiocy, the monstrous mystique of college. We don't have the nerve to complain about too much homework. We don't have the nerve to question the capability of a teacher. And we should. I should, you should. If it's a teacher you like, be honest about your child. Compare notes. His behavior may be different at home from what it is in school. The teacher may not know that he stays up until twelve o'clock at night trying to complete work the rest of the class does easily. Whatever it is, nobody's going to find out nothin' if you don't speak up.

If it's a teacher you don't like, don't be intimidated. (Yes, you *do* have a right not to like a teacher. You can't very well fire her the way you can fire a pediatrician, but you can put the beady eye on her, too, and get her to tell you what she feels about your child. She may turn out to be more intuitive and intelligent than you thought.) Ask your questions, and as tactfully as possible, voice your objections. The worst a teacher can do is loathe you—and your child will probably get into college anyway. At best, the teacher will be sympathetic and helpful, and your child will only have to stay up until eleven at night.

These days, even elementary schools have tremendous administrative problems. They don't have to cope with student riots or faculty dissension, but they are always underfinanced and understaffed. An understaffed school cannot always spot an individual student's little problem in time to prevent it from becoming a big one. But if the student with the little problem is your child, you probably can—after all, he's yours and you know him better than the school does. Trust your own instincts. If *you* suspect that your child has trouble reading and the school insists he has nothing of the sort, take him to a reading clinic and find out for yourself. There are reading clinics all over the country, now. It may be just a passing fad, but it seems to me that every other child you run into has some form of dyslexia—a lovely new word for reading problems. Maybe *dyslexia* and *television* are synonymous!

If your child is falling way behind in French, ask the school to give him some extra help before he sinks forever into the quagmire of irregular verbs. If the school is too understaffed to provide a teacher for him, ask them to recommend a tutor. Your child may consider this utterly humiliating; all kids hate to admit they're being tutored (almost as much as they hate to admit they're getting psychiatric help), but rather than see him irrevocably undermined in one particular area, I would go ahead with the tutoring in spite of his objections. When a kid feels like a failure in one subject, he sometimes loses his self-confidence in all his other subjects as well.

about the children

Do everything you can to combat *grade*-competition and promote *self*-competition in your child. In a progressive school, this is easy to do; in an ordinary school, it's much harder. Parents are competitive about their children, too. If some smug ninny tells you how brilliantly her kid is doing, don't be put down. For all you know, she's lying.

Although schools don't officially accept anything but out-and-out illness as an excuse for absence, be a freethinker. When your child seems tense and overworked, let him stay home for a day and catch up quietly on his own. Whenever I do this, I simply call the school and say, "She's not really sick but she's terribly tired." They've never objected yet.

Even if you're shy about visiting your child's school, do it anyway. P-TA meetings and class meetings are really the best way to find out what the current thought is on allowances, bedtimes, traveling alone, clothes, etc. Naturally, you don't have to do what everybody else is doing, but it's interesting information to have and useful ammunition when your child tries the "but *all* the kids in my class are allowed . . ." routine.

On the traditional parents' visiting day, you should not only turn up, but, especially with a girl, go one step further. Ask her if she has a preference for what you wear. If so, gratify it, unless of course, she has some giddy scheme to show you off in a pants suit. If she doesn't care what you wear, just be underdressed rather than overdressed (suit, skirt and sweater, wool dress, but no pants), and go easy on the make-up and the perfume.

I happen to think there are altogether too many organized extracurricular activities, and it's usually the fault of the parents. Every precious golden nugget of time must be put to good Puritan use—if your kid isn't playing scales on the piano, she's skating; if she isn't skating, she's Scouting; and when she isn't scaling, skating, or Scouting, she's at some unbelievable dancing school where they are teaching her and her reluctant brother how to Fox Trot! (Now *there's* a handy dance to know—I can hardly remember how it goes myself.)

I know dancing school often seems stuffy, irrelevant and anachronistic, but it *is* a way of bringing boys and girls together in fairly large groups where they can learn a good deal about social behavior.

Take music lessons, for instance. We all want to believe our children are talented at something—a serious national defect, that. Why shouldn't some children have *no* discernible talent whatsoever from birth on? And do we have to put the six-year-old's Art Class Masterpieces in the living room? How about their own room having a cork wall? To get rid of the pile-up, suggest a review of the artist's work, and get him to help decide which ones to keep. There's something very schizoid about all this parental talent-scouting anyhow, because for all the pronouncements about how creative their children are, what do the parents say when the children grow up and want to continue being creative? They say, "What do you mean, you want to be a ballet dancer (concert pianist, actor, painter)? You must be out of your mind. It's a most unrewarding life and you can't make any money at it!"

Now that I've gotten that off my chest, it's obviously incumbent upon me to point out that if your child *wants* to take lessons, even if he shows no discernible talent whatsoever, you should let him because it's fun. But before you invest in a Steinway Grand or a Goya guitar, wait a few months to see how long the passion lasts. It may not. And for the energetic type who wants to sample riding, skating, music lessons, and dancing lessons all in one year, you'll have to point out that this is going to put a strain on his schedule and a strain on your budget.

afternoon play groups

Afternoon play groups are one form of extracurricular activity of which I actually approve, especially for city children, and more especially for boys who begin to feel awfully cooped up in apartments if their school doesn't have an all-day program for them. Some groups are better than others; check with the school, other parents, and your own child to determine which one is the best and closest.

These groups often function during Christmas and Easter vacation, too, and they'll give you the choice of paying a lump sum for the whole period, or by the day, which is more expensive. However, if you have the kind of child who changes his mind easily (one day he feels like going, the next day he doesn't), paying by the day is cheaper in the long run.

My final word on extracurricular this and extracurricular that—what about extracurricular reading, sleeping, loafing, looking out the window? Nobody's allowed to do those things any more. In the winter, especially, what do you say we leave our poor little kids alone to feel and think and grow, or even deliberately waste time—because when they're adults, they won't get much chance.

summers

Summers are a different matter altogether. After eight months of having too much to do, now your kids have nothing to do, unless you organize it for them. In the suburbs, this is easy; you can arrange tennis, swimming and riding lessons to supplement informal neighborhood ball games and picnics. (Which you have arranged to supplement informal congregations in your back yard, which in turn you have arranged to supplement, etc., etc. In other words, there's always a lot of arranging to do.) But if you live way out in the country where there aren't any kids around, or in the city where there isn't any tennis, swimming or riding, summer camp is probably the best way to dispose of those long, hot months.

day camp

Day camp is the ideal solution for kids under eight (most sleep-away camps won't take them until they're eight) or for kids who are squeamish about being away from home. Five days a week (or four or three), your child will be scooped up at nine in the morning and returned to you at five—tired, sticky, and happy.

choosing a sleep-away camp

Sleep-away camp is obviously a more complicated proposition. Should it be one month or two? Coeducational or not? A special camp for tennis, sailing, music, French, or the all-round outdoor variety? Your child has to be consulted about all of this. It is, after all, his vacation and he's entitled to his views on how it should be spent. He may have even heard through his classmates about a camp that he's dying to go to; if so, this will save you the trouble of hunting one up. If not, his school, the parents of his friends and/or a professional school-camp advisor can help you.

Once you have zeroed in on your choice, get in touch with the camp in the late fall because most camps are completely full by February. If the owner of the camp offers to come to your house to show you pictures and talk to you, by all means let him. Don't get nervous. He doesn't want to look you over to assess your suitability or anything—he simply wants to show you pictures and talk to you, and let you and your child talk to him.

231

Now for clothes and equipment: You will, around about March, be sent a horrendously long list of items to buy; don't be too depressed—the first year is always the most expensive.

1. The foot locker, sleeping bag, canteen, and other equipment will last for years.

2. The fourteen pairs of underwear, and socks, the seven pairs of shorts and polo shirts won't even last the summer because the laundry loses half of it and your kid loses the other half, so buy exactly what you're told to buy.

3. The camp "dress" uniform or special jacket which is worn only once or twice all summer is the one place where you can economize; try to buy these things, secondhand, from the parents of a child who's outgrown them.

4. In the sporting equipment line, a tennis racquet and balls are a must for most camps, but don't bother with guns, bows and arrows, or fishing poles the first year. The camp supplies them anyway. After one summer, if your child has fallen in love with fishing, for instance, you can give him a pole for Christmas.

5. Go with your child to the camp outfitting place in April. *No later.* Later, the joint will be jumping with screaming kids and mothers, it'll take you twice as long to get everything done. And if you order the stuff early, the store will name-tape it for you; I'm sure I don't have to point out the advantages of that!

If, by any chance, you can't get to the store in April and do have to do your own name-taping, remember to allow three weeks for ordering the name tapes. An indelible marking pencil works pretty well for shoes, underwear and sheets, but there's no easy way out for anything else. Iron-on name tapes come right off. Don't use them.

Even if you have the time and the inclination to drive your child to camp, resist the impulse. Orientation to camp begins on the bus or the train, and initial friendships are made then; if your child arrives separately, he'll arrive lonely. As far as coming home is concerned, if your child wants you to pick him up, fine, but if he's had a good summer, he'll probably much rather come home with his pals.

visiting

Some camps specifically designate one or two parents' weekends and request that you do not show up at any other time; others are more lenient and suggest a time when you might like to appear but are cordial to you at other times, as long as it isn't during the first ten days. Either way, be warned: Although you ought to visit (if you don't, your kid will think you don't love him), it's never a very satisfactory experience. The motel you stay in will probably be horrid; you'll discover, too late, that the state is dry and you didn't think to bring a bottle with you; watching sports events will be boring and buggy; and worst of all, your child will seem to be acutely embarrassed by you. You'll feel as though you've forgotten how to talk to him. In a sense, you have— not because you're losing your parental touch, but because for the first time, you have no shared experiences to talk about. Don't worry. After he's been home for a week, you'll be back in touch with each other again.

home-sickness

It's the rare kid who doesn't feel a twinge of homesickness during the first couple of weeks at camp. Don't be unnerved by wistful or even complaining letters. And in your letters, avoid using the word homesick; the minute you tell a kid that's what he is, you're greatly improving the chances that that's what he'll be. If, however, you are bombarded with "Please, *please* let me come home" letters and sobbing phone calls after two or three weeks, you'd better talk to the head of the camp and consider rescuing the prisoner at the halfway mark, or even right away. I'm sure there are people who feel that "sticking it out" is good for a kid's soul, but I'm not one of them. Whatever the reason is—maybe he's too young to be away, or a little neurotic (so what!), or maybe it's actually a lousy camp or the wrong camp for him—but whatever it is, I think it's cruel and inhuman treatment to make him stay. Better luck next summer.

traveling

Little kids are tireless doers. They are *not* lookers. Unless there's a great World's Fair going on, I doubt there's a city in the world that will fascinate them as much as a long stretch of beach or an endless pile of snow. My mother will be happy to delve further into this subject; as a child, she was dragged from one European city to another every summer. She didn't like it very much. Her parents, on the other hand, probably had a fine time because those were the good old days of governesses and instant baby-sitters, good hotel service and instant laundry. Until I was old enough to have a life of my own, it wasn't much fun, but in looking back over the period, I realize how much my life was influenced and enriched by those early years of exposure to new and exciting sights, sounds, and tastes.

Today, if you're contemplating this kind of trip, you'd first better ask yourself the following questions:

1. Who's going to do all the kids' laundry? 2. How does your three-year-old behave in a restaurant? In that case, how does the idea of eating three meals a day in Chock Full o' Nuts or its equivalent grab you? 3. If you're lost and it's way past their accustomed lunch time, are your little children nice and quiet when you ask directions of a policeman? 4. Is there anything new and riveting about the local zoo, because that's where you'll be spending most of your time? 5. Or does your three-year-old love museums and churches? He *does*? 6. You won't know how to get a baby-sitter for the evening so you won't be able to go to the theater or the opera. Will you mind watching television in your room every night instead? (Some hotels do advertise baby-sitters, but they often turn out to be unavailable when you want them or, for all you know in advance, so ghoulish that you wouldn't dare leave your children with them. And they cost an arm and a leg.)

Okay, joke over. Find yourself the stretch of beach or the pile of snow. Since big hotels and fancy motels charge sixty dollars a day for a room whether it's inhabited by an infant or a senior citizen, here again, I'd like to put in a plug for the Efficiency Motel, or even better, the well-equipped cottage with several bedrooms, a kitchen, and a living room that rents by the week. You'll be cooking breakfasts and making sandwiches for lunch, but you'll save a fortune and, as I implied before, kids don't like eating in restaurants three times a day anyway, it's too confining. By the evening, you won't mind staying home with them; there probably aren't any theaters or concerts to go to, and besides, after

about the children

loping up and down the dunes or the slopes all day, you're as tired as your kids are. *And,* they're still going to get up at seven in the morning—*that* never changes!

Luckily, in the six-to-twelve group, the older the child, the smaller the party. If you want to invite the whole class, go ahead, it's your funeral. It's also unnecessary. Middle-aged kids often prefer not to have the opposite sex at a party.

Written invitations are optional, phone calls are perfectly okay.

Big at-home parties (ten or more) last about three hours. Allow a half an hour for late arrivals and present-opening, one and a half hours for entertainment, and one hour for eating.

entertainment: birthday parties

If you don't want to deal with this yourself and you have the money, there are many available kinds of outside entertainment to import: magicians are still in vogue (although I've always hated them—as a breed, they have such creepy personalities), there are people who bring trained pets, people who come with a movie projector and show cartoons or feature films, people who come and play games. Talented teen-agers can sometimes be found to organize and give the party for you. This is less expensive than professional talent and little kids seem to like this age group as much if not better than very old, old people in their thirties and forties.

home entertainment

If you don't mind coping yourself, or don't want to spend the money for the above services, you can rent your own projector and film, and for free, borrow the services of your husband for projectionist. Or manufacture your own, highly organized bunch of games such as:

Camouflage: Hide fifteen smallish objects in plain view (like a gold wedding ring on a brass andiron); let each kid choose a partner, which is more companionable than going it alone; give each pair a pencil and pad, and dictate the list of hidden objects to them. The pair who finds the most within twenty minutes (or fifteen, or ten, depending on how impatient they begin to get) wins.

Charades: Divide the group into two teams; put each team in a different room; stand in the middle of the two rooms and run it like a relay race: The team who gets through your list of book titles, song titles, or commercial slo-

gans first wins. Don't let the kids make up their own lists—
it'll take them all day.

Spelling Game: On eight-by-eight hunks of shirt cardboard, write big capital letters (one letter per hunk) which,
when lined up in the correct order, will make one big word,
or several smaller anagrammed ones. Each team gets a set of
letters, identical, of course, and each team member keeps his
letter. From your list of anagrams, shout out a word. The
first team to arrange itself, line itself up, with the correct
spelling in the correct order, wins. On a word with fewer
than all the letters, the unused kids have to get out of the
way in a hurry. It's quite a funny game.

Memory Game: Give the kids two minutes in which to
memorize a tray full of small objects—paper clips, stamp,
safety pin—then take the tray away, and the person who
remembers the most things wins.

The Sound Game: Ahead of time, assemble a bunch of
objects with which you can make identifiable noises (opening an umbrella, opening a soda bottle, lighting a wooden
match, running your finger against the teeth of a comb,
filing your nails with an emery board, dialing a telephone,
riffling through a deck of cards). Make the kids close their
eyes and guess what the sounds are, one by one.

Sardines: This is good in rambling and already banged-
up houses only. One person is chosen to hide somewhere,
anywhere, in a totally darkened house. After counting one
hippopotamus, two hippopotamus, up to fifty, the rest of
the group starts looking for him. Anybody who finds him
climbs in with him, sneakily, so the others don't see or hear
where he's gone. Eventually, fifteen children are crammed in
a bathtub, and the sixteenth, the last, and the loser, is the
one to hide next. Marvelous game—I still play it myself.

If you live in the country, have a scavenger hunt. (Each
child has a list of peculiar items to procure—a gum wrapper,
a grasshopper, a pine cone—and the child who completes
the list first wins.) A treasure hunt, in which children,
either singly or in pairs, are given clues which lead them to
other clues which eventually lead them to the hidden treasure, is a swell invention calculated to keep you up all night.
There are many ways to set up a treasure hunt, but two of
them are having the starting clue only lead to the next clue,

236

to the next, and so forth (If you use this method, the clues have to be easy unless you want a bunch of whining, frustrated kids, because if they get stuck on a clue, they have nowhere to go next except home); I prefer the second method: Type out all the clues on one page—one page for each team. Then the team is free to look for the clues it thinks it can find. For instance:

> Men make money
> Wives make tea
> Bees make honey
> French make Brie
> Dog makes Bunny hide or flee
> But only God can make a . . . ?

When the team finally thinks of the word tree, they will find, let's say, the letter F pasted on the bark. When they've collected all of the letters, and written them down in order (Clue 1-F, clue 2-R), they'll find the word *fridge*, which is where the treasure will be hidden. For a more sophisticated group, scramble the order so that once they have assembled all the letters, they must still unscramble them before they get to the treasure. This makes it fairer for everybody because any fool can see that FRI is going to be fridge but GER won't tell you much.

food

Forget the creamed chicken and peas routine. It was always loathsome, nobody ever ate it, and nobody ever will. Instead, try hamburgers and hot dogs, ice cream and cake; pizza, ice cream and cake; hero sandwiches, ice cream and cake; or millions of cold cuts, spreads, different kinds of bread (let the kids make their own disgusting messes and give a prize for the most unusual mess) and ice cream and cake.

To polish off the subject of large, at-home birthday parties, let me tell you just one thing: in order to give a totally successful one, keep the children so busy that they scarcely have time to go to the bathroom! It's all a matter of vast pre-organization. Plan more games than you think you'll need, the leftovers will come in handy next year. Unfortunately, this is not true of the food. And when you give a really good party for kids, you have as good a time at it as they do. Honestly, I swear it!

If you'd rather take three or four kids out than have twenty careening around your house, here are some suggestions:

small parties, not at home, for three or four kids

Boys: Take them to a hockey game, a baseball game, a football game, to the circus, ice-skating, bowling, to a good adventure movie. (No movies with love stuff, it makes them crawl the walls.)

Girls: Take them to a cheery musical, the ballet, the ice show (if these are available), ice-skating, maybe bowling, to a good movie about animals. (Just before they're ready for the people-love stuff, little girls seem to fall in love with animals.)

Food: If you live in the city, both boys and girls like Chinese restaurants, but boys don't like fancy places. Some girls might like the glamour of a big hotel dining room—it depends on your daughter and your bank account.

If you can deliver the kids home after the outing, it's nice but not obligatory.

casual non-birthday entertainment

If your child lives near other children, he'll begin to work out impromptu arrangements for himself at this age. Just make sure the parent of the other child knows where he is and when to expect him home if the date is at your house. Also, when your child unexpectedly turns up with a friend and the house is messy or you're eating leftovers for dinner, don't worry. Everybody else's house has the same dual personality, company and private.

Once the guest has arrived, the kids won't need entertaining for long. Just keep an eye out from time to time to see that they're not dismantling the television set, making joke phone calls, or if they're girls, trying on all your evening dresses and dabbling in your make-up.

overnight guests

Overnight guests are the most fun entertainment there is for kids. But if you think you're dealing with a less permissive mother than you—one who cares what her child eats,

238

about the children

or what time he goes to bed—call her and find out what she has in mind. Then try to make your own child conform or the friend won't be allowed back. Some parents, for instance, never leave a twelve-year-old child alone in a house. If you're planning to be out for even a couple of hours in the middle of the day, make sure this is all right with the other mother.

Once in a while, a youngish child will get homesick in the middle of the night. (To a youngish child, eleven is the middle of the night.) You'll feel as though you've done something wrong. You probably haven't; that's just the way that kid is. The only thing to do is call the parents and let them come and get him, which is hard on your own child. You can make him feel better by telling him how much more independent he is than his friend. It's also hard on you, because you'll wonder what the other parents are thinking. Don't fret; they're probably wondering if their own child is still going to be living with them when he's forty. It has undoubtedly happened to them before, and they know by now that they should have warned you. Conversely, if you're the one with the skittish sleep-overer, you must alert other parents.

If you have the unspeakably bad fortune to have a guest who feels sick in the middle of the night, call his parents and get him off the premises fast. In the middle of the night? You know you wouldn't! Temperatures and colds are bad enough, but the absolute nadir is the kid who says he's going to throw up. Whether he does or he doesn't almost doesn't matter (almost), because it's the anticipation for you and for him that's so agonizing.

ways for mothers to entertain children

Ways for mothers to entertain children break down into three categories: The kind only the child enjoys, the kind only the mother enjoys, and the kind they both enjoy.

Playing with dolls, playing hide-and-go-seek, playing with a Lego set, freezing while your child skates in the dead of winter, going to the boat show when you hate boats, all belong in this first category and, like it or not, you have to do a certain amount of it. And if you do it grudgingly, you might as well not bother at all. Try conning another mother, whose child has similar interests, into joining you on the outdoor excursions. That way, you'll have company and someone to grumble to.

The kind only the mother enjoys usually involve activities that are simply too sophisticated for the child or that go on too long. The attention span of a middle-aged child is obviously greater than that of the younger group but he'll get bored just as quickly at something he doesn't like.

Beware of cultural outings. It's commendable of you to want to imbue your child with a sense of the aesthetic things in life, but a little Rembrandt goes a long way, as does a little Beethoven, and a very little *Swan Lake*. It's a moot point as to which is more discouraging for a child, sitting too long in one place or tramping too long on marble floors where there's nothing to sit down on but a marble bench.

If you can ease your children into the arts without their knowing it's happened, you'll be creating in them a permanently insatiable and lovely mental appetite. So move slowly and thoughtfully when you start.

For boys, is there a Museum of Science and Industry in your area, or a Museum of Natural History, an IBM exhibit? An exhibit of da Vinci's war machines? That's a wonderfully sneaky one—from there you may edge them into etchings, and *then* paintings. Boys love exhibits where they're allowed to touch or where things actually work. I don't blame them. I do, too.

For girls, how about an exhibit of old dolls and old doll-houses, clothes of an earlier period, theater costumes, or Russian crown jewelry?

I wonder why parents inevitably start their children off with ancient Egyptians and ancient Greeks. The Egyptians, except for the heads of Nefertiti and a couple of spooky mummies, are really very dull for a child—wall after wall of two-dimensional foreigners, all facing sideways and all carrying sheaves of wheat. Greeks? Nothing but oversized horses and smooth, white war veterans, amputees all. Romulus, Remus, and Pompeiian pots aren't very jazzy either. When kids are old enough to understand the history behind all of this, they'll like it better, but in the meantime, I'm for showing them modern art, Pop Art, Op Art—or anything at all that's bright and colorful.

The approach to music should be much the same, only here, although bright and colorful is important, the actual period is not. Small kids will go for Mozart, and John Cage will appeal to them about as much as it does to most of us. For musical beginners, the other vital element is noise. All children start by liking loud, fast music and only later do they begin to acquire the patience for the slow, quiet, contemplative stuff. Some of the most gorgeous Brahms and Ravel would be utterly wasted on them. If you're going to take your child to a concert, don't take him to any old concert. Select a program that'll give him and the music a chance.

Into this same category of entertainment that only the mother enjoys, falls a whole bunch of female errands like shopping for your own dresses, having your hair done while your daughter sits around reading old magazines, and including either your daughter or your son in on a lunch with an old friend. If your child understands what's in store for him and still wants to accompany you, fine, but don't delude yourself into thinking that you're entertaining him—you're simply entertaining yourself and dragging him along.

The last category is obviously the nicest: the kind you both enjoy. I guess you arrive at this by cleverly nurturing one of your own pleasures and your child will eventually enjoy it, too. My bag happens to be movies—it amounts to a mania—and I started my kids in early with animal pictures or adventure pictures, took them out (reluctantly) as soon as they were bored, and now it's a mania with all of us. Sometimes we go on movie binges and see four in one night; if there's a good science fiction double feature, we manage to cram in five. On New Year's Eve, we rent a projector, borrow six or seven great old pictures from an endearing and generous friend who has his own private film library and watch movies all night long. We invite a few of our movie-fiend friends over with their children, eat in between reel changes, and never have to worry about what our kids are doing on the wildest night of the year.

A somewhat less unique passion of mine is reading. If it happens to be one of yours, you can always take a child to the children's room of the library on a rainy day and let him loose while you read your own book. Let him get his own library card (a very prestigious event) and he'll begin to make his way there alone. You'll save money on books, too.

Certain chores or projects can be fun. A girl might like to

help you plan meals and go with you, or even go alone, if she's nine or older, to the supermarket. Or you can make a race out of a nasty job. "Helen, you clean your closet, Gordon will clean his closet, I'll clean mine and let's see who wins." Give the winner a small prize, the loser, loud, compensatory praise, and everybody will be happy because you've gotten a dreary necessity over with in a nice way.

Since most kids love to paint, if you're the type who knows about primers and brushes and turp, *et al.,* let them help you paint their own room, or some porch furniture—something that doesn't matter too much if it isn't done perfectly.

The things that you and your children enjoy together are often things your husband will enjoy, too, if he has the time (Saturdays, Sundays, and holidays). There are also some father specialties, like taking a kid of either sex to his office on Saturday if he has a little work to do. Office equipment is great—paper clips, new pencils, fresh pads of paper, typewriters (if the kid is careful and mechanically inclined), and the Xerox machine, which only Daddy should operate.

Boys like to go with their fathers to get the car washed or overhauled; it's something they're going to need to know about someday, anyway

There are loads of stay-at-home possibilities for rainy weekends or evenings. If you like bridge, teach the kids; anybody over nine can learn. Monopoly is still fun if you don't play it too often (when you do play it, stick strictly to the rules and don't get soft-hearted, because the game will go on forever if you lend rent money to your son who keeps landing on someone else's hotel-laden Park Place). If you have several children, many of the games I mentioned in the birthday party section are also fun to play with them.

health:
bedtimes

Bedtimes for middle-aged children vary enormously from family to family. Don't be influenced by what other people do; it never affects your own children unless one of them has an overnight guest with a fussy mother.

Frankly, I don't believe in rigid bedtimes. As a child, I resented them terribly and cheated on them whenever I could. Each year for years, my bedtime was advanced by some ridiculously minuscule amount like fifteen minutes which, when I was ten, forced me into the sack in the middle of the Lone Ranger. I got my revenge by setting the alarm

about the children

for midnight and reading in the bathroom until it was time to get up for school. What I also got was very bad eyes and the reputation for being the kind of child who required a great deal of sleep (four hours really wasn't quite enough, even for me). This idiotic game—popping me into bed early every night to compensate for the sleep they didn't know I'd lost the night before—turned into an unbreakable cycle that didn't end until I was about fourteen.

Some kids need more sleep than others, some kids know when they are tired whereas others refuse to admit it, and any kid can be tired one night and full of energy the next. The best solution is to have a flexible bedtime (between eight and nine, or between eight-thirty and nine-thirty, for instance) and then expect the kids to go to bed exactly when you tell them to, within that time period. If you haven't made a *cause célèbre* out of it, they probably will.

When two kids, close in age, share a room, I find it difficult to make the younger one go to bed earlier. Furthermore, it doesn't work because the older one either awakens the younger one when he gets around to going to bed, or the younger one waits up for him. It's easier to put them to bed at the same time. The older one may complain about the inequality of your decision, but you can remind him of other age privileges that he does benefit from.

health in general

Middle-aged kids are usually pretty rugged. At least they don't get dangerously ill very often and they've just about outgrown the children's contagious disease stage. Just make sure you send them for the obvious checkups—pediatrician, oculist, and dentist.

If your dentist recommends orthondontia, even if it's a borderline case, do it. It's terribly expensive but well worth it. These days, orthodontists don't begin their work until children are preadolescent or in their early teens. As a result, most children, especially girls, are mature enough and vain enough to cooperate with whatever procedure—elastic bands, retainers, wires—is involved. But if your child is a recidivist retainer-loser, you might consider making him pay, at least partially, for the replacements; he'll be a little more careful in the future. The same goes for glasses.

Kids are getting adolescent earlier than they used to. At the first sign of skin trouble, send your sons as well as daughters to the best skin doctor around; you may save them years of anguish.

Buy your daughter her own hair dryer; it will encourage her to wash her hair more often. This is good for the complexion, too. And it's also enlightened self-interest. She won't take yours.

Now is the time when kids, boys especially, break bones, get cut on glass, etc. Without turning into Portnoy's mother, make sure they know all of the run-of-the-mill safety rules. Your husband can teach them about power tools (simple ones, anyway) and electricity; you can make the rules about crossing streets and roughhousing around the house. If they haven't learned about crossing streets by now, you may not have to worry about any of the other problems.

If a middle-aged child has to go to the hospital, he, too, will be happier in a semiprivate room or a ward rather than in a private room.

helping around the house

When it comes to helping around the house, minor tasks are about the most you can expect from these kids. They can empty wastebaskets and ashtrays, take dishes to the kitchen, and pick up their own toys. Girls of ten can make their beds and help set the table. Boys of ten can also make their beds but probably won't. The spread will be on, but what's underneath will look like a relief map of the Rockies. You might be able to persuade them to carry in logs, or collect kindling, but they'll develop a curious block if you ask them to take out the garbage. They won't say no, they'll just forget. Every day.

With boys *and* girls, if you can just get them to be fairly neat and put their clothes in the laundry once in a while, you're doing pretty well. Console yourself with the thought that the neatness problem will get a lot worse before it gets better. Wait'll you hit the teen-age bracket—that's enough to make you move to a hotel.

manners: basic

In the manners department, by now, they know what they're supposed to do, but they often forget. Most of the time, they don't mean to be rude; middle-aged kids are just vague. Remind them, as you do with littler ones, before you go somewhere with them or before they go alone, to say please and thank you. Also get them in the habit of

about the children

writing thank-you notes for presents or for weekends they spend at other peoples' houses. This is a little nicety that has almost gone out of style . . . It has? . . . but I think it's a nice little nicety that ought to stay on. By the way, until you're sure of your child's letter-writing prowess, you'd better check over the letters to make sure they're not toss-offs. People seem to be rather charmed by peculiar spelling, don't nag him about that, but you should try to elicit something slightly more engaging than "Dear Mrs. X., Thank you for the weekend it was swell." As soon as he begins to develop his own prose style, stop looking over his shoulder because then it becomes an invasion of privacy.

There are some other things that kids can now begin to do: They can get up when adults come into a room (old-fashioned but attractive), they can open doors for adults and let them go through them first, they can even give up their seats on buses. I almost hesitate to mention that last one; it's now so rare that your child might get himself arrested for bizarre behavior, but it's worth taking the chance.

I always notice children who have good manners when they come to my house. They do not act like finks, and their friends don't seem to think they're finks. I guess good manners are still an O.K. thing to have.

telephone manners

Telephone manners include the preliminary "hello," "who's calling, please," "just a minute, please," but some other requirements should now be taught. Whereas a little child will run to fetch you to the phone (little children love to run around on any pretext), an older child tends to hold the phone one foot away from his mouth and scream for you. Aside from the possibility that you won't hear him, there is the certainty that he will drive the person on the other end crazy. It's terribly unpleasant, as you undoubtedly know. Do not let your child do this.

Writing down phone messages at this age is a haphazard affair. **How about making it easier for everyone by seeing to it that there is a message pad and pencil firmly attached to something within reach of the phone?**

If you have just moved into a large house or you've decided to install new phones, there is a dandy invention you might consider: the local buzzer system, which any small child can understand. If he's in one part of the house, you're in another, and he's answered the phone, which is for you, all he has to do is push Hold, Local, and buzz the room you're in, or the room nearest to it (the buzzers are loud), and tell you who is on the phone. This will dispose of the screaming problem, and it's wonderfully useful for all forms of family intercommunication—to summon people to dinner and so forth.

While we're on the subject of phones, teach your kids how to make calls as well as receive them. No "Is Tommy there?" Instead, "Is Tommy there, please," or "May I please speak to Tommy?" No early Sunday morning calls unless they're to a family who's famous for getting up early, no calls during dinner, and no calls when the kids are supposed to be doing their homework. This last is the hardest to enforce but important, because if they talk on the phone all night, they're either not doing their homework at all, or they're doing it on the phone with a friend.

Finally, no lengthy phone calls if you're a one-phone family. The boss may be trying to reach your husband. If you have several children, I recommend installing either an extra, private number so that one phone is reserved for incoming calls and the other for outgoing ones, or two consecutive numbers on a rotary system so that if one phone is busy, the other rings automatically. The added expense is relatively minor, the trouble it saves you is enormous.

guests

Much of the information that applies to little kids and your guests applies equally to this age group. When it comes to how, when, and where they should be around, again, it all depends on you, your child, and the kind of guests you're having. If your child thinks he's too old to appear in pajamas, or if *you* think he is, let him wear clean, casual clothes. With the exception of a formal wedding reception, there's no reason to get him all gussied up.

Middle-aged kids can be helpful at parties. They, too, can pass hors d'oeuvres. They can also take the guests' coats, fetch and carry for you and answer the phone. But with added maturity come a few negative aspects.

Now that they've mastered the art of conversation, they may monopolize it, which is fine for an old family friend, but awkward when you're entertaining V.I.P.s or a huge room full of people. Remind your kids to give someone else a

about the children

chance and give them some idea, ahead of time, of how long you'd like them to hang around.

Kids this age may take advantage of the fact that you're all on public display by renewing an old argument, or, if they're younger and energetic, by leaping around on the furniture and riding their bikes through the hall. If possible, avoid an out-and-out fight (a public put-down is painfully humiliating for kids). Raise your eyebrows, roll your eyes, whisper your warning or beckon him to another room where you can deliver it privately. Then, if he persists, I'm afraid you will have to reprimand him right there in front of everybody.

Some kids are innately shy and hate big parties. Others, as they approach their teens, suddenly *become* shy, or moody, or uncommunicative. Or maybe the prospect of passing shrimps and making surface conversation has lost its allure and they'd rather keep to their own quarters. Unless they're of vital assistance to you, I'd let them off the hook. They won't be very congenial if they're making a command performance and besides, it's your party, not theirs—why should they be forced to attend?

quickies for middle-aged kids

When kids persist in writing you notes or gesticulating wildly while you're on the phone, close your eyes. After a couple of times, they'll catch on and leave you alone.

Most children love pizza, hero sandwiches and TV dinners. If you don't, the ideal time to accommodate these culinary predilections is when you are having a dinner party they aren't going to be a part of; it's easy on you and nice for them.

Brilliant stocking presents at Christmas: pencils, pads, Scotch tape, flashlight batteries. (For teen-age kids: stamps, envelopes, scissors, bobby pins, emery boards, ballpoint pens, shampoo, hair spray, razor blades. Why are these brilliant presents? Because the little stinkers are always stealing yours.)

Look out for Five O'clock in the Afternoon. Everybody in the whole entire world is down and out then, but we all forget it. Take a deep breath, maybe a drink, and, most of all, take your time. Actually, this applies to all age groups.

teen-agers

To try to learn how teen-agers feel about all kinds of

things, starting with parents and including friends, food, chores, entertaining and careers, we sent out a questionnaire (which we will call RSP for Rodgers's Small Poll) to a sampling of boys and girls between the ages of thirteen and eighteen. We asked them not to identify themselves—merely to state their age and sex. The questionnaire was sent to kids in the East, the Midwest and the Far West from middle-to upper-middle-class homes, and the results were fascinating. From this highly inexhaustive poll, we gathered that most kids think their parents are O.K. They expect advice from them and frequently even take it. Without exception, they want the same kind of food served at their parties. (Mothers all over the country, get out the chips, sandwiches, Cokes and hamburgers!)

Most kids don't expect to be paid for doing chores, but to a man and woman they hate being asked to take out the garbage. Parents are sometimes "square," "puritanical," or even "weird-looking." Kids are embarrassed by parents who drink too much and fight in public. If there is a kids' party in progress, parents are definitely not invited, but most kids want them to be "in the house." They admire parents who are interested in the world around them and who are understanding about their children.

In answer to a question asking what they considered to be the most important factors in deciding on a career, they spoke as with one voice—that they wanted to do what they would be happy doing, regardless of material gains.

Teen-agers are not all they're cracked up to be. By that I mean they are not all unkempt, uncontrollable, undisciplined, undermotivated and under the covers smoking pot with a partner. Some, but not all. The majority of them strike me as being anxious rather than angry, more often kind than cruel, and more thoughtful than many of us. They may not always be thoughtful *of* us, but they are certainly thoughtful about us, and about themselves, their futures, their war, and their world, which half of them want to change and half of them want to ignore. We may not always know what they're thinking, but surely they must be the most doggedly persistent generation of thinkers this planet has ever produced. They are frequently accused of thinking too much and doing too little; perhaps if the generations

about the children

that preceded them had thought a little more and done a little less, today's kids wouldn't have to think so hard about so many things.

Well, that's what I feel about teen-agers in general. They get my love, my sympathy, and my respect. As for my own kids and their friends, they get love, sympathy, respect, and occasionally, the dubious benefit of my guidance whenever I know how to guide them and they're of a mind to be led.

money

I have never understood what to do about allowances; when kids are still living with you, still basically dependent upon you for all but the most unimportant non-essentials, it seems arbitrary and artificial to hand out little token bits of money here and there. That's not going to teach them about the economics of their future!

My three older children have never gotten allowances from me; they have a little money of their own which they've either earned or received at Christmas and on birthdays. They are quite generous about spending money on each other and on us, and remarkably abstemious about spending it on themselves.

Even though they know I'm rather vague on this subject, they don't seem to take advantage of me. They take buses instead of taxis unless I instruct them to take a taxi, and if anything, they buy fewer and less elegant clothes than they need. They also seem to have acquired a larger general sense of economics: that taxes, schools, rent and doctors are colossally expensive necessities, that cameras, camps, vacations, a second car, music lessons are colossally expensive luxuries. The one thing they haven't been told yet is exactly how much money it costs to provide them with what they have, but I'm not sure I know the answer to that one, myself.

All in all, I like my system. It's unusual, I admit, but unless the children end up in bankruptcy ten years from now, I will consider it a pleasant and successful innovation.

Working on this book with Mary has been an extraordinary experience. It has made me examine my attitudes on many subjects, and it seems to me quite remarkable that although the two of us are so different, the difference turns out to be much more a matter of style and personality than of basic approach. Our values are reasonably similar. Perhaps this is why I disagree with so little of what she says about children. But I do disagree completely on the subject of allowances.

For starters, I think children should be given pocket money allowances at the earliest possible age—not so much to teach them to save (which it may very well do) as to teach them how to spend. The amount, which can be adjusted as they grow older, should be within the average range their friends and classmates are given. And it should be theirs to spend as *they* choose, although they can be encouraged, as time goes by, to set some money aside for birthday and Christmas presents. Now, having just said that children should be free to determine how their money is spent, I will take back 10 percent of that for charity. In these days of tax-free philanthropy, I realize that 10 percent is not very much to give away. But it is a nice round figure that goes back to the Biblical custom of tithing. I think children should be taught to share very early in their lives, because if they are made aware when they are very young, they are much more likely to assume the same kind of responsibility as they grow up. The particular charity doesn't matter. A child should be allowed to pick the one that appeals to him most, put aside 10 percent of his allowance each week, and then, every three or four months, decide where it should go. What is important is that the parents remember, as kids and allowances get larger and money is earmarked for specific expenses, to fix an amount that will cover contributions as well as more "practical" things.

When it comes to clothes allowances, you have to consider not only the teen-ager's needs (and I do mean his need to conform to what everybody else is wearing), but your own ego. I remember when Mary was about fifteen and on a clothes allowance, I reminded her in November to buy evening shoes for a long dress she was going to wear to a dance at Christmas. She forgot and spent the money on books and records. I'd always bailed her out when this had happened before because I couldn't face having her go out looking ridiculous. But I realized she would never learn unless I let her live with her own mistakes, and I was determined not to come to her rescue this time. When about a week before the dance I asked her what she expected to wear and she answered, laughing, "My loafers, I guess," I went into a state of

about the children

near shock at the thought of my daughter looking so awful —probably because I felt I would be criticized. Mary's attitude was great. She didn't blame me nor did she expect to be bailed out. Happily, the story's end saved both faces and egos. At school Mary had been working as a practice-session piano teacher, and in the nick of time, the school came through with her accumulated earnings—just enough to buy the shoes and save the day.

I think it's a wise idea to exclude from a clothes allowance items that are necessary and costly—coats, for example, and the occasional party dress or suit. Also, if you take a family vacation trip for which children need extra or special clothes, you should be prepared to pay for them. Try to make the amount of the allowance realistic, discuss it with your kids, and let them share the responsibility for the final decision.

help around the house

How much help around the house should you expect from teen-agers? This is one of those it-all-depends situations. I have a friend who lives in the country in a large house with a husband, six children, a Great Dane and I think it's four cats (with cats, who counts?). This incredible lady has no outside help. None! Her older girls cook, do laundry, iron, baby-sit for the younger ones—they do everything. However, they are in less demanding schools than the ones my children are in, so they have more time. In vivid contrast, when I was growing up, maids were easier to get, and we seemed to have a lot of them (I mean a lot of them at once, not a lot of them in succession, although later on, during the war, we had that, too). It's not easy to manufacture chores if there's a staff around to do them for you (especially when so many of the chores get done in the kitchen and the cook never wants you in there); my mother had a hard time dreaming up ways for us to grow up unspoiled. She found some, though; when she puts her mind to it, she's a fairly inventive lady.

My own setup lies somewhere between the two extremes. I expect my kids to make their beds, change their sheets once a week, empty laundry hampers, clear and occasionally set the table, get ice, empty the dishwasher and make salad dressing, which is the one culinary skill I have passed on to them thus far. I also ask them to make cookies, which is a culinary skill they haven't yet been able to pass on to me. I do not pay them for any of these things. But I almost never ask them to baby-sit in the daytime with my little boys because I see no reason to penalize them for having a mother who simply goes on and on and *on* having babies. Also, I'm afraid it will turn them off babies altogether, and I'm waiting rather impatiently to be a grandmother. Also, they haven't got the time —too much homework.

One other thing I expect is that they will keep their rooms and closets neat, which I could go on expecting forever. I'm now talking about my two girls, not my son who is extremely neat—don't ask me why.

I do have one wonderful suggestion for those of you with sloppy daughters: Don't waste your breath asking them to clean out their bureau drawers because they'll tell you they've done it when all they've actually done is shift the debris around a little. Instead, about four times a year, set aside some time when you and your daughters are all together, and dump the contents of their drawers and closets out into the middle of the room. (Dumping out is the only successful method I've ever devised for cleaning out.) Then make three piles: one for the thrift shop, one for the rag collection (gray slips make great silver polishers), and one for the garbage can (ratty hairbands and socks with holes make rotten silver polishers). What's left goes either to the cleaners, to the laundry, or back in the closet. And consider yourself the mother of a compulsively neat child if more than one item goes back in the closet.

telephones By now you can count on getting pretty accurate telephone messages and your children are thoroughly adept at both making and receiving calls. With teen-agers around, even two phone numbers are not enough, unless one is very definitely yours and the other is very definitely theirs. Try giving them their own phone, with their own number and listing. Pay the basic monthly charge, make them pay anything over that, and keep track, themselves, of who called whom, long distance.

baby-sitting About this time teen-aged girls take up baby-sitting and there's a certain etiquette to be observed. It goes like this:

Your daughter should look decent. If the parents are going out and she's going to be alone with the children, clean blue jeans are all right, but if she's entertaining the

about the children

children while the parents are giving a cocktail party, they're obviously not all right.

No phone calls, in or out, and no visitors unless specific permission has been given ahead of time. Most parents would really rather not have the baby-sitter's friends around; they probably feel entitled to her undivided attention in the daytime and her undistracted ears at night. Boy friends should never be around; that *really* makes parents nervous.

No mess-making. Parents don't like to come home to soda cans, dirty ashtrays, and squashed sofa pillows.

Your daughter should be sure she has the phone numbers of the pediatrician, the parents and, if you're going to be out yourselves, the phone number where you can be reached. Then, if she can't reach the parents and has a problem, she can always ask you what to do.

If the parents are consistently late coming home, leave dirty dishes and diapers for your daughter to do, have particularly unmanageable or nasty children, or haggle over paying for carfare or an extra fifteen minutes, tell your daughter to resign from the job—tactfully but firmly.

traveling From our questionnaire to teen-agers, we concluded two main things: (1) Going away with your parents and staying in one place is fine as long as there is plenty to do and plenty of people around to do it with. (By people, I assume they mean other teen-agers; in a quiet resort, the rest of us hardly qualify for the people category.) And (2) Going away with your parents and staying in a lot of different places is also fine as long as there is plenty to do and plenty of people around to do it with. (In this case, I think people even includes parents.) This makes it all very simple. Unless you manage to rent yourself a housekeeping cottage on a deserted island, your kids will have no trouble finding other teen-agers in any resort you choose.

But since one of the nicest attributes of this age group is its indefatigable curiosity and energy, you might consider taking them on a whirlwind European trip (if you can afford it) or an excursion to some of the American cities you've never seen yourself or want to revisit. Most kids love restaurants, tolerate, like, and sometimes love museums, and are fearlessly fascinated with the challenge of getting around alone in a new place. In fact, within two days, they'll know more about the transportation system than you do. They can wash out their own laundry, they don't need baby-sitters, and if you want to go somewhere that doesn't interest them or vice versa, they are perfectly happy to entertain themselves. Their most endearing quality is patience; they don't mind standing on lines, they don't complain about bad service, and they have a rather sweet way of making you feel embarrassed when you do. For them, absolutely everything, good or bad, is a stunning adventure. For instance, how would you like to be bumping along in a jeep in the jungles of Mexico and develop a flat tire? Well neither would I, but my son, Tod, who was then fifteen, thought it was the most fun part of the trip—he was able to test out his prep-school Spanish and change a tire on a jeep, so what would have been a nightmare for me was a ball for him.

As you can see, I am a nut on the subject of teen-agers and travel. Because of their enthusiasm and receptiveness, it's the perfect age for globetrotting. They'll never get as good a chance again; once they get to college, they usually feel they should work during vacations. After college, the army gets them. After the army, the jobs and the families get them, and before you know it, they're the ones looking for the good Efficiency Motel for themselves and their three-year-old.

Like most people, my husband and I can't afford two vacations in one year—our own private one which is so vital for us and the big family trip. What we try to do instead is find ways for our kids to go places without us. When Nina was only nine, we sent her all alone to England to stay with friends for six weeks. (The airlines are brilliant in their handling of small children—they may lose suitcases, but I'd rather send a nine-year-old to Tokyo and back than send her alone on a bus across town.) She saw London, Yorkshire, Scotland, experienced a slightly different method of child-rearing, ate new food, and came home with a positively unintelligible British accent that lasted for exactly three days. Then, a couple of years ago, her opposite number from the English family came and stayed with us. *She* saw upstate New York, Greenwich Village, and some of the more sedate cultural attractions of our city. If you can work out this kind of informal student exchange program with friends abroad or in other parts of the U.S., I recommend it highly.

254

Good summer jobs are becoming increasingly hard to find, but there are loads of ways for your kids to *spend* money in the summer instead of coming out even, or earning it.

Chaperoned European tours (very expensive), unchaperoned European tours (planned and executed by your kids and their friends alone, and financed by you, who will worry about them from the moment they leave until the moment they return).

The Experiment-in-International-Living kind of thing, the success of which depends entirely on how amicably your child and his foreign family hit it off. They can exchange letters ahead of time, but you still never know. My husband's nephew once spent a whole summer moldering away in a small town in southern India with a family he grew to loathe within a week.

If the family lives in France, Italy, or Spain, your child will at least come home speaking the language more colloquially than when he left, even if he doesn't like the family. Anyway, it's an adventure.

For boys who love real physical adventure, there are groups which specialize in mountain climbing and living in the wilderness without benefit of sleeping bag, flashlight, insect repellent, or anything else except highly experienced instructors. I'd hate it myself, but with the world crumbling along the way it is, maybe some of us ought to know how to survive and stay fit. Wouldn't Darwin have a bitter laugh!

For boys who love the water, I've only just heard about a semi-cooperative venture in Florida, run by a scuba diver. This intrepid and ingenious fellow and his teen-age gang spend the summer diving for sunken treasure off the Florida coast. One half of whatever they come up with belongs to Florida and the other half is divided equally among the scuba diver and the kids, so that if one guy swims into a stack of gold bricks, the whole outfit is delighted—and rich. This one sounds like fun.

For girls, I can't, offhand, think of anything as intriguing as treasure-diving, but there are places where they can study music, art, ballet, or theater.

Summer stock apprenticeship is still a possibility for both boys and girls, but it's not the way it used to be. In the first place, most summer theaters book traveling shows and the kids never get a chance to act. They spend most of the summer sweeping the stage, being ushers in the theater, answering the box-office phone, wheedling props out of reluctant antique store owners, and if they're very, very, *very* lucky, being the assistant stage manager. In the second place, they sometimes have to pay the theater as much as seven hundred dollars a season for these august privileges and nobody ever pays them so much as a compliment. (And in the third place, it is an absolutely *great* way to spend a summer in spite of everything I've just told you. I don't know why—it just is.)

Going to summer school has lost its stigma. Some of the kids who go actually have to, but thousands of them go for fun, to take courses for extra credit, to take courses that just plain interest them, or to meet other kids. Several of the Eastern boys' prep schools turn coeducational for the summer and provide chaperoned living quarters, food, sports facilities and a wide variety of juicy courses (for quite a lot of money—about nine hundred dollars or so).

I have one remaining thought for the summer. Is it remotely possible or acceptable for kids to do precisely *nothing* for three months? Nothing more momentous, that is, than sleeping late, reading books, talking to their parents, going out on dates? It isn't? That's what I thought, but there's no harm asking.

entertainment Teen-age entertainment is another gigantic topic because parties, group activities and dates are as important to teenagers as education—perhaps even more so.

young teen-agers and big parties Young teen-agers love the *idea* of boy-girl parties but they often don't like being at them and they don't know how to give them. Boys are either very shy, hate to dance, and back out of the party at the last minute, leaving some poor girl with a ladies' sewing circle on her hands, or else they think of themselves as passionate lovers and scare the girls to death. The girls love to dance and aren't as shy, but they are very sensitive about being rejected. Because they don't know how to go about giving and running a party successfully, I'm afraid they feel rejected a good deal of the time. *You have to help them!*

Either telephone or written invitations will do, but written ones give the impression that a good bash, as against a piddling little slapped-together affair, is in store.

Between twenty and thirty kids is a good number. Your daughter will know the girls. Remind her, trying not to sound like Becky Sharp (Scarlett O'Hara?), that there's not much point in inviting a friend who still hates boys and loves touch football. That's only common sense.

If she knows enough boys herself, or each girl can *guarantee* to bring one (the guarantee is about as reliable as a Japanese water pistol), she should dig up some extras anyway because the boys keep defecting right up until the last minute. Do you, yourself, know any mothers who have sons the right age? If so, call them up and ask them if they think their sons would like to come. They can ask their sons privately, which is fairer to the sons, and once they've accepted, they'll probably show up because their mothers will make them. Ah-ha! Although young teen-agers are more timid about party-crashing than older ones, it's a good idea to keep a guest list just in case. Even though you may not need to use it to keep people out, it'll come in handy for welcoming them in—this will make the shy ones feel a little more at home. Maybe.

At this age, it's nice to call the mothers of girls and let them know officially about the particulars. You should also find out what they are going to do about transportation for their daughters: Will they be picked up or are they permitted to be taken home by boys? This is the sort of gesture that gives mothers great confidence in you. It's also rather sensible.

As for the length of the party, from eight to twelve is about right.

For food, refer back to the Rodgers's Small Poll. Or take a good guess; I bet you already know the answer.

Your daughter will want loud music going all night even though nobody is dancing to it. It hides conversational pauses.

Behavior control is solely your responsibility. Do not leave the house for one minute. Under ordinary circumstances, you can make and enforce your own rules in your own house. (If only one teen-age guest is there, you should

about the children

ask him before you offer beer or wine, or before he starts smoking, whether he's allowed to do those things in his own house. If he says no, and he'll probably be honest because he's afraid you'll inadvertently spill the news if he says yes, make him abide by his parents' rules. Should you rat on him if he won't abide by them? I honestly don't know! Mothers don't seem to appreciate ratting when it's to *them* about *their* child, but I've heard many of them say of someone else's child, "If I were his mother, I'd certainly want to be told about *that!*" I'm a coward; I only rat to very good friends who won't get mad at me and who will protect my confidence so that the child won't get mad at me either.)

At a party, even if there are children who are smoking without permission, there is nothing you can do about it. Besides, the brightest kids think it's smart not to smoke. The question of smoking pot and of using drugs is such a serious and widespread problem today that it is virtually impossible for us to give advice. We can only urge you to keep up with the best professional thinking, attend meetings, read all you can, even before you might suspect a problem in your own family. Helping to prevent kids from becoming involved is far better than waiting until there's trouble.

As for drinking, kids that age don't drink the hard stuff, but I think they're even too young for beer. It's okay for your own child alone with you, but en masse, it can lead to raucous carryings-on, and besides, in most states it's against the law.

If you want to make the evening pleasanter for yourself and your husband, invite another couple over. The four of you can lurk in the bedroom, smoking and drinking. You will have to pop out occasionally because some smart aleck will keep turning all the living room lights off, and you'll have to keep turning them back on. If it isn't that kind of trouble, it's the opposite side of the coin: You'll pop out only to find that all the boys are talking to other boys and all the girls are whispering glumly to each other. Unfortunately, there's nothing you can do about it.

What I heartily recommend is that you talk your daughter out of giving the party in the first place. At her age, she'll have more fun and less strain at an all-girl party, although she won't want to admit it. When she gets a little older, she'll know a boy with whom she can give a party. Then he'll corral the boys and everything will be lovely.

When your daughter starts going to parties, if you aren't planning to pick her up yourself, make sure she understands the importance of calling you to let you know if she's going to be late getting home, and that she gives you the phone number of the house where the party is. Then if she *is* late, don't hesitate to call up, no matter what time it is. Other parents are understanding about it, even if you awaken them, and if, by any horrible chance, there's been a car accident, you'll feel pretty stupid if you never even bothered to find out where your daughter was.

dates

Formal dates at this age are rare. If you have theater tickets and your daughter invites a boy to use the fourth seat, that's about as fancy as it gets. On informal dates, for hamburgers or movies or jazz concerts, each kid usually pays for himself unless a boy has officially called a girl and invited her. (Informal dates are usually informally conceived at the last minute.) Supply your son with money for himself and enough to take the girl home, and supply your daughter with money for herself and enough to get herself home in case the boy isn't planning to escort her.

Since teen-age dating rules vary tremendously, depending on what part of the country you live in, how you and your husband feel personally, and the age and maturity of your child, it's dangerous to make any definitive statements about it, but I suppose I can venture a few tentative answers to a few obvious questions:

Should you make a point of meeting a boy who's taking your fourteen-year-old daughter out for the first time? Sure. You may not learn much about his character, but just exchanging pleasantries, discussing the plans for the evening, and reiterating the curfew hour will let him know that you are parents in residence, not vague creatures in absentia.

Is establishing a curfew a good idea? For young teen-agers, yes, although it can be flexible, depending on what the evening plans are. In other words, if a party ends at twelve, you should expect your daughter to come home as soon as it's over, but if a movie ends at nine-thirty and the kids want to have a hamburger and Coke afterwards, you might ask them to be back by eleven.

Is it okay for your daughter to invite the boy in after the date? Yes, if you're up—which you probably are at that hour; no, if you're not.

For older teen-agers, the rules are obviously more relaxed. I don't, for instance, think it's necessary to establish a cut-and-dried curfew, but it is a good idea with both girls and boys for the parents to have some idea of when to expect them. If you don't know when to expect them, you won't know when to start worrying why they're late. As for waiting up for them, I think it's sheer masochism to sit bolt upright in the living room listening for the crunch of gravel in the driveway or the creak of the elevator, but to keep the phone turned on, the bedroom door open a crack, and a sleepy eye on the clock is a compromise measure.

formal dances

This is the time when, if you want your daughter to come out at eighteen (I think it's ridiculous, but maybe you don't), you'll have to start the big social push. It starts long before this—the mothers set the climate before they're even mothers. Whether she likes it or not, your daughter will have to begin going to black-tie functions which she will then faithfully attend every Christmas and Easter vacation until her debut. If you have lived for any length of time in your community and have always been part of that scene, you already know about this. If it's all new to you, or you've just moved to a new town, I think you'll find it too difficult and too degrading to warrant your serious consideration. As a matter of fact, if I may be so bold, I'd like to think it didn't warrant your serious consideration in any community, old or new.

the club dance

The first time your daughter attends a club dance, if it's not a dinner dance, give a dinner party for her and her friends before it, especially if she's nervous, or doesn't know any boys well. Again, either a written invitation or a phone call from mother to mother will do.

When the kids first arrive, you and your husband can sit with them in the living room while they have Coke or to-mato juice, but let them eat alone. Either a seated dinner or a buffet is okay, depending on the amount of help you have, but beware of serving complicated picky little things like squab. Even chicken, unless it's boned, is a nuisance; you don't want spots all over everybody. I recommend roast beef,

about the children

filet mignon, or steak. At a buffet, avoid the things that have to be cut at all—serve stew, which you can think of as Boeuf Bourguignon, with rice and salad. No garlic or raw onions. (I guess a five-year-old could have thought up *that* illuminating tip!)

If this all sounds agonizing to you, maybe you can give the dinner right at the club, but give it somewhere if you can; it's social insurance for your daughter, because boys have to dance with the hostess unless their mothers have forgotten to inform them of this delectable piece of etiquette. If you're the one with the son, remember to remind him.

school dances

You may be asked to chaperone a class dance at some point. If your child is obviously popular and an extrovert, by all means do it; although it's sometimes very dull, somebody's got to do it. But if your child's popularity hasn't been put to the test yet, or if she's the shy type, try to refuse, gracefully. (Your mother-in-law is spending the weekend with you and you haven't seen her in six months.) There is absolutely nothing more embarrassing in the whole wide world than being a wallflower while your mother is watching. It's no lark to be a wallflower in the first place, but parental cognizance makes it twice as humiliating.

church dances

If your daughter goes to an all-girls' school or goes to a coed school but wants to meet more boys, the subject of church get-together dances may come up. In the country, you'll be calling for her by car anyhow, but in the city, even though she may assure you that taxis are available, it's a good idea to call for her unless she's attending the dance with several other girls who have previously agreed to leave when she does and will take a taxi home with her. The same precaution holds for get-together dances with boys' schools.

elderly teen-agers: cars

If you live in the city, your teen-ager does not need a car. Period. If you live in the country, he may think he needs a car but he certainly doesn't *have* to have one. (He'll tell you he does.) If you decide to let him have one, maybe he should help pay for it himself, and if it's a second-hand car, it should be thoroughly checked out and repaired before you let him set a foot in it. The only way to make sure this is done, by the way, is to pay for the checkup and the repairs yourself. He may want to save his money, but you want to save his life.

The other life-saving insurance is to send him to driving school instead of just letting him learn to drive by experimenting, haphazardly, with your own car while you or your husband scream at him in the next seat. A driving school will teach him more quickly and more effectively, and he'll pass the test on the first go-round.

big parties

Big parties tend to be very informal, very last minute-y, and, as I said, Big. Usually too big. When you try to pin your kid down about the number of people coming, he'll suddenly go all vague on you. Look out for that; it means twice as many people as he says he "thinks." If it sounds too big to you, now is the time to stipulate exactly how many bodies you will allow. Later is too late!

With all your precautions, you may still have to cope with crashers. Crashing is customary these days and it's a nightmare. If you see it happening, get your son or daughter to enlist the help of a couple of brutish-looking friends to toss the barbarians out, and if your community is notorious for hoodlum crashers (as distinguished from the kids who just weren't invited), have an actual list of expected guests, and stand at the front door, checking them off as they enter. In some suburban communities, you can even hire an off-duty policeman to help for the evening if you anticipate trouble.

It's hard to believe, but even if all the kids *look* nice, you'd better put away breakables, valuables, loose cash, and liquor.

You can put yourself away, too, in the bedroom again, as long as it seems to be a trustworthy group. Lurk around if you're not sure. Pray a lot.

For food, I refer you once again to the R.S.P.

You can expect the usual loud music—records mostly, but sometimes there is enough local, electric-guitar-type talent in the gang for the kids to make their own live music. If you're in the mood and feeling affluent, you can even hire a group.

Since electric music can be heard in the next county, a considerate move would be to warn your neighbors about the imminent decibel count by dropping them a note of apology in advance, or maybe inviting them over to watch the spectacle for a while and to have a drink.

In New York City, there's a law prohibiting live music after eleven at night or before nine in the morning (with the kind of wing-ding I seem to be envisioning, you could easily end up breaking the law at both ends), but your neighbors are much less likely to report you if they've been graciously and humbly warned. You might even send them flowers the next morning.

While I'm on the subject of law, remember: One pot smoker plus one cop = jail for a lot of people, possibly including your children and you, yourself. Make this abundantly clear to your kids if you haven't already, and throw any and all offenders out of the party *immediately*.

family entertainment

As for family entertainment, here is where all your cautious indoctrination will finally begin to pay off. You can go to the theater and to movies with your kids, take them with you to your own friends' informal parties (ask first, but your friends will be enchanted), and include them in on your own parties, not because you need their services but because at last they've turned into honest-to-God people. As a matter of fact, if you have a really good relationship with them, you'll find you'd often rather be with them than with other people. Sometimes, they'd rather be with other people, though, and this is both sad and wonderful.

losing your grip

Losing your grip, healthily, is what is happening now. There are many aspects of a teen-ager's life that you can't or shouldn't control:

Bedtime.

TV-watching.

How and when or whether or not they do their homework. You still owe it to them and to yourselves to talk to their teachers, to discuss the academic problems, to find out what colleges they recommend, and what colleges your kids like the sound of. If you have a total non-student, take heart, maybe he'll care later on, but if he doesn't, you have plenty of company these days. If you have a child in a private school who is doing badly and the school seems wrong, discuss, quite frankly, with the principal, the possibility of putting him in another school even if there are only two years of high school left. Some principals get insulted—never mind them, it's your child. Find a good scholastic advisor who makes it her business to be well informed about all schools and who, once she is acquainted with you and your child, can recommend alternate educational possibilities. Ask her about boarding schools, for instance.

Crash diets, smoking, drinking, pot, sex behavior. Since you can't be around your kids all the time, you can't enforce your sentiments about any of these things either. You've given them your best advice for years; now there's nothing left to do but sit back and hope they believed you.

Friendships. You never really had a right to tell your children who their friends should be. If you ever did tell them, you shouldn't have, but now you really won't be able to.

Clothes. As for what, in general, is considered appropriate attire for teen-agers, there's a vast difference of opinion on this. We feel one way, They feel another. We think people should look neat, clean, and lovely. They think—well you know what They think, you've seen Them. But as kids get older, the fewer direct, unequivocal confrontations the better. Why? Because either They win or you lose, that's why. So when your daughter comes barreling out of her bedroom in a floppy felt hat, tight blue jeans, and a one-dollar sweater she bought in a thrift shop, ask yourself where is she barreling *to*. If it's only to the kitchen or through the back alleys to a friend's house, then let her go. If it's downtown or to the movies, permit yourself a small sigh, but let her go. If it's to the country club Sunday buffet, simply tell her she can't go anywhere with you, looking like that.

When girls begin shopping alone, some of them turn out to have very good taste and others have none at all. The ones with good taste will want to buy more than you can afford, but that's not an insurmountable problem. The ones with bad taste—well, I don't know. You can go shopping with them and try to steer them in the right direction. You can refuse to buy something outrageously ugly, but once in a while there will be some horrible rag she has *got* to have, so let her have it and close your eyes when she comes into the room.

Incidentally, don't try to pass clothes on from one daughter to another because it doesn't usually work. Teen-age girls, even when they're related to each other and only two years apart, can come in totally different sizes and have totally different dispositions and predispositions.

Another incidentally: If they fit you, borrow your daughter's clothes once in a while and see how *she* likes it. If she

about the children

doesn't mind, you two may be on to a good economical thing, clothes being what they are these days.

A third incidentally: Although the age at which you put your child on a clothes allowance will vary, depending—like everything else to do with teen-agers—on his or her maturity, no matter when you initiate this unpleasant bit of parental training, you are going to have trouble with charge plates. Your child will lose them in stores and forget to tell you about it until too late. Or your child will get them home safely but lose them around the house. Or your child will charge three hundred dollars' worth of stuff when the clothes allowance is only fifty dollars a month and then you'll have to return most of it.

So, if your child is on a clothes allowance, give him (or her) cash, and if your child is not on a clothes allowance, let him charge specific items to your account, but hang on to your charge plates unless he's a very mature, very careful human being.

Boys? They cannot be controlled. I happen to like the way my son dresses, but if I didn't, I wouldn't, and that would be that. He has never worn an overcoat in his life because at the age of six, he decided that only snobs wore overcoats—good guys wore parkas. He has never owned a pair of black shoes, or a blue suit, or a blazer. Come to think of it, he doesn't even own a pair of shoes that tie, unless you count sneakers.

Political opinions are theirs, all theirs, and you can't do a thing about them. They won't necessarily be taken as a reflection of your own because everybody knows about kids being independent thinkers. If you're ever asked by some conservative what your kid was doing at an antiwar rally, you can say you haven't the foggiest idea but you respect his right to be there. Nobody dares disagree with that because it's supposed to be one of the basic tenets of our American philosophy. Unless your child is physically disruptive, nobody worth anything will ever blame you for what he says or thinks, although he may feel sorry for you!

I seem to have come full circle—right around again to the subject of what a teen-ager thinks. If he's a vociferously indignant liberal, he'll tell you right away. About politics. But that's not all he's thinking, and if you care to find out

about the children

some of the rest, you must obey one cardinal rule: Talk to your kids. Once in a while, stay up late with them even if you're all tired the next day, and really *talk* to them—about their friends, their friends' relationships with their parents. Find out who's doing what and how your kids feel about it. And I don't mean stay up late and make "pals" of them. You don't have to tell them everything about yourself and your friends or let them in on all kinds of adult personal revelations; first of all, they're not ready for most of it, and secondly, they're up late talking to you because they trust you *as parents* and value your opinions *as parents.* You've created a congenial atmosphere, and they will be receptive to what you have to say, but they want the answers to their questions and problems, not yours.

Sometimes, most of the time, you don't *have* the answers —you and me both.

Ah, ladies, I don't know why I'm trying to tell you about children. I don't know any more about them than you. Maybe less. At any rate, all I'll ever be able to talk about is my own five, and I can't even do that with authority right now because they're not baked yet. Furthermore, they won't be baked for many more years. And what's even more furthermore is that when and if they all turn out, decades from now, to be humane, beautiful, kind, decent, honest, considerate and *useful* people (or, God help me, selfish, neurotic, twisted, amoral little gargoyles) will I have had much or anything to do with it?

I know one thing, though: That four-year-old, the one I keep referring to, the TV addict, the nay-sayer, the "ship"-shouter, my next-to-youngest (at least that's what I *think* he is) —that four-year-old is completely toilet-trained, day *and* night. But every night, unless we're out, which isn't too often, or unless my husband beats me to it, I go into his room at about eleven and pick up those thirty-four pounds and carry them to the bathroom dead asleep, the skinny legs wound around my middle, the skinny arms flapped over my shoulders, the damp head wedged into my neck somewhere. I stand up this loose-limbed, narcoleptic bundle on the bathrug, face it toward Mecca, and when it's finished, lug it back to bed. Because I like to. Maybe he's already too old for me to be doing such a thing. By next year he surely will be. But

about the children

until then, right or wrong, that's what I do at eleven o'clock, and I bet I'm not alone in this either. I bet all over the country women are lugging four-year-olds to the bathroom because we *all* like to. It seems like a nice, *right* thing to do for a kid that age, and if it seems right, maybe it is right. For children of all ages, if it seems right, maybe it is right is the only truth I'm sure of. I think.

I know I'm straying from the main line of the book, yet I feel there is something I must add. Mary says her children aren't "baked yet." I know what she means. She is talking about that moment when parents realize that, having done their best, they must let go and trust that the years of their influence will pay off. However, I don't like using the word "baked." To me, it means completed, and I hope that more and more people will recognize that growing and maturing should be a never-ending process. For some people, unfortunately, it is true that education stops when they leave school. But—thank goodness—for most, intellectual curiosity and the capacity to learn continue throughout their lives. These lucky souls—lucky in the sense that they were given the kind of education that stimulates a lively interest in the world and its people—are usually happier and healthier than the ones who have been "baked" and whose interests have been allowed to cool and even freeze in rigid patterns.

In this most confusing world, consistency in the parents' attitudes and reactions is the only way children can know what to expect. I can remember my own bewilderment as a child when my behavior could, and usually did, bring out in my impulsive mother a wide range of reactions. It all depended on her mood at the time. On one day I would be warmed by her approval, only to discover that the same act could on the next day get me into big trouble.

If you point out to your fifteen-year-old that the use of pot is illegal and therefore cannot be permitted, even though he thinks he can handle it, you weaken your case considerably by breaking the speed limit in your car simply because you feel you are a skilled driver. Similarly, bending the tax laws or abusing expense account privileges sets a pretty bad example. I feel rather strongly about this point, because my own adolescence was spent during the Prohibition Era, when I learned at an early age that great numbers of otherwise law-abiding citizens, holding the Prohibition Act in contempt, broke the law quite openly. It was not only a bad influence on the young, but it was also the beginning of organized crime in this country.

Even without television, any bright twelve-year-old learns a whole new language his parents don't understand—the vocabulary of rockets and space, computers, physics, the new math. But today's parents are faced for the first time with a generation that has grown up with that tireless baby-sitter, the TV tube. The kids have been influenced not only by lullabies and fantasy, but through television they have been exposed to an incredibly wide range of "live" experiences.

On the evening news, they have seen people die for real in Vietnam. They have seen heart transplants. They have seen astronauts set out to explore the moon. They have seen children dying of starvation in Biafra and in the U.S.A. They have seen race riots and looting, statesmen and their assassins murdered, *live*. The debating sessions of the U.N., drug addicts, homosexuals, revolutions, three-ring circuses—both the Barnum and Bailey kind and the political conventions. They have watched Congress investigate the Mafia and the Senate censure its own for corruption in high places.

Older generations never saw such things. They were protected, even naïve. I can remember being sharply criticized by the mother of a small girl to whom Linda flashed the news that there was no Santa Claus. The children were then about five, and the fact that this particular mother didn't want her child to know about Santa seems to me somehow related to the fact that the same girl gave birth to an illegitimate child when she was only fifteen.

Having learned that it is no longer possible to hide knowledge from the young, we have taken the first step. Now we must work with this aware generation, decide what can be changed and do it. We, the elders, are the disillusioned. The young have not been allowed to have any illusions; the great majority of them care deeply about their world and how it is going to be run. They have marched in peaceful protest against the war in Vietnam and risked being beaten up by the forces of law and order.

It seems increasingly clear that the disorders all over the country are not just a problem of racial tension. Neither are

about the children

they solely due to the so-called generation gap. They are, I think, the problems of the engaged and the disengaged. The elders want it all put back the way it was, and the young know they must do better.

Perhaps they will forgive me if I find it difficult to like all their superficial symbols of rebellion. Stacked up against injustice, corruption, hate, poverty, and war, however, wearing shoes, combing hair, and bathing are certainly unimportant. These minor irritations become important only when they loom so large to the older generation that they create the wall that separates people of good will from the young. Chronologically, I belong to the disengaged group, but more and more, I find myself on the side of the kids—not the organized agitators, but the ones who care. I like the things they care about.

YOU,
YOURSELF, AND
YOU

Throughout this book we've talked about women as "wives" and "mothers"—both are words that relate them closely to husbands, to children, to homes. And that is as it should be since most of a woman's life revolves around her family. It absorbs her greatest energies and gives her her greatest pleasure. This one chapter, however, is different because it is just about her and what she can do with the time she somehow finds to call her own.

Unlike a man's time, the hours a woman has to herself cannot be inviolable. She has to teach herself to take them when and where she can find them and make the most of them. Maybe the fact that she can't count on them makes such moments particularly precious.

A woman whose marriage is happy accepts the fact that her best-laid plans are automatically canceled when a child suddenly gets sick or a repair man has to be waited for or a baby-sitter doesn't show. It doesn't have to be a major disaster. With everyone safely packed off to school and her husband on his way to the office, she may be settling down with a book she's been looking forward to when suddenly the phone rings: A child with a sore throat is on his way home. He needs care and company, and that is that. A working wife who isn't her own boss has to be sure to find a job where such priorities are understood. Even volunteer work—if it requires being at a certain place at a certain hour each week —can be difficult unless a woman knows she is covered in case of emergency absences.

What about our own emergency absences? What happens when I get sick? *Nothing* is what happens when I get sick, nothing at all. Nothing goes to the cleaners, nothing goes to the A&P, nothing makes the plans for the weekend and sometimes nothing even answers the phone, so I rarely get sick for more than about two days at a time—like most women with a big household and small children, I simply can't afford to. I am a living, breathing medical phenomenon: the only two-day Hong Kong flu case, the only two-day pleurisy case, the only five-day walking pneumonia case. All of these illnesses were eked out over a period of fifteen years, you understand.

A few years ago, I had a spinal fusion which I anticipated with great relish because it meant three and a half to four weeks in the hospital with good books to read and nobody yapping at me. And guess what? They threw me out after only two and a half weeks, a record for the hospital, a ghastly disappointment for me. All these rapid recoveries are a testament to my doctors, yes, but they are also a testament to my megalomaniacal fear that everything, everything, everything will fall apart without me. This is utter nonsense, of course. So what if nothing goes to the cleaners and nobody answers the phone till the tenth ring? The really important things like which child has a temperature and which child has to be picked up at school are handled admirably by my husband and other members of the household in my absence.

If we were smart, we women, we would all make a point of being absent once in a while—healthily absent. One afternoon a week, one whole day a week, even two whole weeks a year away without husbands; this is what's called Getting Out from Under and we all need it badly. Without it, we succumb to a much more serious illness than the physical ones. I call it January-February-March Disease, and it can go on all year if you don't take care of yourself. Its symptoms? Irritability: "Mummy, is it all right if I . . ." "Can't you see I'm taking a bath, no, it is not all right whatever it is." Lack of imagination: Suddenly you cannot for the life of you think of anything for dinner but meat loaf, which you just had the night before. And most debilitating of all, depression: Life is one long wretched series of routines, each of which you carry out with abysmal ineptitude. Getting up in the morning is a drag, even after eight hours of sleep. You are getting stupider by the year because you never have enough time to read and when you do, you fall asleep over the book; in a minute nobody will bother to talk to you, including your own children. (Good, that'd be a relief anyway!) You are getting fat. The winter is too long and too cold. You hate your face. Your husband must hate your face . . .

Everything culminates in an agonized, silent scream of self-doubt: What am I doing? What am I getting up in the morning *for*? How is it that I have healthy children, a hard-working husband, all those wonderful material possessions, don't live in war-torn Indochina, and I'm still depressed?

January-February-March Disease is what it is. Part of the cure is to find something you love to do and then *make* the time to do it. Or have lunch with a friend and ask her how *she* feels about getting up in the morning these days, and you'll discover you have plenty of company, which in itself is part of the antidote.

Admittedly, when the children are small, the time a woman can find for herself may be only part of a day or a few hours each week. But for those few hours she should be her own woman—not "the wife of . . ." or "the mother of . . ." but herself. Impossible, says a young wife counting the children, the laundry, the errands that have to be done before she picks up her husband at the station. Possible, I maintain—if you're determined and adaptable.

making time for yourself

Today the aim of a wife is the same as it has always been: to make things comfortable and pleasant for her family. Ideally, she'd like to have everything beautiful and in near-perfect order, too. Given the money, when nannies and maids roamed the earth (they never did stay in one place very long, even in those days), order was an ambition within reason. These days housekeeping is more and more like politics: the art of the possible. And—miracle-working appliances notwithstanding (they've yet to invent one that can put in nose drops or feed a child successfully)—perfection simply isn't. So you make choices. If you have to pick between good-looking, or perfect, and comfortable, you choose comfortable because it makes your family happier.

You start by reminding yourself—firmly—that there's clean and there is clean. (Some things are actually cleaner today with less effort than they've ever been before: clothes and china, for example, done in machines with water hotter than hands could ever stand.) And then there are some

you, yourself, and you

cleaning chores that with few helping hands available are simply not worth the hours they take. Among them, I'd list polishing brass and silver, waxing floors, ironing sheets and linens. With these, you have two choices: You figure a way around them (lacquer the brass, use stainless steel, buy no-iron sheets) or let them go for longer than you might have in ready-maid days gone by. What you choose to do is up to you. If you like polishing things (which, as a matter of fact, is a mindless task that I really rather enjoy once in a while), go right ahead. But do your best to eliminate work you find boring. A third alternative would be to spend all your free hours cleaning, straightening, and maintaining—a course guaranteed to make and keep you a very, very dull person.

Somewhere along the way, I've attained a reputation for being a perfectionist that I haven't really earned—in one department at least. For the truth is, it isn't sheer love of perfection that makes me organize things. The fact is I'm lazy. I like to know where I can find what I need without having to look for it. When Mary and Linda were teen-agers, they found it much easier to take my fountain pen (they knew where it would be) than to find their own, lost deep in their stocking drawers. If I make notes about supplies running low, it is to avoid finding myself in the kitchen with wet hands and no paper towels—and I don't like having to trot all over the house to check every closet to find out what's about to run out. I organize to have more time for baking bread or doing needlepoint or reading—or maybe taking a walk.

When it comes to things that have to be coped with day by day, I'm an inveterate listmaker: of calls that must be made, supplies that must be ordered, errands that have to be done. As a matter of fact, when the project is really complex—like Christmas or redecorating the apartment—I've been known to make lists of lists just for starters. But all the jokes of my family and friends aside, lists do help you organize and make the most of the time you have. And besides, even on a gray day, it can boost your morale considerably to check back and find that there really are things crossed off.

Whatever the scale or style of your household, there are certain chores that have to be done on a reasonably regular basis. Besides meals, the list includes housecleaning, laundry (home-done, sent out, and dry cleaning), maintenance (regular, as in clothes-mending, and emergency, as in washer breakdown) and marketing. The easiest way to take care of these is with some sort of schedule—however loose.

Taking it from the top, it is probably best to make some kind of peace with housecleaning first. What and how much you do when will depend to some extent on your stamina and the amount of help you have, but feelings come into it, too. If you have help and if it pleases you to see everything bright from attic to basement and/or you want to get the whole horrid business out of the way, it's likely you'll find it worth all the effort it takes to get the job done in one day. If that's too much to cope with, you can split the work down the middle and twice a week have half a gleaming house to glory in for a few minutes before the kids swarm in to reverse the cleaning process. Or your system might call for doing a room or two a day on a more or less regular basis through the week. Whatever timing you settle on, make things easy for yourself. Is having the silver tea service out on display worth the polishing it takes? I put all my ceremonial silver away years ago, and the pieces we use are kept covered in drawers to slow the tarnishing process. Use low-maintenance materials wherever possible. Not one floor in our house in the country needs anything more elaborate than soap-and-water care, and after all those years of waxing and polishing, it is a positive joy!

The same approach goes for laundry. The more of it you have to do yourself, the more you should go out of your way to buy no-iron clothes, sheets, and table linens. They are worth every penny, provided you also take the time to read tags and laundry directions carefully so you won't wash away or melt superfinishes. I'm all for reading tags and directions carefully, but unless you have a mind like a steel trap, you're not going to remember them six months later and neither will your cleaning woman or laundress or whatever she is. Great big sweaters will shrink down to premature infant size, snow-white acetate polo shirts will develop instant jaundice in the dryer. The solution is to identify the tags (Mr. Smith's permanent press shirts, Mrs. Smith's polo shirt) and tape them to the inside of the cabinet door nearest the washing machine. Best of all, tape them in the cabinet where you keep the soap. In similar fashion, I tape stove instructions near the stove, mixer instructions near the mixer, etc. As I've already told you, I don't understand directions and never read them, but sometimes somebody else does and will.

As we've said before, Monday washday is a thing of the past. Still, some people find it easier to collect and cope with laundry once or twice a week; others prefer to do a load each day. Once a week, you can pack off special washables that need to be sent out as well as clothes for the dry cleaners.

About maintenance, what can I tell you—except that it's always there? When it's the emergency kind, a list of service men you have used and whose work you like is a big help. It will also save you future aggravation if you have the patience to keep trying different men till you find the right one for your jobs. Chronic maintenance, as in mending, just has to be faced and done. Somehow. By someone.

Which brings me to the subject of help. Because if you loathe mending as much as I do, you may just want to allocate part of your budget to hire someone who'll come in every now and then to do it for you (an ad in the local paper or a call to the women's exchange might unearth somebody's grandmother who loves to sew). Whether you have help full time or on a regular part-time basis, the man or woman who'll mean the most is the one who can take over the jobs you dislike doing. Try to work out a specific list of things you want done and a routine for anyone who comes in regularly. Invest some time of your own in the beginning to make sure the person or people you've hired understand your house and your appliances and have the cleaning things that they like to work with. Be available to answer questions that are bound to come up those first days, and be emphatic about any special products you want used. Encourage them to ask before plunging ahead when in doubt.

You can be as emphatic as you want, but I've yet to find a cleaning woman who doesn't insist on her own particular brand of cleaning powder, ammoniated floor liquid, wet mop, dry mop, and ironing board cover. This is fine if your cleaning woman sticks with you, but if you run through six or seven in a month (which can happen to even the most benevolent employers these days), you end up with enough cleaning equipment to sanitize Madison Square Garden.

Don't expect me to come up with an answer for this—there isn't one. You might, though, consider weeding out the unfinished but currently unpopular brands every once in a while.

For most of today's young wives, shopping for food means going to the supermarket once or twice a week plus occasional ordering by phone (see MR on settling in). I strongly suggest planning your menus in advance and making a list before you set foot in the market because, if you're like me, even then you'll be irresistibly tempted to buy extras (without a list, I'm hopeless). You can still take advantage of "specials": Put them in the freezer and plan around them the next week. It is worthwhile investigating to find out when the store receives its deliveries so that you can plan accordingly. Large markets generally receive produce, meat, and nonperishables several times a week, though not necessarily all at once. Late mornings or early afternoons of delivery days are usually your best bets since shelves are fullest then. True, but late morning and early afternoon are the worst possible times from the standpoint of crowds. Every mother's son (I mean that quite literally) is in there then with his mother and his animal crackers and his screams of delight or anguish. It's a detestable experience. I'd rather shop early in the morning and come home with nothing but bruised apples and packages of bologna. If it is possible, marketing once a week in advance of the weekend is the most efficient. Thursday afternoon when stocks are full and crowds light is probably best of all. Failing that, try Friday morning. By Saturday morning, meats and produce have been pretty thoroughly picked over.

If you have the storage space, ordering in quantity and by phone saves considerable time with it comes to household items like soap, facial tissues, toilet paper, cleaning supplies and food staples. And buying in quantity is often cheaper.

The phone is worth a thousand steps when you are searching for a particular item or a special kind of service. And I also find it invaluable when it comes to getting information, making arrangements, or communicating for quite specific purposes. I don't ordinarily use it just for visiting. I realize, of course, that for a young mother who can't get out, the phone provides a way to keep in touch with friends and gives her a break in the day. But I'm afraid that one more place where my generation gap really shows is in my feelings about the use—or misuse—of the telephone.

The ring of a phone bell is a kind of peremptory summons that cannot be ignored. When you call, whoever is on the other end must drop whatever she is doing to answer—whether she is having lunch or entertaining friends or baking bread or reading. And a lengthy call at any one of these times may not be any more welcome than an unexpected visitor would be (the telephone caller probably wouldn't dream of dropping in without notice).

For young mothers in search of time for themselves, there remains the most important department to cope with: the children, of course. Mothers of preschoolers aren't likely to be able to set up reliable weekly schedules for getting away without some kind of regular help (and even then, it's tough —households full of small children being more emergency-prone than others). But there are ways of stealing a few hours or an afternoon here or there. Young wives who live in apartment houses or congenial housing developments may find it possible to set up cooperative plans whereby one mother takes over the care of several children for an afternoon a week on a rotating schedule (providing, of course, that the kids get along well together). That gives everyone a chance to go to the hairdresser, visit friends, shop, explore a museum or spend a few hours on a hobby. Making time for yourself is difficult, but it is possible, and after the kids are in school even part of the day, it is even more possible.

fashion

Now with your life smoothed out a bit, you can begin to contemplate some frivolities. One of them is fashion. While I am not one of the group that believes Clothes, with a capital "C," are worthy of enormous expenditures of money or time, I do think they are important. When a woman knows she is looking her best, she feels better, more self-assured, about everything. And I do think that matters.

The world of fashion is curious, special, and not really mine. Its essence is change. That is what the whole industry is about. Hems are down, or up, upper, UP! Hips are there or nowhere; bosoms, out or in. And women's shapes are supposed to behave accordingly (which, of course, they can't). Since change is the name of the game, ironclad rules about what's right or wrong are out of the question. And even the Beautiful People make mistakes. I remember a book about fashion that came out a few years ago. It was written by a woman of great taste who stated firmly that while alligator bags were extremely smart for daytime and travel, they were never, never appropriate at night. The presses had barely stopped rolling when the "in" thing for evening was suddenly the small alligator bag. So, while I will go far enough out on the limb to suggest that I don't think slacks will ever be correct for funerals (I have already heard that "The bride wore culottes . . ."), I'm not willing to go much beyond that where specifics are concerned. About clothes in general, however, I will risk a few convictions.

Today, as never before, fashion is to do your own thing. Even men—once so buttoned up in their button-down shirts and gray flannel—are getting a chance to have some fun with colors and fabrics and new cuts in clothes. Startlingly enough, their women go right along, coaxing and flattering their formerly short-haired husbands to let their hair and sideburns grow "just a bit longer." And women's designers, who once traveled parallel, if not identical, courses from year to year, are now taking off in all sorts of divergent directions.

The old status symbols—the mink coat, the real jewels— are out. Now the smartest furs are "fun." The correct little string of Oriental pearls, so right for so many years, stays home while the ten-millimeter fakes make the best parties. (Put your old-fashioned jewelry away in the safe-deposit box so that you won't have to pay insurance on it. And forget about it for the present—it's only a question of time before it will be "in" again. Thirty years ago, little Victorian earrings for pierced ears and snake bracelets were considered quaint and were worn only by "arty" ladies with no pretensions of chic. Furthermore, dealers won't give you much if the jewels are out of fashion unless they have good-sized stones.) Now everyone with an appetite for glitter can satisfy it with a fabulous collection of "jewels" (impossible with the real stuff) —beads, shells, gold coins, glass, plastic, wampum, or whatever—to loop into great necklaces. And antique finds— Renaissance, Georgian, Victorian, even pre-Columbian and

African—fill the need for unique pieces at prices within reason.

Fashion is more available and more varied than it ever has been in history. American manufacturers and stores buy top designs from Paris and Madrid, Florence and Rome, and make moderately priced copies widely available. The trend puts "now" fashion within everyone's reach; haute couture names are appearing on boutique clothes everywhere. (I do deplore the current vogue for literally wearing your favorite designer's name or initials on your sleeve or scarf, coat pocket, luggage or shoes; I belong to the school that thinks advertising should be paid for.)

Remarkable new fabrics—washable and drip-dry—make the most delicate colors practical even for travel. (I actually prefer light-colored clothes for travel because they're not such lint-picker-uppers.) The cost of clothes has risen relatively little in comparison to other necessities—food, rent, transportation, hospitalization, and even movie tickets. Today it is also much easier to find simple well-designed clothes at modest prices. (Years ago, the simplest clothes were always the most costly.) So you can often afford the fun of buying current fashion and discarding it when the time comes without feeling guilty.

*what's
right for
you*

This new freedom puts a great responsibility on a woman to censor her own clothes and accessories. With so many different looks to choose from, it is up to her to select the ones that are really flattering to her and those she feels right in. She must look at herself critically from all angles—top to bottom and sideways. She should learn how her clothes should be fitted to bring out the best and minimize the worst features of her shape. Dresses that have belts or well-defined waistlines seem to me to be most becoming when the line dips toward the center back and rises gently to center front. Similarly, because of an optical illusion, I suspect, hemlines that are slightly lower in the back tend to look even.

Not every girl, or even every young and pretty girl, should wear pants suits or miniskirts; she should have the long, slim, straight legs that go with them. On the other hand, small girls in midi-length skirts sometimes look as though they were standing in a hole. Remember that dark colors are the most flattering to legs and, for that matter, to bodies.

Whatever you wear, be sure that it's comfortable, and that you can forget about it once you have put it on. There is nothing more distracting than a woman who is constantly tugging at her skirts or clutching at a neckline that's too low or a scarf that is awkward to handle. Wrap-arounds are murder on a cold windy day. Make sure when you're having clothes fitted that you can sit down and move in them. And take into account the height of the heels you'll be wearing with the dress.

what to wear when

The occasion and the audience always have a great deal to do with what is right to wear. The perfect outfit for a school visit is probably not the thing you'd wear for lunch at the Plaza. Ask yourself for whom you're dressing and give yourself honest answers. Children tend to be embarrassed by their mothers being "too dressed up." Mary and Linda always used to tell me just what to wear—including what perfume—on their school's visiting days.

If you're going to meet a lot of your husband's business associates, make sure that he likes the way you look before you leave the house (he's the one you want to please most anyway, or he should be). If he hates fur-trimmed dresses, don't buy one. Anything extreme makes most men nervous —if it's worn by the woman they're with.

When your husband gets home in the evening, you don't have to greet him in a sweeping at-home costume, but I do think your hair should be brushed and your face looking its best—it will make you feel better, too. I also think that daytimes, when you're alone with the housework, is the time for rollers and greasy creams if you use them. It's silly and not at all necessary to look that way at night.

In your own home, anything in which you feel comfortable and look your best is fine, though I would rule out chiffon and ostrich feathers for a hostess who plans to do her own cooking and serving. And she should be considerate enough of her women guests not to say, "Oh, we're not dressing—just anything simple," and then appear in her sequined lamé.

Black-tie evenings take a bit of analyzing. If it's a concert or an evening at the theater, a short dinner dress that won't dust the aisles or get crushed in narrow seats makes most

you, yourself, and you

sense because it's the most comfortable. For a dinner party, you can take your choice—either short or long. One old rule that still holds, I think, is that it is always better to be under- than over-dressed. So save ball gowns for really big parties, the kind to which men once wore white ties.

accessories

Fashions in accessories change more drastically and faster than any others. And they make the difference between looking really right or just missing. Shoe designs change dramatically—and often. And there is nothing that spoils a "look" so noticeably as wearing a pair of shoes that is "out."

Choosing accessories is a matter of finding things that are both fashionable and becoming—and personally, I think becoming is the more important of the two. Take hats, for example. There was a time when a woman didn't feel dressed without one, and unless she was wearing something on her head she didn't feel she could enter a place of worship. As I write this, kids are having all kinds of fun with everything from Anzac campaign hats to crocheted helmets and stocking caps—for them any hat is great if that's how it looks on. Yet women on the whole are wearing hats less and less. And although I'm sure custom varies in different parts of the country, fewer and fewer women seem to feel hats are required even for church. So in answer to the question "When?" where hats are concerned, I'd say a hat is fine whenever it's becoming, makes you feel happy, and your husband doesn't mind.

Being married to a man who feels that no woman has ever been improved by a hat, I have a hard time with them. On some of my best friends—not me—those large floppy numbers are very pretty and very feminine, too. For practical reasons I find turbans (the kind that cover all my hair) very useful for trips to the hairdresser. And I love fur hats because they're so terribly flattering and also because they keep my ears warm in these days when hairdos leave them without any fur of their own.

Even in summer, when I can't use the cold as an excuse, I feel uncomfortable without gloves in the city. In the country, except for special events, I don't think they're necessary. And I have strong feelings about corsages. So often they add one touch too many. As far as I'm concerned, the only way to wear a corsage is with its ribbons off, in a vase on a table.

281

Make-up can be a big help or a terrible liability. Here again, the first thing it should be is appropriate (false eyelashes are out at the P-TA). And it should always seem, to the beholder, more artifice than applied art. The most difficult make-up of all is the one that looks like no make-up. At the hairdresser's I've sat and marveled at models who arrive pale and mousey, watched them set out creams and jars, brushes and tubes, and—after using a palette more varied than Rembrandt's—leave forty-five minutes later as raving "natural" beauties. Most of us don't go in for this kind of maquillage, but it is startling to watch and realize the great potential friend every woman has in make-up used with skill.

Beauty products are so glamorously presented, they smell so good and they promise so much that most of us find them irresistible. The best of them will do your face no harm, but they can do great damage to your pocketbook. When it comes to actually caring for your skin, dermatologists will tell you that there are basically only two things you can do that have any value: one is to clean it thoroughly and the other is to lubricate it. What preparations you use will depend on what works best for your particular skin. But whatever you use, I'm convinced that if women spent as much time cleaning their faces as they do putting on their make-up, they'd benefit enormously.

How do you learn the tricks? There are several ways. You can take a make-up lesson at a salon, where you'll learn the basic techniques that do most for you plus variations for day and evening. Cosmetic companies often assign trained demonstrators to department store locations where they will be happy to suggest products they think will be most helpful and show you how to use them. Since styles in make-up change, it's a good idea to consult such professionals for a refresher course every season or so. Remember, too, that your skin tones vary with the time of the year and exposure to the sun, and you should adjust your make-up accordingly. And since no two skin textures or colorings are identical, it is also a mistake to assume that because a certain foundation or lipstick does marvelous things for your best friend, it will work miracles for you.

In the perfume department, all of us have known women who trail vapors that are overwhelming. It should never be that obvious. It should be subtle. What people often fail to realize is that a perfume that smells wonderful on one woman may actually smell rancid on another. It's a matter of chemistry, and for this reason I never give perfume as a gift unless I know what the woman herself likes. Better none than the wrong kind.

hair

Hair is terribly important. It can spoil the whole picture. Too bleached, too blue, too bouffant—too anything is wrong. Individual styling is essential to start with since the "in" idea is not necessarily becoming to all shapes of faces. Furthermore, differences in texture, natural wave and amount of body make it impossible to give two women identical hairdos. Then there is color. Gone are the days when changing your hair shade had to be obvious. Bleaching and dyeing are done so skillfully today that you would be foolish not to use either to your own flattering advantage. But hair coloring should be used as it was intended—to enhance your looks, not to stun the people you meet. It is never as important to be A Blonde as it is to have your hair a shade that suits your skin tones. You may look better with light hair than with dark; then again, you may not. What looks best on you may change from year to year as your skin tones do.

wigs and hairpieces

The growth of the wig industry has put wigs, hairpieces, and falls within everyone's reach, and unlike the time when wig-wearing was a kind of disgrace (you did it only if you didn't have hair, and you never *admitted* you wore one), now wigs in all lengths and all versions are enthusiastically accepted fashion accessories. Today's are more natural, they're more comfortable, they fit better, and they make it possible to try all sorts of styles that would be impossible to do with your natural crop. Some years ago, knowing how Dick felt about my cutting my own long hair, I bought my first wig. It was such a smashing success that I finally decided to have my real hair cut like it. Disaster! It didn't look like the wig; the texture wasn't the same, and to make the whole thing worse, the wig no longer fit since it had been made to wear over my long hair. Since then, I've gone through a series of hairpieces that have spent most of their time in boxes on shelves because for me they were just too much trouble to use. But recently I bought a new wig that's light, fits well, is comfortable and is absolutely marvelous—great for traveling, for days when I can't get to the hairdresser, or for no reason at all. Fashions and fads aside, hair—your own or a wig—should look like hair and be becoming. That's all that really matters.

MR's fashion advice

I'm back again. Did you miss me? Did you wonder where I'd been hiding for the last seven pages? In the closet, too ashamed to come out. In my closet are many garments—most of them unsuitable, some of them totally unwearable—and many ill-assorted shoes. With a little luck, I might find a matching pair, but they probably won't go with any of my clothes. I am a frump. Are you a frump? If not, you may skip the next few paragraphs, but if the shoe fits—and you can't find the other one . . .

FASHIONS FOR FRUMPS

First, a little character analysis: The paradoxical thing about you is that you spend easily as much time and money on how you look as does a nonfrump. Maybe even more. (In the half hour when I'm looking for the other shoe, DR is up, dressed, and out of the house, looking like my younger sister.) But you enjoy it less. In fact, you don't enjoy it at all because you have no Confidence in Yourself. You would love to look nice, but you don't know where to start. Start with your closet. Take absolutely everything out of it. What a fascinating accumulation! Relics of the forties, the fifties, and the sixties—you could open a costume museum.

Throw out any dress you haven't worn in a year because I promise you you're never going to wear it again. Curb the tendency to hang on to it just because it was so expensive or because it might come back into style seven years from now. Maybe it will, but in the meantime it's been collecting dust, taking up space in your closet, and who knows what your figure will be like in seven years—you might be fatter or thinner, and whatever it is won't fit you anyhow. So give it to the Thrift House and get a nice tax deduction on it. The same goes for shoes: you're allowed to hang onto one old pair to wear in the rain.

Call up your best well-dressed friend (how will you know

if she's well dressed? You'll know, you'll know. Even a frump recognizes well-dressed when she sees it) and invite her over for the afternoon. Model the meager remainder of your wardrobe for her. If she says the green is terrific but too long, give her some pins and let her pin it up for you. If she says the purple thing looks terrible and purple isn't your color anyway, believe her. No matter *what* she says, believe her. You haven't got much to lose so you might as well go for broke.

By the end of the afternoon, you'll end up with practically nothing to wear, but you're no worse off than you were in the morning when you had a whole closetful of nothing to wear. At least now you can sweep the floor of the closet.

Your natural instinct will be to rush right out of the house to go shopping. Don't do it, not yet. You have to make a careful analysis of your social life first. For instance, there's no point in stocking up on sporty ensembles if you almost never go anywhere in the daytime, or party dresses if you almost never go to fancy parties. On the other hand, if it seems that your social life consists mostly of going to other people's houses for dinner, then you need several versions of "the little black dress"—or its equivalent.

You are now ready to go shopping, but be prepared: It's going to be harder for you than for a nonfrump because you'll be intimidated by saleswomen, unsure of your taste, and overwhelmed by the infinite variety of little dresses. Take your trusty friend with you—she'll steer you to the right departments of the right stores and reinforce whatever humble, embryonic opinions you're beginning to form. She'll also remind you to get the shoes and the bag to go with the dress; forgetting the accessories is a common frump failing.

A couple of extravagant-sounding suggestions: When you've found a great dress, get three of it if you can, in three different colors. As a reluctant shopper, this saves you hours of agonizing indecision and if the dress is becoming, no one except you and your best friend will notice that you have several. If they do, the worst they'll think is that you're rich.

If the hems are too short or too long, let the store dressmaker do the alterations for you; it'll be forever before you get around to it yourself.

What's going on with your hair? Nothing much? You've worn it that way for ten years and you *like* it? Well, you're probably right. (Ha, ha, fooled you that time, didn't I!) You see, the frump mentality is timid. You mustn't put yourself in the hands of one of those spindly-fingered fanatics—he'll chop all your hair off (having sworn to you that he was only going to shape it a little), or talk you into a fun fall for three hundred clams which you will never wear because it'll make you feel as though you're wearing a hat. Or he might talk you into paying a three-hour visit to the colorist upstairs—another spindly-fingered fanatic who'll turn you Nordic. For sixty dollars. And six weeks later, because your hair is now half Norse, half Nubian, you're back in there again for another sixty dollars. A year later, all your hair falls out.

No, no, my dear, if you like your hair the way it is, go to your best friend's hairdresser—he'll do what *she* tells him because she has authority—and have a genuine shaping. As for color, the most adventurous step for you is very light streaking, or frosting, or whatever they call it, because then if you don't like it or if you do like it but don't make it back to the hairdresser for six months, people won't notice when it grows out.

Make-up? False eyelashes are probably not for you. You'll blind yourself or glue your eye closed forever putting them on. And never mind that pale lipstick. Maybe it's okay for eighteen-year-old models, but it'll make you look as though you'd burned your mouth kissing a steam iron.

Now that you've put together yourself and your small but totally coordinated collection of clothes—nine usable items in place of thirty-nine no-goodniks—you'll have no trouble deciding what to wear. You can get out of the house as fast as my mother, having inspected yourself carefully for spots and ripped hems. There's very little to choose from, but what there is is right. Congratulations, you are all set. You are no longer a frump!

Ah, that's the trouble with us frumps. We always think we're all set. (As a matter of fact, thinking you're all set is the sign of a true frump.) But the next thing you know, it's spring or summer or fall or something, and it's time to start the whole horrendous weeding-out process all over again. I wonder where I put the other shoe . . .

you, yourself, and you

But to get back to you and your "spare" time, for purely restorative purposes, there's nothing that can match a real vacation—even a vacation alone. Health spas are growing more popular, especially with young mothers whose lives are so pressured all year round. The cost varies widely depending on the frills, and the spas nearer home save you money on transportation. Women who can manage this yearly feel that the refreshment they get from a week of supervised diet, rest, and exercise is well worth the price.

Your husband probably won't mind as long as you don't abandon him to a household full of children and laundry and details he doesn't know anything about and couldn't handle if he did because he's in the office all day. So before you go away, you'll have to do the following:

Find a competent baby-sitter to look after the children. If you can't find such an animal, send the children to your mother, if she'll have them. If she won't you'll have to stay home.

Give your competent cleaning woman (or whoever you have working around the house for you) full instructions about the chores you usually perform for your husband. If you're the one who puts the shirts away, she won't know how and where unless you tell her.

Make provisions for getting your husband fed—either by the competent cleaning woman or by friends who know you're going to be away and would love to invite him for dinner. In case he feels like staying home alone, stock the freezer with a few TV dinners or, if you're DR, blanquette de veau and fancy soups.

Leave a detailed fact sheet behind you with phone numbers of doctors, laundry, cleaners, etc., in case he wants to call them, and information about where you can be reached, in case he wants to call you.

By the time you've done all this, you may conclude that it's all more trouble than it's worth—it depends on how much you want to get away.

But when your children are little and it's difficult to get yourself out of the house at all, let alone a week, a break in routine or an hour spent doing something you enjoy can do wonders for your morale. You don't have to leave home to close your door, put your feet up and read a book. And while you won't be able to devote hours at a stretch to grown-up pastimes, half an hour while the washer is running or during the children's nap can make it possible to get away to your own world for a short time.

. . . in
the world
outside

If you can actually get out of the house, all sorts of beautiful possibilities open up. When I find myself with a few extra hours, my steps almost automatically turn toward the Metropolitan Museum where I rent a walkie-talkie tour of a gallery I don't know well. With the perfect guide—a voice that tells me what I'm seeing and stops when I push the button—I stroll through at my own pace. An hour or so later, I'm back outside feeling as though I've had a real vacation. Another day I might head for Grant or Mott Streets, where there are all sorts of Italian and Chinese food stores, or the Greek groceries on Ninth Avenue, or a spice shop—shopping, sniffing, exploring whole other worlds.

Depending on what gives you most pleasure, the choice is endless: a movie you've wanted to see, lunch with a friend, (adult conversation for a change), a ramble through the Botanical Gardens or—as long as I don't have to do it—an afternoon at a gym. I admit to a total lack of self-discipline when it comes to exercise. Except for croquet, I hate it. I don't mind at all if something I'm doing—like making a bed or packing or walking *to* someplace—involves physical activity. But yoga, isometrics, bicycling, push-ups—they're not for me. I'm incapable of exercise for exercise's sake. On the other hand, sinful and sybaritic though it may be, every once in a while I do think it's fun to give yourself over to a whole day of beautification in one of those sweet-smelling salons, have yourself a massage (someone exercises *you*), pedicure, facial treatment and make-up, a hair styling (new cut, perm, streaks, set, what-have-you) and manicure. Probably clutching a costly package of new cosmetics, you emerge with no dough and a very happy face, looking and feeling radiant.

If this is too frivolous for you and you can manage some regular time off, how about lessons—in sewing, Italian, anthropology, math? (You may even find out what the kids are talking about.) Undoubtedly you'll have to miss a session now and then, but it won't be disastrous. And it's fun to learn something new.

Though I have never been able to muster much enthusiasm for the kind of social ladies' clubs that exist for bridge playing and luncheons, if you like to play bridge and there's a group in your community, by all means take advantage of it. The point is that a vacation needn't be two weeks long and cost a lot of money. A day away out of the rut, doing something you enjoy, can return you to the battle refreshed and ready to cope.

It's the change that is restorative. When I'm tense or have problems on my mind, I find that doing something I don't do every day is marvelous therapy; for me, concentration brings a special relaxation. I love doing things with my hands: cooking, sewing, needlepoint. I find all of them an enormous satisfaction and pleasure. And it seems to me that such wifely arts are enjoying a renaissance right now.

crafts Fashions in crafts change just as fashions in clothes do. For years, only your grandmother crocheted; now suddenly all the mod kids are turning out seven-foot scarves and wooly hats, and if anyone ever gets around to giving us some "today" colors and designs, who knows—we might even bring back the afghan. In days when fewer and fewer girls seem to be doing much sewing, my granddaughter Nina has become interested in it and has made herself some lovely things. Skills don't go out of style—it's simply a question of updating designs. Unfortunately, manufacturers of craft kits and materials too often lose sight of their responsibility to keep up with current trends. As a result, many highly skilled women are being steered in the wrong direction by dull designs and drab colors. I also think manufacturers of needlepoint materials should take it upon themselves to supply directions for mounting. The cost of mounting makes needlework too expensive for women who would otherwise enjoy it tremendously. Most of us could probably manage pillows and possibly even some picture frames if we were told how.

The thing to remember about taking up any craft is that the person you should be trying to please is you. As long as what you want to try is something you enjoy, that's just fine. You'll probably find, as I have, that you get most pleasure from doing things you do reasonably well. For example, I don't paint because loving paintings as I do makes me hypercritical, and turning out bad ones would only make me miserable. On the other hand, I'm quite comfortable living with my needlepoint.

collecting

Collecting, too, can be an absorbing and refreshing hobby. It repays you in pleasure and growing interest for all the time you invest. It can lead you off into all sorts of interesting paths—to study, to travel, to search and research—that take you away from everyday worries for minutes, hours, even days at a time in almost the same way a real trip organized by a museum might. As your knowledge grows with your collection, you enjoy the fun of becoming an expert even though your field is small.

Some people are born collectors—they're the kids whose pockets are always full of pebbles and bottle tops and stubs of "good-colored" chalk. There's a name for those kids: they're called Boys. In the pleasantest sort of way, others have collecting thrust upon them—through the gifts of friends. A collection of ours that grows each Christmas was born when an old friend gave us a family of Scandinavian straw angels the year Dick wrote *I Married an Angel*. Over the years only their halos have aged, and I've made new ones for them out of gold and silver paper. And our collection of croquet things—which now includes engravings, cartoons, and a number of enchanting little books on rules and strategy—was started by friends who came across bits of croquetery in their browsing and, knowing how much we love the game, have brought them home to us.

You can, of course, take up collecting quite deliberately. Lots of people do. And the ones who enjoy it most have always seemed to me to be those who've chosen to concentrate on something unfashionable or at least on something that no one they know is collecting. For one thing, it makes the sport less expensive and very specially yours, and while the items are harder to discover, it's so great when you make a find. Whether it's thimbles or antique stoves, the most valid reason for collecting is that it gives you pleasure.

The "unfashionable" rule holds even if you're thinking in terms of investment because most things that were good in their time eventually return to fashion. We have friends, for example, who started buying nineteenth-century paintings and *trompe l'oeil* years ago when nobody else was interested.

290

They did it for the world's best reason: because they liked these particular paintings. And now that styles have shifted once more, they not only have lots of company but an extremely valuable collection. Anyone who wants to collect primarily as an investment should probably give serious thought to the beautiful early eighteenth-century English furniture that hasn't been "in" for years. It's all bound to come back one day. But for anyone in a two-room apartment, buttons are better than armoires.

gift-giving

A peripheral benefit of collecting is that a friend who is wild about Wedgwood or toy soldiers or even eggs (my sister-in-law Wilhelmina has collected dozens—marvelously carved or colored or painted) is wonderfully easy to shop for when Christmases or birthdays come around. Gift-giving, I think, can be one of life's great pleasures if it involves creativity and imagination on the giver's part. If that sounds scary, I don't mean it to. There are only two things to keep in mind really: first, finding something you know the person will like, and second, something you'll like giving. Since gifts are to please, not to educate, the tastes of the receiver should always come first. If you love antique trivets and she loves contemporary ornaments—especially if they're made of Lucite, you keep looking till you find something in Lucite that you like, too—and if, in the course of your shopping you unearth the perfect William and Mary trivet, buy it anyway and save it for a later occasion and a friend who will love it as you do.

I have never had much patience with people who claim that it's impossible to find a present for so-and-so because "she has everything." Quite often such people are easier to shop for than almost anyone else on your list. For one thing, their tastes are usually very catholic, they are interested in and pleased by many different kinds of things. And they're more fun to shop for because you don't have to be hamstrung by the necessity of finding something *useful*. For them, the monetary value of a gift truly doesn't matter. The perfect present may be anything from an old cookbook to a beautiful shell you've found on the beach and set on a clear plastic square—or a set of bright-colored shopping bags in different sizes filled with paper wrappings, tags and string.

The gifts you can find time to make yourself are often

291

treasured most by the people you love, but they can be embarrassing, too. So unless your last name is Picasso, resist the temptation to paint a picture for art-collector friends. Instead, do some needlepoint (it's a small art that can usually be tucked in somewhere), bake a cake or bread, or cook and freeze a meal that includes a dish you know they like especially. A sturdy box covered in a particularly handsome paper is another often-welcome present to make (give parents or grandparents a set—one with each child's name on it—to store favorite photographs in). If you don't like to do things with your hands, make a gift of your time—for x hours of baby-sitting so a friend can get out to lunch or the movies.

It used to be obligatory to give brides fine china or crystal or silver, but that is a thing of the past. (Many girls "register" their choices of china, glass and silver, and while this certainly makes it easier for the giver, it always makes me feel that the bride doesn't trust her friends' taste and I might just as well send a check.) Today's bride, I think, is often happier with a gift of some beautiful kind of kitchen equipment that is not only useful but that doesn't require the kind of maintenance she doesn't have time to give it. I never send things that have to be polished—silver or copper or brass— any more. And I never have presents monogrammed because I don't mind at all if the kids want to exchange them in case of duplication or in case there is something else they'd find more useful than whatever it is I've chosen.

I don't for a minute mean that I always give presents that are instantly exchangeable. The part of gift shopping I like best is picking up appealing things that remind me of special people, whenever and wherever I'm lucky enough to find them, and saving them for Christmas or birthdays. Not only is it a good feeling to know you've got something that is particularly right all ready and waiting, but my serendipity buying plan helps eliminate last-minute worry and rush—especially during the holidays. Museum gift shops are among my favorite places because their things are unusual and beautiful, their prices are modest, and their profits help support other museum activities.

gift-wrapping

I buy gift-wrappings the same unscheduled way. All year I like to accumulate things to make packages pretty—flowers, ribbons, papers, tags, florist's wire to wrap in ribbon and bend into intriguing shapes. I scout stationery stores, ten-cent stores, notions departments and trimming shops (New York's wholesale hat district is a great place to hunt birds, berries, flowers, ribbons and assorted bees and butterflies). And my favorite Japanese store has new paper items to offer me every time I stop in.

Wrappings can give almost as much pleasure as the gift itself. And you can spend a fortune on them—but you don't have to. Instead, develop an eye for spotting and saving things that come into your orbit. I am a shameless salvager —of scraps of bright fabric, small toys, gadgets, buttons. Last year a marvelous grinning alligator that came on a box of candy for Dick was a smashing smiling success on Adam's Christmas present. New wrapping papers come in exciting colors and textures. I like least those printed with angels and bells and happy birthdays. Solid colors leave you freer to design your own package, to try surprise combinations. How about black and white tissue, half and half, on one package, a pink-orange split on another, or trimming shiny white paper with black velvet ribbon? I love velvet ribbon, but it is expensive, so I never tie it all the way around; instead, I cut short tabs, put something pretty—a bird or a flower or a "jewel"—on top and sing prayers of thanks to the transparent-tape people with every present I wrap.

How about if you detest wrapping and are no good at it? I say let the store do it, or let your little kids do it, or you do it and *say* your little kids did it. In self-defense I have to think it's what's inside that counts.

volunteer work

Presents and wrappings are things you do both for yourself and the people you love. But there is another kind of giving that is terribly important, and that is the gift of time to your community. American women are unique in the time and quality of service they are willing to volunteer to their favorite causes. In many other countries, a woman's contribution to a charity may stop with allowing her name to appear on its letterhead or buying a couple of tickets to a ball. Here she goes to work. She is quite willing to study, take courses, acquire paraprofessional skills. Often she works on an almost semiprofessional level. And I don't know what would happen to cities like New York without the time and talent such women contribute.

In volunteer work as in anything else, I think you do best and give most doing a job you enjoy. Some people are happiest working with people, others prefer paper work. Some work best in large, well-organized groups with specific tasks assigned to them. Others prefer the freedom to approach jobs their own way and are willing to assume the responsibility for their decisions. And while some women are bored doing routine work, others actually enjoy it. The important thing to realize is that—in the world of Good Works—there are jobs that make use of all sorts of tastes and skills. I have never been any good at fund-raising on a direct person-to-person basis, but over the years, I have been able to persuade performers to appear at benefits, thereby making it easier to part potential contributors from their money. During World War II, instead of being a very bad nurse's aide (which I certainly would have been), I worked for the Writers War Board to persuade authors to supply dramatic material—sketches, skits, monologues and sometimes even cut versions of their full-length plays—for the entertainment of the Armed Forces. Knowing writers and some of their problems, I felt suited to the job and I enjoyed it.

Even while your children are small and you can't leave home regularly, you can help by writing letters and making phone calls. If you like working with children, there are all kinds of badly needed jobs to be done in schools and community centers. If, on the other hand, you prefer working with adults, there are fascinating programs which help students and professional people from foreign countries learn idiomatic English through informal talk sessions with volunteers. You might offer to help out at a local historical society or museum—all of which are desperately short-handed—or do some recordings for the blind, or put a special skill like sewing or cooking or music to work at a settlement house. And noncommercial radio and TV stations are often in need of help.

politics

Politics is another field with openings for all sorts of talent. To me, one encouraging happening in the sixties was the way young people—most of them too young to vote—took the very constructive step of working for candidates they believed in, did jobs that would otherwise have gone undone for lack of money. During elections and in between,

you, yourself, and you

the nonpartisan League of Women Voters educates and encourages citizens to get involved in and concerned about the men and women who represent them in local, state and national government.

In short, any woman—whatever her talents—should be able to find a volunteer job she likes and from which she can gain the double satisfaction of feeling needed and being part of the outside world.

working wives

There are, however, some women lurking in the under-brush who are possessed with—no, I mean possessed *by*—a more ravenous appetite for living than the satisfaction of hearth and home, even combined with a volunteer job, can possibly provide. Not that they don't love their husbands and children or appreciate the need for volunteer work— they do, but it's not enough for them. Quite bluntly, they want to work and they want to be paid for working; unless their husbands are violently opposed to it, these are women who absolutely *should* work. If they don't, they are going to suffer from the January-February-March malaise all year long. Kick around in the underbrush, and you'll flush out countless wives who are bored to death by their own little children, wives who detest cooking and housework, or wives who simply like having a little extra money to play around with. But will they admit it? They wouldn't *dare!*

In our society, domestic ennui is not an acceptable reason for a married woman to work. Financial need is acceptable, a creative talent (But it had better be successful!) is accepta-ble, putting to use some previously acquired professional training (a lady lawyer, for instance) is usually acceptable, but working just for the fun of it because you don't want to hang around the house or be a Gray Lady before you're a gray lady? That's not acceptable if you dare explain your motives.

If this sounds like you, the solution is really perfectly simple. As long as your husband understands, just go out and get yourself a swell little job in a bookstore, or in real estate, or in a travel agency, or in school administration work— part time or full time (whatever the home traffic and your own energy will bear)—and enjoy your freedom, your extra money and yourself. When other people ask you why you work, tell them quite truthfully that you're doing it "for fun." They'll never believe you. They'll think you're bravely concealing a grave financial crisis and will probe no further.

Then there are the real career women—the doctors, lawyers, teachers, trained technicians, creative writers or painters—who want to work, not necessarily to avoid anything at home, but to pursue something that passionately interests them outside of it. As I've already said, society seems to be more tolerant about the married woman with talent or professional training (maybe because her need to work comes from a positive rather than a negative motive), but this kind of woman has to learn to be tolerant of herself. The demands are tremendous; if she expects to play all her roles to perfection, she'll end up more miserable than if she never worked at all.

I have worked for years—sometimes part time, sometimes full time, always free lance, but never free time. When you have a career and a husband and children, even if he's a generous and understanding one, which mine is, there is no such thing as free time. And my life is a series of don'ts— things I don't do, people I don't see, things I don't have time to worry about, or try at least not to worry about.

Those of you who work have probably long since compiled your own list of don'ts, but for whatever it's worth, here is mine:

Don't stay up late; no matter how much fun you're having, you still won't be able to get up in the morning.

don'ts for working wives

Don't wait until the last minute to decide what's for dinner. More than anything else, you have to be well organized. Plan a whole week's menus in the bathtub, shop at the supermarket early in the morning when it and its shelves are empty, and if your family doesn't fancy bruised apples and bologna, use a market that delivers. Sure it's expensive, but you're working. You can afford it.

Don't rely on your memory for *anything*. For instance, insist that your older children, who make their own plans, tell you about them and *write them down*, complete with phone numbers and addresses. The reason for this is simple: As a working mother, you will be household-detail-ridden much of the time when you're not working. You'll be in the tub planning menus when your child tells you she is spend-

you, yourself, and you

ing Friday night at a friend's house. You'll say, "Mm-hm," and then promptly file this golden nugget of information in with your mental list of frozen spinach and giant-size boxes of detergent. By eleven o'clock Friday night, you will be calling every mother in the neighborhood, maybe even the police, and when you locate your daughter, who has not run away with a hippie or been hit by a bus after all, you will scream at her before she gets a chance to say more than hello. And then you will feel v-e-r-y f-o-o-l-i-s-h! (Generally speaking, look out for mm-hms—it means your mind is wandering.)

With small children, arrange their social schedules well in advance—afternoon play groups are great for working mothers. Search for a housekeeper who is thoroughly reliable, intelligent and good-humored so that the kids aren't utterly devastated by your absence. Working mothers have to be much more meticulous about the competence of their substitutes than non-working mothers; references have to be checked twice as diligently. And I don't know about the rest of you, but when I'm not around, I'd much rather have someone with my kids who has fun with them and plays with them than someone who compulsively polishes the silver.

Now that you've provided as adequately as possible for your kids, don't feel guilty about the amount of time you spend away from them. I am not a psychologist, but *they* say the quality of your time is more important than the quantity and I choose to believe them. To come home exhilarated and enthusiastic about your day, your job, and therefore, yourself, will make you a much better mother in the long run than the self-sacrificing harpy who stays home to be with the children whom she secretly resents. But when you do come home, manufacture a chunk of time for them and really give it to them. No talking on the phone to your friends and no mm-hming; that's a cheat and they know it. If your son wants to drag out the whole hideous Erector Set and make a battery-powered oil-driller out of it, well that's what you have to do. Even if it means emptying three flashlights to find the batteries because you certainly won't find them in the Erector Set where they belong.

When you have a job, you'll find that a lot of things aren't

you, yourself, and you

where they belong—you're going great if you find them at all. Don't worry if you don't find them. Most of them will turn up eventually. Maybe they're under the bed . . .

Don't look under the bed! You might find the flashlight batteries, but you positively will find clumps of dust, pencils, a stocking with runs in it, balled-up Kleenex, a three-week-old wedding invitation for yesterday (you forgot to go and you even forgot to answer—quick, quick, send a present!) .

If you're looking under your daughter's bed, you'll find a fossilized apple core, a *dirty* stocking with runs in it and, if your luck is running, her bite plate. Seventy-five dollars worth of plastic and titanium rutile has been under that bed for months. By now, she probably has her buck teeth back again. You haven't even noticed. Good Lord, what kind of a mother are you anyway? You hate yourself! Don't.

Just order new batteries from the hardware store, and don't look under the bed. Or under the fridge, or on top of the bookcase, or in the junk closet. If you thought you had junk in there before, you will hardly believe what's in there now . . .

Don't worry about this either. I'm not advocating out-and-out household filth, but cleanliness (and neatness) are not really next to godliness, and if you're going to have a career, something has to give somewhere—you simply cannot be a perfectionist. There's always Sunday, or Spring Cleaning (you're going to pay someone else to do that because you're working and can afford it) , or guests coming for dinner the next night which is a super-inducement to clean up the surface mess in a hurry. You may, by the way, find yourself wishing you didn't have to have any dinner guests; a fancy dinner is just one more thing on your overburdened mind, one more added complication. So make a simple dinner. Your friends know you've been out working all day; they'll think you're a versatile genius if you manage to slap some cold cuts and a salad on the table. Or if you have higher culinary aspirations, do some cooking over weekends when you're free and store a few meals in the freezer.

And one final caution: in the midst of your electrifying career, don't forget that you are still your husband's wife, and if he doesn't mind living in a less than perfectly run establishment with a lady who insists on retaining her own

you, yourself, and you

identity and feeding her own ego, he's a pretty emancipated fella, even by today's standards. He should be rewarded not penalized for his enlightened attitude. Don't get me wrong. I think we are absolutely entitled to our own identities and egos—but if we're smart, we won't nurture them to the detriment of our husbands'. Not if we want to hang on to our husbands, we won't.

Take money, for instance. If you earn only a little, I don't think it matters what you do with it, but if you earn a lot, it's a mistake to think of it as Your Money to be put in Your Account and to be spent as You see fit. You'd be much better off to decide, with your husband, how you're going to dispose of it.

When your husband comes home at night, it is not tactful to tell him all about Your Day before he gets a chance to tell you about his.

If he wants to go to the theater and you're exhausted, go anyway. If a child wakes up in the middle of the night, it's still your job to go see what's the matter and if you find yourself thinking, "I'm just as tired as he is, why doesn't he get up?" you're taking advantage of the double standard we women are always complaining about. After all, he *has* to work, whereas you're working because you want to.

The life of a career wife is often a frantic, fragmented mess. It doesn't take long to figure that one out, it's a question of whether or not you have the emotional stamina for it. Sporadic fits of despair ("I'm doing a million things at once and none of them well . . . utter disaster!") are to be expected, but if the sporadic fits lengthen to a permanent state of self-loathing, it's time for you to quit. There's nothing the matter with being a plain old wife and mother, and it's a lot easier on the people you live with. If, on the other hand, you can somehow manage to juggle all the little pieces, and please most of the people most of the time, you have every right to say to yourself, "Look at me! I'm a housekeeper, a bookkeeper, a homemaker, a moneymaker, a superb organizer, a lovely mother, a devoted wife and a fascinating person. I am the Compleat Woman of Today!"

And so you are, if you think you are . . . which is what DR and I have been trying to convey, lo, these many pages. The Compleat Woman is *any* woman who knows what she is and likes what she is. You can work, or not work; you can give a banquet or a make-your-own sandwich lunch; you can have a living room full of eighteenth-century antiques, you can have all plastic furniture. As Oscar Hammerstein once said,

> "Now you can do
> Whatever you want,
> Whatever you want to do,
> Here you are
> In a wonderful world
> Especially made for you . . ."

*the
quality of
life*

How you fit all your world together gives your life its distinctive style and is a kind of art. Today what we think of as Art has a capital A and the name of a sculptor or painter attached. But it hasn't always been that way. For centuries, beautiful things have been made by people with no names at all—glass blowers in Egypt fashioned exquisite vases; Greek peasants, 3,000 years ago, shaped oil lamps; unknown itinerant artists wandered along the Hudson in the 1800's and painted the people and places they saw. In all civilizations, men intent upon doing the best work they could have made useful things beautiful—pots, lamps, cosmetic jars. One of the loveliest things I have ever seen is a 3,000-year-old handle for a whetstone I gave to Dick last Christmas—so simple, but made by a man with an eye for beauty whose aim was only to create a useful object. He and men like him were not artists but craftsmen, and museums are full of the beauty they put into everyday things—wine bottles, handles and toys. Fortunately, there are still people creating beauty through a determination to create quality.

A woman can shape her life to have that kind of beauty—always trying to do her best. With each day's decisions she makes a statement. The way she runs her house, what she does with her spare time, the things she chooses to make part of her surroundings, how she feels about the issues of our time and how involved she becomes—the sum of all these becomes the quality of life she creates for her husband, her children and herself.

you, yourself, and you

APPENDIX

PARTY
CHECKLIST

ALWAYS

China
Silver (flatware,
    serving pieces)
Glassware
Linens
Serving dishes
Candles
Flowers
Vases
Chairs
Tables
Cigarettes

Matches
Soft drinks and mixers
Liquor
Ice
Money (for extra help)
Pitchers
Hot plates, trivets,
    warming trays
Light bulbs
Soap and hand towels
Hanging space
    for coats

BIG PARTIES

Coat rack
Coat checks
Hangers
Bar
Paper towels (for
    guests' bathroom)
Large coffee urn

Table tops (for bridge
    tables) or folding
    tables
Platters with food
    warmers
Extra ashtrays

STORES
FOR THE SHELVES
(CANS OR GLASS JARS—
NO REFRIGERATION
NEEDED)

SOUPS

Chicken broth   Black bean
Chicken gumbo   Borscht
Madrilène   Clam juice
Beef consommé   Tomato juice

MEAT

Cooked canned ham, corned beef, pot roast,
    turkey, or chicken
Salami
Beef stew, Stroganoff, and hash

FISH

Herring (two or three   Sardines (boneless)
    kinds)   Smoked salmon (in tins)
Rainbow trout   Tuna (white chunks)
Mackerel in white wine
Mussels

VEGETABLES

Artichoke hearts   Mushrooms (several
Artichoke bottoms   varieties)
Hearts of palm   Tomatoes (in quarters)
     White asparagus

FRUITS (CANNED)

Bing cherries   Mandarin orange sections
Sour pitted cherries   White peaches
Lichee nuts

DRIED FRUITS AND VEGETABLES

Apples   Raisins
Apricots   Mushrooms
Prunes

JAMS AND JELLIES

Apple jelly   Currant jelly
Apricot jam

MISCELLANEOUS

Assorted herbs and spices (dried)
Black olives
Cake (the kind that keeps in tins or plastic containers)
Capers
Cheese (Parmesan in one piece for grating,
   and other cheeses)
Crackers
Ginger root (keeps best in a sherry
   or Madeira wine in refrigerator)
Horseradish (refrigerated)
Melba toast
Mustard
Oil
Onions and shallots
Pasta (assorted sizes and varieties)
Pâté
Quail eggs
Rice (plain, herbed, and saffron)
Tomato paste
Truffles
Vinegar (wine and tarragon)

STORES FOR
THE FREEZER

COMMERCIALLY PACKAGED FOODS

Assorted fruits (especially raspberries and strawberries)
Assorted vegetables, herbs, and spices
Bread doughs
Cakes (and cheese cake)
Crêpes (sweetened and unsweetened)
Ice cream, sherbets, and water ice
Pasta (cannelloni, lasagna, ravioli, tagliatelle, tortellini,
   ready for final cooking)
Quiche

UNCOOKED FOODS

Chicken breasts   Small steaks
Shrimp   Veal scallops

TIME-SAVERS

Chopped chives, parsley, tarragon, etc.
Lemon juice
Tarragon butter, lemon butter, etc.

EMERGENCY SUPPLIES

Bread, muffins
Butter, margarine
Egg whites and yolks

FIRST COURSES

Cheese soufflé   Soups
Crabmeat, lobster
   (cooked)

MAIN COURSES

Beef stew	Stuffed cabbage
Chicken or lamb curry	Veal Marengo

LEFTOVERS

Cream	Roasts (beef, chicken, duck, lamb, veal)
Hollandaise sauce	Whipped cream

DESSERTS

Chocolate roll
Pastry shells
Soufflés

MENUS

DINNER MENUS

Smoked salmon (with capers and lemon wedges)
Veal birds   *Pouilly-Fumé*
Cold asparagus with vinaigrette sauce
Apple tart

Seafood Armoricaine,
    cucumber sandwiches
Roast of beef   *Red Burgundy*
Artichoke bottoms, purée of carrots
Parslied potato balls
Mixed green salad, cheese
Hot fruit with custard sauce

Prosciutto and melon (pear may be substituted
    if melon is out of season)
Danish chicken with rice (chicken with a   *Chablis*
    basic velouté sauce with horseradish
    and a bit of sugar added to it)
Purée of mixed vegetables
Green salad, cheese
Ginger roll

Greek lemon soup
Roast leg of lamb   *Bordeaux*
Spinach, kasha
Raw mushroom salad, cheese
Oranges in red wine

Artichokes vinaigrette
Roast duck   *Burgundy*
Snow peas, potato balls
Lingonberry pancakes

Asparagus with hollandaise sauce
Veal piccata   *Bordeaux*
String beans, fettucini
Apricot roll

Chicken soup with a pinch of ginger
Veal Marengo   *Muscadet*
Pasta with peas
Water ice with berries

New England clam chowder
Frankfurters and sauerkraut   *Beer*
Lima beans, boiled potatoes
Apple tart

Sorrel soup
Pork roast   *Pouilly-Fuissé*
Baked tomatoes and artichoke hearts
Roast potatoes
Salad, cheese
Chocolate Bavarian cream

Filet of sole mousse, lobster sauce
Cucumber sandwiches
Short loin of beef   *Burgundy*
Truffled rice, tiny peas
Endive salad, cheese
Pears in red wine, Madeleines

Rainbow trout with mustard sauce
Saddle of lamb with kidneys   *Red Chianti*
Broccoli, kasha
Crêpes with apricot purée

Assorted hors d'oeuvres
Blanquette of veal with rice   *Rosé*
String beans
Raspberry water ice with lichee nuts

Smoked trout with horseradish sauce
Ham with Madeira sauce   *Pouilly-Fumé*
Purée of spinach, herbed rice
Strawberry tart

Cheese soufflé
Roast lamb with coffee sauce   *Bordeaux*
Baked eggplant, onion sauce
Asparagus with vinaigrette sauce
Jelly roll

DINNER MENUS (*continued*)

Pâté
Roast beef hash
String beans with almonds   *Burgundy*
Tomatoes with basil
Caramel custard

Black bean soup with sherry and crabmeat
Roast chicken tarragon   *Orvieto*
Purée of mixed vegetables, parslied potato balls
Spinach and bacon salad
Peaches in red wine

LUNCH MENUS

Hot borscht
Curried chicken, shrimp and lobster with rice   *Verdicchio*
Chutney
Cucumber salad
Oranges and tangerines in red wine, cookies

Gazpacho
Cold poached bass and shrimp with green sauce   *Chilean Riesling*
Mushroom and artichoke heart salad
Yogurt "Coeur à la Crème" with berries *

Sorrel soup
Feta cheese and crackers   *Soave*
Zucchini (poached in wine or raw) stuffed with
   lobster salad in green sauce
Mixed fruit

Senegalese
Cold poached salmon with dilled mayonnaise   *Chablis*
Tomatoes stuffed with cucumber
Lemon ice with blueberries

* Allowing one 8-oz. container per person,
use plain yogurt; put it in a colander that has been lined
with cheesecloth, and let yogurt drip into a bowl
in the refrigerator overnight. Lift yogurt in cheesecloth,
and put into heart-shaped mold for several hours.
Unmold and serve with cream and sugar
and surrounded by fruit.

Red caviar soup (jellied Madrilène with a spoon-
    ful of red caviar and a dash of sour cream)
Cold tarragon chicken   *Gewurztraminer*
Artichoke vinaigrette
Green salad and cheese
Trifle

Lamb broth with dried mushrooms and barley
Meat loaf   *Anjou*
Baked asparagus and tomatoes
Cheesecake with berries

Clam bisque
Stuffed cabbage   *White Burgundy*
Tiny peas
White peaches with raspberry sauce

Black bean soup with sherry and chopped
    scallions
Filet of sole with crabmeat (or shrimp)   *Pouilly-Fumé*
Raw mushroom and tomato salad
Apricot tart

Chicken gumbo with crabmeat
Quiche   *Beer*
String bean salad
Peaches and strawberries (fresh or frozen)
Crumb cake

Pasta
Boeuf à la mode en gélee   *Sangria*
Mixed green salad
Strawberry mousse

Manhattan clam chowder
Eggs Florentine
Boysenberry ice

Mussels vinaigrette
Risotto with chicken livers   *Bordeaux*
Green salad
Strawberries Romanov

Cressonière soup
Cold poached eggs in aspic with ham
Leeks vinaigrette
Stewed pears with kirsch and almond slivers

Beef consommé with eggs (beat a whole
   egg into a can of consommé
   and bring just to the boil)
Baked snapper and   *Chablis*
   crabmeat with sauce mousseline
Artichoke vinaigrette
Mixed fruit

MENU
FOR A LUNCH
OR A LATE SUPPER
BUFFET

Cold Polish ham   *Beer, rosé,*
Beef salad   *Sancerre*
Mixed green salad
Spinach-cheese pie
Ginger roll
Chocolate roll
Strawberries with orange juice

Some kind of bread should be offered with all these meals. I particularly like French, Italian, rye and, with smoked fish, pumpernickel. Crisp crusted rolls, croissants, toasted English muffins, and popovers are other favorites, but the choice will depend on the menu. Hot coffee is usually served at the end of the meal, but wine is optional, and, for summer lunches, iced tea or coffee is fine with lunch.

TABLE SETTINGS

Dinner plates (approximately ten inches) should be used for the main course, but it's useful to have plates in different sizes that can serve more than one purpose. Luncheon plates (about nine inches) can easily be used as fish plates or for special vegetables, such as asparagus, artichokes or leeks. Eight-inch plates are just about right for salad or dessert. It's nice to have both the creamed-soup cups (also useful for jellied or other cold soups) and soup plates. Bread and butter plates are usually about six inches in diameter, but there are some charming three-inch ones for butter only that take up very little space when your table is crowded. In addition to the water goblet, there are several traditional sizes for wine, but it is perfectly all right to use just one kind provided it is large enough—holding six to eight ounces.

1. Setting for a menu calling for fish, meat, salad, and two wines with a service plate or a first course on the table. The forks go to the left, the knives to the right, in the order of their use— first used on the outside, i.e., fish, meat, and salad forks. The napkin is placed to the left of the forks. The dessert spoons and forks may be brought to the table on the dessert plates and the spoons for the coffee on the cups and saucers. The water goblet goes above the knives with the red wine glass next to it; the white wine glass goes on the outside since it is generally used first. When place cards are used, they should be put directly above the plates. The butter plates and knives are eliminated from this rather formal setting.

2.   *Setting for a menu calling for soup, meat, salad, dessert, and one wine. The forks to the left, the knives to the right, in the order of use, the first used on the outside—soup spoon to the right of the knife. The dessert spoon and fork are placed at the top of the setting because it makes clearing simpler, although they may, of course, be brought in on the dessert plates. The butter plate and knife go above and to the left of the forks. The spoons for tea or coffee may be brought with the cups and saucers. Since there is no service plate or first course on the table, the napkin is placed in the center. The water goblet goes above the knife and the all-purpose tulip-shaped wine glass stands to the right of the water glass.*

A NOTE ON THE TYPE

———————

THIS BOOK *is set on the Linotype in Baskerville.*
The punches for this face were cut under the supervision of George W. Jones,
the eminent English printer and the designer of Granjon and Estienne.
Linotype Baskerville is a facsimile cutting from type cast from the original
matrices of a face designed by John Baskerville, a writing
master of Birmingham, for his own private press. The original face
was the forerunner of the "modern" group of
type faces, known today as Scotch, Bodoni, etc. After his
death in 1775, Baskerville's punches and matrices were sold in France
and were used to produce the sumptuous Kehl
edition of Voltaire's works.

———————

This book was composed by Kingsport Press, Inc.,
Kingsport, Tennessee, printed by RAE Publishing Co., Cedar Grove,
New Jersey, and bound by H. Wolff Book Manufacturing Co.,
New York. Architectural drawings and diagrams by Joyce Steinglass.
Typography and binding design by Ruth Ansel.